Journal of the Society of

# Christian
# Ethics

VOLUME 38, NUMBER 2 • FALL/WINTER 2018

# Contents

## Book Reviews

# Preface

The essays in this issue were presented at the annual meeting of the Society of Christian Ethics in Portland, Oregon, in January 2018. The theme of this meeting was "Christian Ethics: Retrospect and Prospect." Each of the essays in this issue addresses in some way this double-sided coin. Each deals in a distinct way with the continuing influence of the history of Christian ethics on the present, looks to the future of the field, or combines both views to develop a constructive vision of what Christian ethics may become.

David Gushee's presidential address, "Christian Ethics: Retrospect and Prospect," offers an overview of the theme, rehearsing the development of Christian social ethics as a field over the past century and a half as well as reflecting on the changes that have taken place as the field has moved from its ecclesial-formational roots, to the development of the social ethics model, through the Hauerwasian critique, and moving toward a liberationist vision of the future of the field. Drawing on his own experiences, Gushee offers a reflection on the possibilities and limitations of each of these types of Christian ethics, and how they have affected him as a scholar and as a Christian.

In a departure from the usual way that plenary addresses are assigned at the annual meeting, Gushee invited the three working groups of the society to each offer a reflection on how the field of Christian ethics has evolved from the perspective of their own communities. We have published here the corresponding essays that represent the state of the field as interpreted by the African American, Asian American, and Latino/a working groups.

The contribution by the African/African American Working Group surveys the progenitors and major themes that have emerged within the African American tradition within Christian ethics. It addresses the problems of hostility and marginalization that this tradition has faced within the field of Christian ethics, and within the Society of Christian ethics specifically, and poses some trenchant questions to the society about the future of the place of an African American hermeneutic within Christian ethics.

The Asian American Working Group's contribution similarly offers a retrospective survey of the development of a distinctly Asian American approach to the practice of Christian ethics. It then addresses the dual issues of what precisely a distinctive Asian American ethical perspective is and how this perspective is grounded in the marginalization of Asian Americans, a marginalization that is often obscured beneath the image of Asian Americans as "model minorities."

The Latino/a Working Group also seeks to identify key themes that mark its distinctive contributions to the field of Christian ethics, rooted in a historical survey of the development of the field and an articulation of key themes within the tradition. Among the issues this essay addresses are those of migration and the immigrant experience, the role of Afro-Latinx scholarship in the field, and the question of where queer Latinx voices fit within the tradition.

Collectively, these working group reflections offer a striking portrait of where the Society of Christian Ethics has been and where it may go in the future. They also serve as a reminder that the society has often failed, despite its rhetoric and good intentions, to fully embrace the voices of minority scholars in the field. Prospectively, the question of whether this will be remedied remains to be seen.

The remainder of the essays in this volume represent concurrent session papers that were presented during the conference. Brett McCarty's "Medicine as Just War?" looks at the legacy of James Childress within the field of Christian ethics, examining how his approach to bioethics was informed by his work in the area of just war theory, while Nathanial Van Yperen's "Nature Elicits Piety" examines the continuing relevance of James Gustafson's theocentric ethics for the development of ecological ethics. Van Yperen connects this to the question of wildlife conservation in the American West.

Matthew Elia's "Ethics in the Afterlife of Slavery" takes on the task of examining what Saint Augustine's rhetoric of "mastery" in the context of Roman society has to say about the way in which his theology can be received in a postslavery world. M. Therese Lysaught and Michael McCarthy, in "A Social Praxis for US Health Care," look at the relevance that the development of new approaches to Catholic bioethics for Catholic social teaching, particularly in those areas in which issues of justice and social marginalization connect to the US health care system.

In "Aesthetics and Ethics," Susan A. Ross examines the contributions of communities of women religious in the moral formation of students through development of an aesthetic sensibility, which allowed them to understand their responsibility to create a world that was both good and beautiful. Janna Hunter-Bowman offers a critical assessment of practices of nonviolent peacemaking in "Constructive Agents Under Duress." Through an analysis of the multiple eschatological theories present in the work of John Howard Yoder, she argues that a careful distinction between messianic and gradualist conceptions of eschatology can allow for a more effective conception of the relationship of church and state for the purposes of nonviolent peacebuilding. Finally, David

Lantigua's "Liberal Domination, Individual Rights, and the Preferential Option for the Poor in History" considers the ongoing legacy of liberal individualism in the dispossession of the poor in Latin America, and considers the continuing importance of the turn toward the poor in theology for stripping liberalism of its mythological power over political and economic life.

Each of these essays engages in a distinct way with the conference theme, yet together they offer a portrait of a discipline with a rich history and a live, though contentious, future. By considering both the retrospective and prospective dimensions of Christian ethics, they allow us to consider the continuing contributions of this history, and how this future should be shaped.

*Selected Essays*

# Christian Ethics: Retrospect and Prospect

*David P. Gushee*

This SCE presidential address attempts an interpretation of the history of American Christian ethics that is simultaneously an intellectual autobiography. Seven types of Christian ethics receive attention: ecclesial-formational, Protestant social ethics, Niebuhrian, Catholic, evangelical, Hauerwasian, and liberationist. The discipline is described as methodologically fractured and professionally endangered, especially in the case of its founding strand, Protestant social ethics. The essay ends with a call for mutual respect and support among Christian ethicists, sustained attention to one another's work, and shared efforts to advance the discipline.

## Prologue

This essay attempts an interpretation and mapping of the discipline of Christian ethics that is simultaneously a personal intellectual autobiography and an honest confession concerning those voices to which I have not adequately attended. At one level, it is a review of the rise and fall of American Protestant Christian social ethics. At another, it is a cri de coeur concerning our internal divisions and the imperiled state of our discipline. I offer these reflections in service to my colleagues and our discipline, and to those in the church, world, and academy who rely on us to do our best work.[1]

## Ecclesial-Formational Christian Ethics

The first expression of Christian ethics that I experienced came through my mother and the Catholic faith in which she raised me. When she tried to teach me the way of life appropriate to a Catholic Christian, she was doing Christian

David P. Gushee, PhD, is Distinguished University Professor of Christian Ethics at Mercer University, 3001 Mercer University Drive, Atlanta, GA 30341; gushee_dp @mercer.edu.

*Journal of the Society of Christian Ethics*, 38, 2 (2018): 3–20

ethics. The version she taught me was an awkward combination of western Pennsylvania Irish Catholicism and the groovy post–Vatican II vibe of my northern Virginia parish. I rejected it when I was fourteen years old.

A map of Christian ethics should begin with efforts such as those of my mother. *Christian ethics happens wherever Christians offer moral instruction to those in their care, and Christian believers attempt moral discernment, rooted in their confession of Christ.* Let us call this "ecclesial-formational ethics." It is offered in parental talks and Sunday sermons, in private prayers and small group meetings, in ethicists writing monographs and friends talking together. It is any serious effort to help Christians try to align their story with the story of what God has done in Jesus Christ.[2]

Ecclesial-formational Christian ethics is close kin to traditional Jewish and Muslim ethics, and it bears a resemblance to any ethic aiming at moral formation within a religious community. There is an obvious family resemblance between any ethics in which God is held to be the source and ground of ethical obligation, believers understand themselves to be obligated to adhere to God's will, and faith leaders are held responsible to God for properly exercising teaching authority.[3]

Long before there was an academic discipline known as Christian ethics, there were Roman Catholic, Eastern Orthodox, and Protestant Christians seeking faithfulness to Jesus Christ.[4] This was the primal expression of our discipline. It happened every day *back then*; it happens every day, *even now*.

## The Birth of American Protestant Christian Social Ethics

Even after my Catholic childhood and then my conversion at sixteen to a morally serious version of Southern Baptist Christianity, it took me a long time to recognize that what my parents, priests, and pastors were doing was an expression of Christian ethics.

That is because when I pursued my "call to Christian ministry" in 1984, I attended Southern Baptist Theological Seminary. At Southern, I fell hard for Christian ethics under Glen Stassen and decided to pursue it as my vocation.[5] I did my doctoral work at Union Seminary in New York, where I worked with Larry Rasmussen and Beverly Harrison and wrote my dissertation on the moral implications of Christian behavior during the Holocaust, finishing in 1993.[6]

I did not know that what Southern and Union taught me as Christian ethics was only *one version of Christian ethics*. I will call it "modern American Protestant Christian social ethics." It did not always exist. Gary Dorrien has detailed its history in his magisterial *Social Ethics in the Making*.[7]

Modern American Protestant Christian social ethics was born committed to a very different project than ecclesial-formation ethics. Its vision was, as

Dorrien says, "to transform . . . society in the direction of social justice."[8] This version of Christian ethics emerged in the late 1870s, when the first classes and professorships in "Christian sociology," "practical ethics," and "social economics" began to appear.[9] Its aim was to bring the resources of Christian faith to bear on "the social question," the urgent social evils attendant to the rise of modern industrial capitalism.

The first American Protestant social ethicists were the seminary professors Francis Greenwood Peabody (Harvard), William Jewett Tucker (Andover), and Graham Taylor (Hartford and later Chicago Seminary). Princeton Seminary established the first chair in Christian ethics in 1871, and Union Seminary (New York) offered its first course in Christian ethics, taught by George Prentiss, in 1877.[10]

History did not remember them. It did remember higher-profile figures in the Social Gospel movement. Among those is Walter Rauschenbusch.[11] In undertaking new research on Rauschenbusch, I have concluded that he was the true founder of modern American Protestant social ethics.[12] I have also concluded that large chunks of his vision flowed unconsciously into me through my teachers.

A seventh-generation pastor of immigrant German stock, Rauschenbusch inherited a strict Protestant ecclesial-formational ethic reminiscent of the stern Christian personal ethic and nonexistent social ethic that Southern Baptists first taught me. Rauschenbusch's pastorate in gritty late-nineteenth-century New York taught him that he needed a more holistic, more fully biblical ethic that could address the structural evils consuming the lives of his flock:

> The morality which the [Jewish] prophets had in mind . . . was not merely the private morality of the home, but the public morality on which national life is founded. They said less about the pure heart for the individual than of just institutions for the nation. We are accustomed to connect piety with the thought of private virtues; the pious man is the quiet, temperate, sober, kindly man. The evils against which we contend in the churches are intemperance, unchastity, the sins of the tongue. [Yet] the twin-evil against which the prophets launched the condemnation of Jehovah was injustice and oppression.[13]

For a modern social ethic, Rauschenbusch turned to the core sources of Christian thought: scripture and tradition. His methods of assessing these sources and many of his conclusions came to shape modern liberal Protestantism and Christian ethics.

Rauschenbusch treated scripture as an inspired yet human product, containing various strands of material differing in moral significance. All scripture must be tested by the life and teachings of Jesus, a thoroughly Jewish figure who was steeped in the Hebrew prophets and who offered a message of God's dawning kingdom. Jesus was not merely a good man or an earnest social reformer. He was the Son of God, who called people to God. But in doing so, he called them to create a new kind of social order.[14]

The Kingdom of God, said Rauschenbusch, was the religion of Jesus. It looks like love, justice, and social salvation, equality, dignity, and brotherhood.[15] Pursuing the Kingdom of God should be the mission of the church, even if it leads toward the Cross, as it did for Jesus.[16]

Rauschenbusch did more than any other figure to popularize a theology centered on the Kingdom of God, understood as a transformed real-world social order. This vision continues to captivate many Christians today, and it stands at the center of my own most widely read work.[17]

For Rauschenbusch, the Kingdom of God, thus understood, is the central concept, norm, and mission of Christianity. But instead, said Rauschenbusch, the historic church turned Jesus into the basis for a "system of speculative thought" and "the founder and organizer of a great ecclesiastical machine."[18]

Rauschenbusch thus offered a takedown of nearly the entirety of Christian tradition, detailing how kingdom vision deteriorated into the hope of personal immortality; the church fixated on its inner life;[19] otherworldliness sapped Christian moral energy, and asceticism, sacramentalism; and dogmatism calcified.[20] It all got encrusted in ancient writings that became mystified as authoritative, hindering the church from recovering Jesus' own mission.[21]

But now the church must again find its kingdom vision. This requires tackling "the social problem," with the churches inspiring cultural change and policy reform.

Rauschenbusch's policy proposals were reformist, addressing worker's rights, social insurance, health care, consumer protection, and urban living conditions. The broader project was attacking self-interested economic ideologies that grind up human beings and go unchallenged in the name of liberty.[22] This agenda remains with us in progressive politics and in Christian ethics. One long-standing expression of it is Christian socialism.[23]

Rauschenbusch is the most important creator of modern American Protestant Christian social ethics, which ended up producing a certain kind of ethicist. Such ethicists

- understand "the Christian Gospel" to address major social problems and not just personal salvation;

- attempt to gain critical competence in Christian scripture and tradition, but also relevant aspects of government, social science, and specific policy issues;

- present detailed social reform and public policy proposals;

- tend toward peripatetic activity, playing multiple roles as scholars, teachers, pastors, activists, and denominational officials; and

- exude a powerful spirit of moral earnestness and urgency, fired by their strong sense of vocation and the seriousness of modern problems.

This was the inspiring and strenuous version of Christian ethics in which I was formed. It has produced important work for over a century. I have attempted my share of social-ethical work—in this regard, I take greatest pride in my efforts to resist US-sponsored torture after the September 11, 2001, terrorist attacks on the United States.[24] But perhaps because it was the founding tradition of modern Protestant Christian ethics, Christian social ethics took a long time to remember that it was only one strand of the discipline, not the whole of it.

## Mainline Protestant Social Ethics after Rauschenbusch

After Rauschenbusch came Reinhold Niebuhr. At Union, I imbibed everything Niebuhr wrote.[25] I came out of my doctoral program wanting to imitate his pattern by writing a book a year and authoritative national opinion columns every week. I tried it for a long while.

I used to think that the differences between Rauschenbusch and Niebuhr mattered a lot—Social Gospel idealism versus Christian realism and all that. But their similarities were more important.

Certainly, there *were* profound differences. Many of them were contextual, related to the chronically apocalyptic conditions of Niebuhr's era. In America, cultural Protestantism was fading, Enlightenment optimism was dying, and reformist hope was giving way to despair.

In response, Niebuhr made three key moves. First, in theology, he made a move toward Christian tradition by recasting a neo-Augustinian pessimism about human nature that seemed richly theological compared with what the Social Gospelers had offered, though it only somewhat masked the ad hoc nature of his theology and the continuing liberal presuppositions of his thought. Second, in ethics, he derided pacifism, moral suasion, and "sentimental" liberalism, employing a cold-eyed realism about power relations that was initially informed by a sympathetic application of Marxism—but finally tended toward skepticism about the prospects or even the desirability of attempting major social changes in the direction of greater justice. And third, in strategy, Niebuhr dominated the field through his omniscient-sounding and ubiquitous commentaries on policy issues, commentaries that reflected and helped shape American elite opinion during the catastrophic times in which he lived. In the end, Niebuhr became such a hero to the midcentury American establishment that he both appeared on the cover of *Time* and was awarded the Presidential Medal of Freedom.[26]

I want to highlight important shared characteristics of Rauschenbusch and Niebuhr, which were carried forward in our discipline through at least the late 1960s. They together helped create a tradition that was

- *American*: It was undertaken by Americans and focused especially on the problems facing our country.

- *mainline Protestant Christian*: It was led by clergy-scholar-activists from the mainline Protestant denominations.

- *liberal*, in three different senses: It was governed by the assumptions of American liberal democracy, aimed at achieving liberal outcomes, and rooted in liberal rather than revelational theology.

- *oriented toward social ethics*: It was ethics that addressed public social concerns with fine-grained policy analyses and proposals, rather than the moral formation of individual Christians or churches.

- *indelibly stamped by the social location of the white male*: It was an ethics from the center, even if the ethics offered was sometimes aimed to aid nonwhite males on the margins of power.

I now see that, based on my own social location and training, upon graduation in 1993 I was able to seamlessly enter that unbroken line of *American Protestant social ethics* that can be traced from the 1870s, dominated the field at the time of the founding of the American Society of Christian Social Ethics in 1959 (later renamed the Society of Christian Ethics, SCE),[27] and remained central for decades afterward.

## Roman Catholic Social Ethics

The character of our guild was gradually but profoundly affected after Vatican II when Catholic moral theologians began joining Protestant ethicists in the SCE. They did not come from nowhere. While the early Protestant social ethicists were doing their work, Catholics were pursuing similar ends in their own way, first through the 1891 papal encyclical *Rerum Novarum*, which launched the development of modern Catholic social teaching, and then through the work of John Ryan and his successors.[28]

The defining experience of the first generation of Catholic ethicists to affiliate with the SCE, and of their new Protestant colleagues, was the lengthy, bruising Vatican effort to remove Charles Curran from an official teaching role because of his writings about sexual ethics.[29] But, of course, the Catholics brought with them more than post–Vatican II controversies. They also brought the rich and comprehensive Catholic moral tradition into what had been mainly a Protestant social ethics association.

The Curran affair reminds us that the earliest Catholic ethicists to join the SCE often challenged moral norms taught by the magisterium with what could be described, sympathetically or not, as a liberalizing agenda. But even when these Catholic scholars challenged the tradition, their arguments were usually made from within the tradition. This itself was instructive to Protestants, whose theological sources and framework often seemed to be themselves a matter for debate.

Ironically, I first encountered Catholic social ethics through courses with Glen Stassen at Southern Baptist Seminary. He was deeply appreciative of the Vatican II documents on social-ethical issues, and he introduced us to modern Catholic social teaching.

Half a decade later, I found myself working on the staff of the progressive evangelical Ron Sider. This was during the heyday of Joseph Cardinal Bernardin in Chicago, with his popularization of a "seamless garment ethic" or "consistent ethic of life."[30] Sider was also enamored of Pope John Paul II, who was then, and remains, deeply influential among US evangelical Christians, the community with which I increasingly identified after 1990.[31] For a long season, I tried to be a seamless garment Southern Baptist evangelical, offering a holistic, sacredness-of-life ethic rather than the narrowly focused abortion-and-euthanasia agenda that came to dominate conservative Catholic and evangelical social ethics.[32] That split, as we all know, remains with us to this day.

## Evangelical Social Ethics

Trying to be that John Paul II kind of evangelical ethicist dominated my vision for about twenty-five years. To speak truly of my encounter with the discipline of Christian ethics, I must camp out a moment with the evangelicals, a neglected part of our guild.

"Evangelical," or "neo-evangelical," was the term retrieved from history in the 1940s by Christian leaders within the fundamentalist side of American Protestantism. These men sought to bring an antimodernist Protestantism cautiously into conversation with broader intellectual currents.[33]

Beginning in the late 1940s, Carl Henry offered a first tentative engagement of evangelicals with the broader Christian conversation about contemporary social problems.[34] Later, in the 1960s, Francis Schaeffer became known for his extensive popular engagement with moral issues raised by contemporary culture.[35] Both did versions of American Christian social ethics; those versions turned out to be politically conservative, eventually informing the agenda of the late 1970s Christian Right.

But simultaneously, progressive evangelicals like Jim Wallis and Ron Sider offered a very different social-ethical vision.[36] These men were the evangelicals who captured my loyalty. I did not then realize what a small minority of (white) evangelicals they represented, perhaps because their progressive evangelical brand was overrepresented in our SCE guild in such luminaries as Stephen Mott, Darryl Trimiew, Allen Verhey, and Christine Pohl.[37]

The largest Protestant denomination in America remains the Southern Baptist Convention. There was once a progressive Southern Baptist ethical tradition; I was trained in it. From the 1940s to 1960s, its leaders were T. B. Maston, at Southwestern Seminary,[38] and Henlee Barnette, at Southern Seminary.[39] Eventually, Glen Stassen became the central figure, until he left for the evangelical Fuller Seminary in 1996. These schools also had robust doctoral programs in ethics, and their aging graduates still seed religion departments across the Baptist South.

These progressive Southern Baptist outposts were intentionally destroyed by the fundamentalists who took control of the Southern Baptist Convention in the late 1980s. Today, Southern Baptist clergy are largely instructed in ethics by scholars who are not trained in our field and have had no contact with the SCE. Not coincidentally, Southern Baptists are a bulwark of an increasingly reactionary, politicized white neofundamentalism. I have personally abandoned both Southern Baptists and "evangelicalism" as a result.

## The Hauerwas Revolution

Into this scene came Stanley Hauerwas in the early 1980s. His work offered a sustained and powerful critique of the dominant Christian social ethics tradition.[40]

Hauerwas's corpus as a whole offers a negation of the Protestant social ethics tradition.[41] He rejected the focus on America.[42] He routinely critiqued mainline Protestantism, both its theology and its social activism. He challenged the confidence of Christian ethics in the meaningfulness of a reformist public policy agenda within American liberal democracy.[43] He revalorized premodern Christian tradition, helped open space for the recovery of a focus on major historic thinkers like Aquinas and Augustine, and participated in excavating the ethical implications of sacramental theology.[44] In short, he offered a reclaiming of the ecclesial-formational Christian ethics that Rauschenbusch critiqued while repudiating the social ethics tradition that Rauschenbusch pioneered.[45]

In his wake, Hauerwas has opened space for many scholars who are interested in something other than liberal social ethics. Christian ethics research today demonstrates a much deeper connection with traditions in theology and moral philosophy—with doctrine, liturgy, historic figures,[46] discipleship, and character—than it has since the birth of the modern discipline in the 1870s.[47]

There is an aspect of the (post-)Hauerwas project that still involves doing Christian social ethics. I am thinking of current explorers of premodern, preliberal Christian politics, who tend to demonstrate an appreciation for the political theology of premodern European Christendom—or at the very least, a desire to help moderns enter that world, understand the goods that were lost when it disappeared, and gain an appreciation of ancient resources that can inform a postliberal, postmodern future.[48]

This recovery of premodern Christian political theology reminds us that ecclesial-formational Christian ethics was not the only kind of Christian ethics on offer before 1870. There was also Christian social ethics, but for about 1,500 years this was social ethics done in the context of a church–state alliance. It emanated from Europe and eventually underwrote a massive colonial enterprise.

This combination in some Christian ethics after Hauerwas—a *turn* away from liberal Protestant social ethics toward ecclesial-formational ethics, and a second *turn* away from liberal democratic modernity toward premodern Christianity, even Christendom—is alien to the tradition in which I was trained. I honor its scholarly achievements, note its staying power, and acknowledge my tendency toward suspicion. This suspicion appears to be shared by many who believe that Christian ethics needs to go in a completely different direction.

## Liberationist Christian Ethics and the Work of Minoritized Scholars

In a scalding 1920 essay, "The Souls of White Folk," W. E. B. Du Bois writes: "Of [white folk] I am singularly clairvoyant. I see in and through them. I view them from unusual points of vantage. . . . I see these souls undressed and from the back side. I see the working of their entrails. I know their thoughts and they know that I know."[49]

In Donald Trump's America, the land of #MeToo and #BlackLivesMatter and #LockHerUp, of #BuildThatWall and #JewsWillNotReplaceUs and the #MuslimBan, my soul feels undressed. I am discovering that I am part of a white American Christian male problem being unmistakably unveiled in our cultural moment.

I need to disclose another aspect of my story. When I wrote a book in 2014 making a theological argument for full LGBTQ inclusion in evangelical Christian churches, it cost me my place in evangelical life.[50] For the first time in adulthood, I personally tasted rejection, exclusion, and, finally, a ghostly invisibility. Though I realized that my new friends had spent most of their lives drinking far worse suffering down to the dregs, my own marginalization had a very bad taste.

As I read a newly emerging body of LGBTQ evangelical literature, as I hung out with infinitely precious young LGBTQ Christians trying to keep body and soul together, as I processed my own feelings of hurt, I learned that the view from the trampled underside offers extraordinarily valuable insights.[51] I eventually realized, with sorrow, that until these experiences *I had never adequately attended to the marginalized voices in my own discipline.*

I had been trained for better. After all, I had gone to Union Seminary in New York, where I studied with James Cone, the founder of black liberation theology, and with the pioneering feminist ethicist Beverly Harrison.[52] But at the time, I mainly responded with polite silence and inner resistance, and then I went on to pursue my highly rewarding career as the imagined Reinhold Niebuhr of evangelicalism.[53]

It was only after tasting my own bitter marginalization that I woke up to a new world. One might call it repentance. But repentance is a process, like peeling an onion, and each time I think I am getting somewhere, I discover how much farther I still have to go.

I have homework to do for the rest of my career. I need to dig far more deeply into African American ethics,[54] feminist ethics,[55] womanist ethics,[56] Latino/a ethics,[57] Asian American ethics,[58] Native American ethics,[59] and LGBTQ ethics.[60] I need to become just as conversant with these rich bodies of literature as I am with the other strands addressed in this essay. This is the standard to which colleagues of color challenge me, and all of us.

I now think the liberationists who used to unnerve me at Union Seminary were mainly right in what they affirmed. Liberation ethics is a primary and indispensable contribution to Christian ethics. It is the unique product of historically marginalized people, people who can identify with the experience that Howard Thurman names as having their backs against the wall.[61]

This phrase resonates a bit differently right now. We have heard a lot recently about women of all colors, and a few men, who have had their backs literally pressed against the wall by sexual predators, rapists, and criminals. They demand liberation. They are right to do so, as are people of color protesting the risk of being shot at routine traffic stops; and advocates for toddlers taken before US immigration courts; and LGBTQ people who know that Roy Moore, arguing for their criminalization, very nearly became a senator; and Native Americans at Standing Rock; and so very many others.

Liberation ethics challenges every strand of Christian ethics. To the American Christian social ethics tradition, it questions the purported goodness of our nation and the prospects for justice to be delivered by tinkering with our systemically unjust political order. To the ecclesial-formational tradition, it asks whether our churches are interested in forming people who will resist injustices directed at our neighbors.

Although social location is not everything, how much it does matter is continually revealed. Men do not do so well when put in charge of adjudicating sexual predation against women, as in the case of John Howard Yoder.[62] White people, including icons like Rauschenbusch, tend to miss a lot when it comes to the racial dimensions of social problems.[63]

Liberation ethics does not represent the entirety of the contribution of minoritized scholars. The work of such Christian ethicists spans every kind of methodology and interest. Liberationism was a first mode and a persistent one—but having pried open the doors of the guild to previously excluded scholars, it has opened space for scholars to explore all kinds of other interests. This is all to the good. Much-needed renewal in Christian ethics is made possible through their exciting new contributions. At a time when much American Christianity seems to be both fading and toxifying, this is where energy and hope are to be found. But the rest of us must pay attention.

## Where Do We Go from Here?

Christian ethics as a discipline now has multiple layers and lineages. There is no consensus, and no imaginable recovery of one. There are significant fractures among us, some of which have become personal, and in relation to which we should earnestly seek reconciliation.

Christian ethics today also faces serious labor challenges that demand our attention. Some of them are not unique to our field, but we must address them.

*The academic labor market now reflects structural injustices that demand moral response.* Seventy percent of course hours in higher education are now being taught by contingent faculty.[64] We who were granted tenure and rank are being challenged to face the fact that *their* $3,000 courses are what make *our* professorships, salaries, and sabbaticals possible. This is a justice issue of the first order, and contingent faculty are requiring that the rest of us pay attention, as we must.

*A related justice concern is the overproduction of doctoral degrees.* PhD-granting institutions bear culpability for not adjusting their admissions sufficiently in response to obvious market trends. It is wrong to train more doctoral students than a discipline has any hope of placing. But nobody coordinates doctoral admissions for the whole profession, and each school pursues its own interests.

What happens to unemployed or underemployed Christian ethicists matters a great deal, both to those directly affected and to the field itself. The future production of knowledge may be left to a tiny favored elite who obtain that small minority of full-time jobs in which scholars are given time to read and write. We face a tragic and unjust waste of the intellectual potential of many colleagues, and a truncation of scholarship in the field.

These realities make it even more troubling that *the discipline seems especially vulnerable to cutbacks.* The SCE 2020 Committee found that positions for Protestant ethicists were already in decline.[65] Our guild needs to advocate for Christian ethics as a discipline, Protestant ethics in particular, and to resist the disappearance of teaching slots.

Many younger ethicists are responding to market realities by cross-training in various methods or fields. The weakening market especially for confessional

Protestant ethicists is creating a feedback loop that causes many young Protestant scholars to write in a comparative or religious studies mode so they can find jobs but which then threatens to further weaken Protestant ethics. All this cross-training is impressive and could have creative implications for future scholarship. It is also kind of sad.

I urge us to recall that *there are Christian ethicists who do not participate in the SCE but could if we provided an environment in which they felt welcome.* If we are a community devoted to high-level scholarly exchange in Christian ethics, many voices should be welcomed. But to the extent that the liberal-to-liberationist ethical commitments of our majority dominate our ethos, those who do not share these views will feel unwelcome. This reflects broader national tensions.

The staggering events of the past two years in the United States reveal many things. Among them is that we need more faithful churches and a renewal of American public life. *We need all strands of Christian ethics to do their best work, in conversation with one another.* We need better character, better government policies, better professional ethics, better sexuality and gender relations, better race relations, better pastors, and better churches. We need more love and justice, more integrity, and more truth. Surely our discipline can help, in all its expressions.

There will never again be a consensus way of doing Christian ethics as there was in the heyday of twentieth-century Protestant Christian social ethics. We will be less white, less male, less mainline Protestant, less liberal, and perhaps less fixated on America and its policy problems. Besides the externally imposed threats to our discipline, we face the critical internal challenge of avoiding a permanent fracture between a radicalized multiracial "left" and a neotraditionalist, largely white, "right." That would essentially replicate the great and tragic political fracture that is sundering not just our country but also Europe. We have the resources to do better. We must do better. It begins by listening to each other. Let us continue our good work, with gratitude for our rich history and a steadfast commitment to each other and to the compelling vocation to which we have all devoted our lives.

## Notes

1. While taking full responsibility for this essay, the author gratefully acknowledges these colleagues who reviewed one or more drafts: Patricia Beattie Jung, Brian Brock, Miguel De La Torre, Gary Dorrien, Matthew Elia, Stacey Floyd-Thomas, Matthew Gaudet, Stanley Hauerwas, Grace Kao, Larry Rasmussen, Isaac Sharp, Cristina Traina, Darryl Trimiew, Sara Wilhelm Garbers, Reggie Williams, and Diane Yeager.

2. I am grateful to colleague Brian Brock for this helpful formulation.

3. I am asserting a kinship between all theocentric-communal ethics, especially but not exclusively in the Abrahamic traditions. See Charles Mathewes, *Understanding Religious Ethics* (Chichester, UK: Wiley-Blackwell, 2010).

4. Because I will not return to the Orthodox, here I simply note the following key books: Vigen Guroian, *Incarnate Love: Essays in Orthodox Ethics* (Notre Dame, IN: University of Notre Dame Press, 1987); Joseph Woodill, *The Fellowship of Life: Virtue Ethics and Orthodox Christianity* (Washington, DC: Georgetown University Press, 1998); Stanley Samuel Harakas, *Living the Faith: The Praxis of Eastern Orthodox Ethics* (Minneapolis: Light & Life Publishing, 1992); and Christos Yannaras, *The Freedom of Morality* (Crestwood, NY: St. Vladimir's Seminary Press, 1984). My limited reading in Eastern Orthodox ethics suggests that it largely remains focused on ecclesial-formational ethics, but see Aristotle Papanikolaou, *The Mystical as Political: Democracy and Non-Radical Orthodoxy* (Notre Dame, IN: University of Notre Dame Press, 2014).

5. Glen H. Stassen, ed., *Just Peacemaking: The New Paradigm for the Ethics of Peace and War* (Cleveland: Pilgrim Press, 2008); Glen H. Stassen, *A Thicker Jesus: Incarnational Discipleship in a Secular Age* (Louisville: Westminster John Knox Press, 2012). Stassen spent much of his professional time leading peace activist efforts and training graduate students. He was my indispensable mentor.

6. David P. Gushee, *The Righteous Gentiles of the Holocaust: A Christian Interpretation*, 1st edition (Minneapolis: Fortress Press, 1994).

7. Gary Dorrien, *Social Ethics in the Making: Interpreting an American Tradition* (Chichester, UK: Wiley-Blackwell, 2011).

8. Ibid., 1.

9. Ibid., chap. 1.

10. Ibid.

11. Christopher H. Evans, *The Kingdom Is Always but Coming* (Grand Rapids: Eerdmans, 2004). Also see a new three-volume collection of the key works of Rauschenbusch: William H. Brackney, ed., *The Works of Walter Rauschenbusch* (Macon, GA: Mercer University Press, 2018).

12. I worked simultaneously in 2017 on two documents: a lengthy introduction to the ethics of Walter Rauschenbusch, and this presidential address. David P. Gushee, "An Introduction to the Ethics of Walter Rauschenbusch," in Brackney *Works of Walter Rauschenbusch*.

13. Walter Rauschenbusch, *Christianity and the Social Crisis* (Louisville: Westminster John Knox Press, 1991; orig. pub. Macmillan, 1907), 8.

14. Ibid., chaps. 1 and 2.

15. The most mature version of Rauschenbusch's theology of the kingdom is found in *A Theology for the Social Gospel* (Louisville: Westminster John Knox Press, 1997; orig. pub. 1917), 139–45.

16. Walter Rauschenbusch, *The Social Principles of Jesus* (New York: Grosset & Dunlap, 1916).

17. David P. Gushee and Glen H. Stassen, *Kingdom Ethics: Following Jesus in Contemporary Context*, 2nd edition (Grand Rapids: Eerdmans, 2016).

18. Rauschenbusch, *Christianity and the Social Crisis*, 91–92.

19. Ibid., 142.

20. Ibid., 178.

21. Ibid., 159.

22. Ibid., chap. 5.

23. Or economic democracy. Dorrien, *Social Ethics in the Making*, 88–89 and throughout.

24. See David P. Gushee, *The Future of Faith in American Politics: The Public Witness of the Evangelical Center* (Waco, TX: Baylor, 2008).

25. The first book project I ever worked on involved a comprehensive dive into the scholarly and popular works of Reinhold Niebuhr as I assisted Larry L. Rasmussen on his *Reinhold Niebuhr: Theologian of Public Life* (London: Collins, 1989). Niebuhr's four most important books were *Moral Man and Immoral Society* (New York: Scribner's, 1932); *An Interpretation of Christian Ethics* (New York: Harper & Brothers, 1935); and *The Nature and Destiny of Man*, 2 vols. (New York: Scribner's, 1941, 1943). See Robin W. Lovin, *Reinhold Niebuhr and Christian Realism* (Cambridge: Cambridge University Press, 1995); and Robin W. Lovin, *Christian Realism and the New Realities* (Cambridge: Cambridge University Press, 2008).

26. Dorrien, *Social Ethics in the Making*, 268.

27. The only historian of the SCE so far is Edward LeRoy Long Jr. See his *Academic Bonding and Social Concern: The Society of Christian Ethics, 1959–1983* (Saint Cloud, MN: Religious Ethics Incorporated, 1984).

28. On Ryan, see Dorrien, *Social Ethics in the Making*, 185–98; John A. Ryan, *Economic Justice: Selections from Distributive Justice and a Living Wage*, ed. Harlan R. Beckley (Louisville: Westminster John Knox Press, 1996); and David J. O'Brien and Thomas A. Shannon, eds., *Catholic Social Thought: The Documentary Heritage* (Maryknoll, NY: Orbis Books, 1992). More recently, see Christina A. Astorga, *Catholic Moral Theology & Social Ethics: A New Method* (Maryknoll, NY: Orbis Books, 2014), 237–304; and Meghan J. Clark, *The Vision of Catholic Social Thought: The Virtue of Solidarity and the Praxis of Human Rights* (Minneapolis: Fortress Press, 2014).

29. Dorrien, *Social Ethics in the Making*, 534–44.

30. Joseph Cardinal Bernardin, *Consistent Ethic of Life* (Kansas City: Sheed & Ward, 1988).

31. See Ronald J. Sider, *Completely Pro-Life: Building a Consistent Stance* (Downers Grove, IL: InterVarsity Press, 1987).

32. See David P. Gushee, *The Sacredness of Life: Why an Ancient Biblical Idea Is the Key to the World's Future* (Grand Rapids: Eerdmans, 2013).

33. The story of modern evangelical ethics is told by David P. Gushee and Isaac B. Sharp, eds., *Evangelical Ethics* (Louisville: Westminster John Knox Press, 2015), which anthologizes key contributors.

34. Carl F. H. Henry, *The Uneasy Conscience of Modern Fundamentalism* (Grand Rapids: Eerdmans, 1947); Carl F. H. Henry, *Aspects of Christian Social Ethics* (Grand Rapids: Eerdmans, 1964).

35. For Schaeffer, most famously, see Francis Schaeffer, *How Should We Then Live? The Rise and Decline of Western Thought and Culture* (Wheaton, IL: Crossway Books, 1976).

36. An early, seminal work by Jim Wallis was *The Call to Conversion* (San Francisco: Harper & Row, 1981), and a key work from Ron Sider was *Rich Christians in an Age of Hunger* (Downers Grove, IL: InterVarsity Press, 1977). Each has gone on to write dozens of other books.

37. See Stephen Charles Mott, *Biblical Ethics and Social Change* (Oxford: Oxford University Press, 1982); Darryl M. Trimiew, *Voices of the Silenced: The Responsible Self in a Marginalized Community* (Cleveland: Pilgrim Press, 1993); Allen Verhey, *Remembering Jesus: Christian Community, Scripture, and the Moral Life* (Grand Rapids: Eerdmans, 2002) (Verhey was a beloved ethicist in the Dutch Reformed tradition, and this is perhaps his best-known work); and Christine D. Pohl, *Making Room: Recovering Hospitality as a Christian Tradition* (Grand Rapids: Eerdmans, 1999). For Pohl's work on women and evangelicalism, see Nicola Hoggard Creegan and Christine D. Pohl, *Living on the Boundaries: Evangelical Women, Feminism and the Theological Academy* (Downers Grove, IL: InterVarsity Press, 2005).

38. Southwestern Baptist Theological Seminary (SWBTS), in Fort Worth, was and is a massive training ground for Baptist ministers in the Southwest. T. B. Maston was the seminal center-left ethicist at SWBTS. He trained generations of progressive-leaning scholars and pastors. See his *The Christian Church and Contemporary Problems* (Waco, TX: Word Books, 1968).

39. Henlee Barnette was the larger-than-life Christian ethicist who led the progressive wing of the Southern Baptist Theological Seminary faculty from the 1940s through the 1970s. His doctoral dissertation was on Walter Rauschenbusch. See his *Introducing Christian Ethics* (Nashville: Broadman Press, 1961). In a highly controversial move at the time, Barnette invited Martin Luther King Jr. to Southern Seminary the year this book was published.

40. Stanley Hauerwas is the author of over twenty-five books on Christian ethics. His publishing career began in the early 1980s and continues in his purported retirement today. His works that had the deepest impact on me include *A Community of Character: Toward a Constructive Christian Social Ethic* (Notre Dame, IN: University of Notre Dame Press, 1981); *The Peaceable Kingdom: A Primer in Christian Ethics* (Notre Dame, IN: University of Notre Dame Press, 1983); *Resident Aliens: Life in the Christian Colony* (Nashville: Abingdon Press, 1989); and, more recently, *The Work of Theology* (Grand Rapids: Eerdmans, 2015).

41. In personal correspondence with the author, Hauerwas suggests his greater affinity for the Social Gospel than what I suggest in this paragraph, especially in its focus on Jesus and a passion for justice. Still, I believe the claim is accurate in the sense in which I outline it in this paragraph.

42. Hauerwas regularly repeated this claim. One place to see it in print is here: https://peacetheology.net/anabaptist-convictions/hauerwas-on-jhy/. See also Hauerwas, *Work of Theology*, 57.

43. See Stanley Hauerwas, *A Better Hope: Resources for a Church Confronting Capitalism, Democracy, & Postmodernity* (Grand Rapids: Brazos, 2000). His overall challenge of pretty much all the assumptions of liberal modernity, including Enlightenment rationality, free market capitalism, the centrality of the state, patriotism, war, social justice projects, and the valorizing of democracy has won him unlikely friends and foes. The present author sees an interesting connection with the pugnacious "radical orthodoxy" project launched by John Milbank, *Theology & Social Theory: Beyond Secular Reason* (Oxford: Blackwell, 1990), as well as other efforts to recover premodern Christian traditions.

44. Hauerwas opens the door to the continuously surging recovery and reconsideration of Thomas Aquinas and Augustine by Protestants. On the latter, see Eric Gregory, *Politics & the Order of Love: An Augustinian Ethic of Democratic Citizenship* (Chicago: University of Chicago Press, 2008); and Paul J. Griffiths, *Lying: An Augustinian Theology of Duplicity* (Grand Rapids: Brazos, 2004).

45. See Brian Brock and Stanley Hauerwas, *Beginnings: Interrogating Hauerwas*, ed. Kevin Hargarden (London: Bloomsbury / T&T Clark, 2017), 167. On the dying Christendom theme, see also Hauerwas, *Work of Theology*, 113.

46. All kinds of historical figures are being retrieved for consideration in dissertations and monographs. See, e.g., William J. Danaher Jr., *The Trinitarian Ethics of Jonathan Edwards* (Louisville: Westminster John Knox Press, 2004). It is most unlikely that a new Christian ethicist in 1974 would have written such a text.

47. Most introductions to Christian ethics now emphasize Christian character, community, virtue, and other Hauerwasian themes rather than just focusing on contested social problems. See Russell B. Connors Jr. and Patrick T. McCormick, *Character, Choices & Community: The Three Faces of Christian Ethics* (New York: Paulist Press, 1998); Victor Lee Austin, *Christian Ethics: A Guide for the Perplexed* (London: Bloomsbury, 2012); and Timothy F. Sedgwick, *The Christian Moral Life: Practices of Piety* (Grand Rapids: Eerdmans, 1999).

48. Among the scholars who are exploring preliberal political theology to inform a renewed liberal politics or a new postliberal politics are Alasdair MacIntyre, John Milbank, Oliver O'Donovan, Charles Mathewes, and Eric Gregory. See Alasdair MacIntyre: *After Virtue: A Study in Moral Theory*, 2nd edition (Notre Dame, IN: University of Notre Dame Press, 1984); Oliver O'Donovan: *From Irenaeus to Grotius: A Sourcebook in Christian Political Thought*, co-edited with Joan Lockwood O'Donovan (Grand Rapids: Eerdmans, 1999); and Charles Mathewes: *The Republic of Grace: Augustinian Thoughts for Dark Times* (Grand Rapids: Eerdmans, 2010). In a private communication that I have permission to share, Hauerwas took special pride in opening a bridge from Christian ethics to philosophers with religious interests—such as Alasdair MacIntyre and Jeffrey Stout—who specialize in addressing the strained context for meaningful moral conversation that is found in late modernity. Jeffrey Stout, *Ethics after Babel: The Languages of Morals and Their Discontents* (Princeton, NJ: Princeton University Press, 1988).

49. W. E. B. Du Bois, *Darkwater: Voices from within the Veil* (Mineola, NY: Dover, 1999), 17.

50. David P. Gushee, *Changing Our Mind* (Canton, MI: Read the Spirit Books). The first edition appeared in October 2014. Within the year, it was clear that I was no longer welcome in evangelical intellectual life. Within two years, it was clear that my relationship with Jesus Christ and therefore my eternal salvation were in question.

51. See Justin Lee, *Torn* (New York: Jericho Books, 2012); Matthew Vines, *God and the Gay Christian* (New York: Convergent Books, 2014); and endless blogs and articles. Of course, there was already a massive literature on Christian theology, queer theology, and the ethics debate over "homosexuality." I had not seriously engaged it before 2014, though I have done so since then.

52. Beverly Wildung Harrison, *Making the Connections: Essays in Feminist Social Ethics*, ed. Carol S. Robb (Boston: Beacon Press, 1985); see Dorrien, *Social Ethics in the Making*, 421–46.

53. These and other aspect of my biography are discussed in more detail in my *Still Christian: Following Jesus Out of American Evangelicalism* (Louisville: Westminster John Knox Press, 2017).

54. Modern (male) African American Christian ethics could be said to begin with Howard Thurman's *Jesus and the Disinherited* (Boston: Beacon Press, 1996; orig. pub. 1949), then move through Martin Luther King Jr., James Cone, and successor voices of black liberation theology, and then on to Peter Paris, Samuel Roberts, Darryl Trimiew, Riggins Earl Jr., Noel Erskine, Deotis Roberts, and Victor Anderson, with emerging voices today such as Reggie Williams. Much of the most important work related to African American ethics is not actually done by "ethicists" but by historians, theologians, and church leaders.

55. Christian feminist theology and ethics, often identified with the work undertaken by white women, began with radical and liberal voices such as Mary Daly, Beverly Harrison, Sharon Welch, Carter Heyward, Carol Robb, Mary Hunt, and Karen Lebacqz. The first feminist theologian who captured my serious attention was Rosemary Radford Ruether. See her *Women and Redemption: A Theological History* (Minneapolis: Fortress Press, 1998), among other works. (I mainly read her work on Christian anti-Semitism.) More recently, one must identify the massive contribution of Lisa Cahill in multiple areas (family, peace and war, global justice), as well as Margaret Farley in sexual ethics, via her *Personal Commitments: Beginning, Keeping, Changing* (San Francisco: HarperSanFrancisco, 1986). The debate over integrating Christian tradition with feminist commitments today seems most lively in Catholic ethics—e.g., in the work of Cristina Traina and Barbara Hilkert Andolsen. For introductions, see Lois K. Daly, ed., *Feminist Theological Ethics: A Reader* (Louisville: Westminster John Knox Press, 1994); and Susan Frank Parsons, *Feminism and Christian Ethics* (Cambridge: Cambridge University Press, 1996).

56. "Womanist theology/ethics" is the primary term for a major strand of scholarship written from the perspective of African American ethicists and theologians. In ethics, central early

figures included Katie Geneva Cannon, Emilie Townes, Marcia Riggs, and Cheryl Sanders. A bit later came Traci West, Joan Martin, Rosetta Ross, Cheryl Kirk-Duggan, Cheryl Gilkes, Angela Sims, and Stacey Floyd-Thomas. Today's newer voices include Keri Day, Melanie Harris, Shawn Copeland, Monique Moultrie, Thelathia Nikki Young, and Eboni Marshall Turman. For early, seminal works, see Katie G. Cannon, *Black Womanist Ethics* (Atlanta: Scholars Press, 1988), and Emilie Townes, *In a Blaze of Glory: Womanist Spirituality as Social Witness* (Nashville: Abingdon Press, 1995). A key collection is *Womanist Theological Ethics: A Reader*, ed. Katie Geneva Cannon, Emilie M. Townes, and Angela D. Sims (Louisville: Westminster John Knox Press, 2011).

57. Latina/o ethics generally describes ethics written by people of Hispanic origin who live in the United States. Because much Latino/a theology/ethics claims connections to the liberation theology written in the Latin American setting in the 1960s and 1970s, tracing this tradition can be complex. The most prolific Latino ethicist is undoubtedly Miguel A. De La Torre, author of more than thirty books. See his *Doing Christian Ethics from the Margins*, 2nd edition (Maryknoll, NY: Orbis Books, 2014); *Latina/o Social Ethics: Moving Beyond Eurocentric Moral Thinking* (Waco, TX: Baylor University Press, 2010), in which I am called out for ignoring non-European American voices; and my favorite, *The Politics of Jesús: A Hispanic Political Theology* (Lanham, MD: Rowman & Littlefield, 2015). Other pioneering voices within Christian ethics proper include Eldin Villafañe, *The Liberating Spirit: Toward an Hispanic American Pentecostal Social Ethic* (Grand Rapids: Eerdmans, 1993); and Ismael García, *Dignidad: Ethics through Hispanic Eyes* (Nashville: Abingdon, 1997). Latina ethicists include the pioneering Ada María Isasi-Díaz and Maria Pilar Aquino. See Ada María Isasi-Díaz, *Mujerista Theology* (Maryknoll, NY: Orbis Books, 1996); and Ada María Isasi-Díaz, *En La Lucha: A Hispanic Women's Liberation Theology* (Minneapolis: Fortress Press, 1993). Today, leading SCE Latina/o ethicists include, besides those named so far, Rubén Rosario Rodríguez, María Teresa Dávila, Victor Carmona, Teresa Delgado, Robyn Henderson Espinosa, and Nichole Flores.

58. Asian/Asian American ethics has been the last underrepresented group to crystallize in the guild of Christian ethics. Important voices include Grace Ji-Sun Kim, *Embracing the Other: The Transformative Spirit of Love* (Grand Rapids: Eerdmans, 2015); Hak Joon Lee, *The Great World House: Martin Luther King Jr. and Global Ethics* (Eugene, OR: Wipf & Stock, 2017); Hak Joon Lee, *We Will Get to the Promised Land: Martin Luther King Jr.'s Communal-Political Spirituality* (Eugene, OR: Wipf & Stock, 2017); Grace Yia-Hei Kao, *Grounding Human Rights in a Pluralist World* (Washington, DC: Georgetown University Press, 2011); Ilsup Ahn, *Just Debt: Theology, Ethics, and Neoliberalism* (Waco, TX: Baylor University Press, 2017); Jonathan Tran, *The Vietnam War and Theologies of Memory: Time and Eternity in the Far Country* (Malden, MA: Wiley-Blackwell, 2010); and Christina Astorga, *Catholic Moral Theology and Social Ethics: A New Method* (Maryknoll, NY: Orbis Books, 2013). An important collected work is *Asian American Christian Ethics: Voices, Methods, Issues*, ed. Grace Y. Kao and Ilsup Ahn (Waco, TX: Baylor University Press, 2015).

59. Native American Christian ethics is almost unknown, which is sadly symbolic of the tortured relationship between Native Americans and Christianity. George E. ("Tink") Tinker is a visible Native American scholar who relates to, and challenges, Christian ethics. See his *American Indian Liberation: A Theology of Sovereignty* (Maryknoll, NY: Orbis Books, 2008). See also Randy S. Woodley, *Shalom and the Community of Creation: An Indigenous Vision* (Grand Rapids: Eerdmans, 2012).

60. LGBTQ literature is massive and growing, but remarkably little of it has been written thus far by self-identified Christian ethicists. See Patrick S. Cheng, *From Sin to Amazing Grace: Discovering the Queer Christ* (New York: Seabury Books, 2012). As noted, my most extensive engagement with LGBTQ literature to this point is from the current (ex-)evangelical conversation.

61. Thurman, *Jesus and the Disinherited*, viii.

62. John Howard Yoder brought Anabaptist theological and social ethics into the contemporary Christian conversation. His presentation of a Jesus-centered, discipleship-focused, pacifist vision was deeply influential. See his *The Politics of Jesus: Vicit Agnus Noster* (Grand Rapids: Eerdmans, 1972). And it turns out that he was a serial sexual predator who theorized his mistreatment of women as therapeutic experiments in Christian sexual ethics, with offenses of breathtaking duration, scale, scope, and harm, and with persistent, recalcitrant resistance on his part to changing his behavior or facing accountability. See Rachel Waltner Goossen, "'Defanging the Beast': Mennonite Responses to John Howard Yoder's Sexual Abuse," www.bishop-accountability.org/news5/2015_01_Goossen _Defanging_the_Beast.pdf. Hauerwas offered a lengthy reflection on Yoder's sexual misconduct in "In Defence of 'Our Respectable Culture': Trying to Make Sense of John Howard Yoder's Sexual Abuse," ABC Religion and Ethics (Sydney), www.abc.net.au/religion /articles/2017/10/18/4751367.htm. When I saw in the Goossen piece that my teacher Glen Stassen was also involved in premature efforts to return Yoder to good standing in Christian life, this matter hit awfully close to home.

63. Ralph E. Luker, *The Social Gospel in Black and White: American Racial Reform, 1885–1912* (Chapel Hill: University of North Carolina Press, 1991), 316–22; Ronald C. White, *Liberty and Justice for All: Racial Reform and the Social Gospel* (San Francisco: Harper & Row, 1990). Rauschenbusch also had major blind spots when it came to women. See Janet Forsyth Fishburn, *The Fatherhood of God and the Victorian Family: The Social Gospel in America* (Philadelphia: Fortress Press, 1981); Wendy J. Deichmann Edwards and Carolyn De Swarte Gifford, eds., *Gender and the Social Gospel* (Urbana: University of Illinois Press, 2003).

64. American Association of University Professors, "Background Facts on Contingent Faculty Positions," www.aaup.org/issues/contingency/background-facts.

65. SCE, "2020 SCE Committee Report," https://scethics.org/sites/default/files/SCE%20 2020%20Report%20Final_1.pdf.

# Life in the Body: African and African American Christian Ethics

*Eboni Marshall Turman and Reggie Williams*

African and African American Christian ethics comprises an assemblage of disciplines and traditions that address the embodied experiences of black people and provide moral guidance for life in community. Its progenitors helped to establish it as a field of ethical inquiry despite marginalization and hostility and in contrast to dominant ethical traditions that privilege concepts over encounters with embodied life. African and African American Christian ethics privileges embodied encounter as the location for determining a moral hermeneutic in order to recalibrate our understanding of communal relationships toward healthier norms, for the sake of the entire community's survival and wholeness.

IN JANUARY 2018, THE AFRICAN/AFRICAN AMERICAN WORKING Group was asked to give an account of its current status and to offer reflections on the questions guiding the field of African/African American Christian ethics at the annual meeting of the Society of Christian Ethics in Portland, Oregon. The African/African American Working Group was the first working group to form in response to the findings of the SCE's 21st-Century Committee. Its purpose is compelled by three goals: (1) to support the professional development, research, and publications of African/African American Christian ethicists; (2) to convene concurrent sessions and focused interest group discussions at the annual SCE meetings related to African/African American approaches to ethics; and (3) to seek ways to nurture, cultivate, mentor, and support African/African American doctoral students in ethics toward the successful completion of their degrees and first job placements. What follows is the response presented at the January 2018 meeting. The essay prioritizes progenitors of African American Christian ethics,

Eboni Marshall Turman is assistant professor of theology and African American religion, Yale Divinity School, 409 Prospect Street, New Haven, CT 06511; eboni.marshallturman@yale.edu.

Reggie Williams is associate professor of Christian ethics, McCormick Theological Seminary, 5460 South University Avenue, Chicago, IL 60615; rwilliams@mccormick.edu.

*Journal of the Society of Christian Ethics*, 38, 2 (2018): 21–31

whose prominent themes include the moral problem of whiteness, black woman-ist interventions, and intellectual racism. We also point to a necessary moment of resistance within the SCE as a starting point for serious consideration of the import and significance of African American Christian ethics.

## Progenitors and Major Themes

What is important to African American Christian ethicists? At the outset of this discussion, it is significant to note that the category is not homogeneous. The primary strands of African American Christian ethics—historical, politi-cal, ecclesial, and aesthetic—engage distinct methodologies that guide criti-cal analysis. To this end, this field of Christian ethics is an interdisciplinary endeavor that is compelled by the broad traditions of black and black woman-ist theological inquiry. Although the breadth of African American Christian ethics cannot be overstated, several shared emphases are identifiable within its various strands: community, experience, interdisciplinarity, liberation, and hope.

Peter Paris's probing account of the black Christian tradition—that "dis-tinctive principle of coherence which forms the bedrock of black American religious experience"—offers extensive representation and analysis of the afore-mentioned themes.[1] A former president of the SCE (1991), Paris is a progenitor of twentieth-century African American Christian ethics. His most recent vol-ume, *African American Theological Ethics: A Reader*, offers a genealogy of seminal nineteenth- and twentieth-century African American religious scholars that features many of the prominent works of African American Christian ethi-cists (some of which have been included in the bibliography that the African American Working Group composed for the 2018 annual meeting). Given the interdisciplinary nature of African American theological ethics, however, Paris is also careful to note African American scholarship that does not fall within the traditional canon and yet has unquestionably shaped the field. Martin Delaney's *The Origin of Races and Color* (1879); Ida B. Wells-Barnett's *The Red Record and Southern Horrors: Lynch Law in All Its Phases* (1892); Anna Julia Cooper's *A Voice from the South*; W. E. B. Du Bois's *The Souls of Black Folk* (1903); Carter G. Woodson's *The History of the Negro Church* (1921); Benjamin E. Mays's *The Ne-gro's God as Reflected in His Literature* (1938); and E. Franklin Frazier's *The Negro Church in America* (1963), among others, stand as foundational and represen-tative works of scholarship that grapple with African American sociopolitical development, quests for freedom and liberation, and confrontation with con-cepts that undergird white racist pursuits of an idealized society. Their rigorous engagement with common life through the ethical indicators of moral conflict, moral agency, autonomy, political identity, and power have directly aided the formation of religious and moral thought and action that guide historical and contemporary black churches, as well as the many textures of African American Christian ethics.

## The Moral Problem of Whiteness

African American Christian ethics takes embodied life and social encounter as the starting point for determining Christian moral faithfulness. Attempts to give an account of the Christian moral life that minimize or ignore embodied encounter lead to the historical problems of domination and oppression that are characteristic of the formation of white supremacy in the Western world. White supremacy is a compound form of oppression that centers white hetero-patriarchy as the divine ideal around which to build ideal communities. In the academy, white supremacy has been the defining hermeneutic to organize the concept of morality and to press conformity to an abstract, hegemonic idealized figure as the template for both human beings and for the Christian. One's humanity and Christianity are measured in aesthetic proximity to this hegemonic ideal by devotion to abstract concepts and ignoring embodied realities. Within the field of African American Christian ethics, attention to embodied life helps to disrupt hegemonies that would privilege abstract ideals for moral discernment over embodied encounters with real life, to the detriment of historically marginalized people.

Said differently, religious devotion to abstract concepts of morality can be described as remnants of the fall into sin. They are the result of the creature who has become focused on self rather than community and who is obsessed with pursuing individual piety and no longer capable of a seamless relationship with God, fellow humans, and the rest of creation. What remains is a concept of human personhood as autonomous and self-possessed—one that is not designed for social encounter but has been retooled as an enclosed hermeneutical circle of self-reflection, a category of *sicut deus*, or "like God," in possession of the knowledge of good and evil. But this is not actual knowledge of truth; this is reframing reality and relationality. African American Christian ethicists recognize this relational distortion of the pious *sicut deus* as the theo-ethical representation of white supremacy. The Christian claims about God as an autonomous, sovereign figure serve to stabilize a white masculine fetish who, to quote Du Bois, views himself in "ownership of the Earth forever and ever, Amen!"[2] Because the devotion is to abstract concepts of morality, embodied reality offers no filter to the imagination of the white sovereign masculine whose word gave to the world hegemonic ideologies of human difference, describing all of humanity in relationship to himself. Consequently, this white sovereign masculine is the template human; he is the one gifted with the image of God and burdened with the task of saving the world. He is a Christ figure; he crafts a God in his white, masculine, pious image and demands that the world worship him. The theoethical task within African American Christian ethics includes the uncoupling of whiteness and God for the sake of a new anthropological principle that endeavors to remove obstacles that prohibit human capacity for community and right relationship.

For African American Christian ethicists, the Gospel is the good news of liberation for the oppressed, and it emphasizes concrete embodied encounters. Where such a focus is absent, the Gospel is distorted and the corresponding Christian discipleship is harmful. Historically, Christian ethics that ignores embodied encounter has instead privileged abstract concepts and principles as the point of departure for determining the moral life. The result has been theoethical apologetics for violence done to minoritized bodies. African/African American Christian ethics demonstrates that healthy theological ethics works to prioritize the well-being of the community by prioritizing embodied life as the departure point for determining a moral hermeneutic. It does so by attention to the everydayness of social encounter, in a hopeful pursuit of liberation. This makes sense of understanding the way of Jesus as the way of justice, and justice as the content for Christian moral faithfulness.

## Black Womanist Ethics

Over the past thirty-three years, womanist theological ethics has called attention to the voices of black women who are commonly silenced and rendered invisible in the field of Christian ethics. Katie G. Cannon, the matriarch of womanist theological ethics, emphasized the significance of black women as the moral pillars of the black church and community. Black women have historically cultivated and mobilized black life in the United States and throughout the diaspora. Although the current landscape of womanist and black feminist theoethical discourse is enlivened by the work of thinkers like Emilie M. Townes, Traci West, Cheryl Kirk-Duggan, Angela Sims, Stacey Floyd-Thomas, Melanie Harris, and Keri Day, among others, it was Cannon's essay "The Emergence of Black Feminist Consciousness," delivered at the 1985 meeting of the American Academy of Religion, that first highlighted the theological and ethical implications of the interrelationship of white supremacy and male superiority for the lives and life chances of black women.

Womanist ethical inquiry—which was born at the interstices of black women's lived experience, black feminist theory, black liberation theology, and feminist liberation theology and ethics—addresses the "aggravated inequities of the tridimensional phenomenon of race, class, and gender oppression."[3] Cannon's trailblazing work offers a critical hermeneutical intervention to the field of Christian ethics. Building on the literary genius of Alice Walker and Zora Neale Hurston, Cannon's corpus links the triple jeopardy of black women's lived experiences with the struggle for racial justice inherent in the prophetic black church tradition. Having adapted the word "womanist," which first appeared and was defined in Walker's 1983 classic *In Search of Our Mothers' Gardens: Womanist Prose*, Cannon exposed the need to theologically and ethically contend with the compounded and intersectional nature of oppression.[4] A lack of attention to the intersectional nature of oppression renders some bodies invisible. Centering one strand of oppression alone—like race, on one hand, or gender, on the other hand—and ignoring the natural interdigitation of racism, sexism, classism, and heterosexism does not go far enough to address the problem of idealized humanity. It leaves the suffering of the multitudinously jeopardized, whom the womanist systematic theologian Jacquelyn Grant would identify as the oppressed of the oppressed, unaccounted for in the struggle for liberation.[5]

In contradistinction to the monovocality of the experiences of black men and white women, multiple and variegated strands of identity—race, gender, class, and sexuality—are woven together in the lives of black women. Accordingly, it is out of the experience of being simultaneously race, gender, and class subordinated that womanist ethics, grounded in the faith and moral wisdom gleaned from black women's lives, emerges as a corrective to normative Christian ethical discourse working to recalibrate humanity from harmful, hegemonic ideals. It opposes and endeavors to dismantle all oppression, while envisioning and constructing a hope-filled future amid the mandate of survival and the struggle for liberation.

## Racism as Uneven Intellectual Geographies in the SCE

Serious consideration of black womanist justice as the content of Christian witness and moral faithfulness lends itself to a critical assessment of the rationale for the African/African American Working Group in the Society of Christian Ethics. A womanist ethical analysis of the African/African American Working Group employs black feminist thought as a primary theoretical underpinning for the task of black womanist ethics, given the consistent challenges to the value and import of the working group and other clusters that explicitly attend to the intellectual concerns and flourishing of minoritized Christian ethicists. Black womanist ethics helps to highlight the uneven intellectual geographies and the moral problem of the geographic displacement of black intellectual life and discursive territorialization in the SCE. Such intersecting moral dilemmas make sense of the paradox of the working group as both a marginal/ized space *and*, as womanism prescribes, a retreat "for reasons of [black] health."[6]

Engaging the dilemma of discursive territorialization in the SCE through the black feminist lens of Katherine McKittrick also serves to deepen understanding of how marginal, though not *necessarily* marginal, spaces must become *central* to how Christian ethicists across racial/ethnic distinctions know—as much as how the working group is central to how racially minoritized, namely, black and/or African/African American Christian ethicists know—what is really going on.[7]

In her 2008 presidential address to the American Academy of Religion, then-president and womanist ethicist Emilie M. Townes exhorted the academy to "[grow] our scholarship large."[8] Townes contends that such growth is determined by a certain hospitable aptitude that welcomes "new conversation partners" to critically challenge and expand the boundaries of our research, teaching, and service. Such hospitality is not based on the will to "control or dominate—but to allow the richness of insights and experiences beyond what we know and don't know to fill our scholarship with deeper meaning, to beget more piercing analysis, to offer more trenchant critique, [and] to be more relevant to the schools in which we work and the folks who are influenced by what we do."[9]

Although Townes's address intends to underscore the possibilities of interdisciplinarity for the broad tasks of religious and theological inquiry, the ethical challenge and dilemma her comment uncovers for reflection on intradisciplinary fragmentation, and the moral failure it engenders is particularly useful. Such fragmentation recapitulates the texture of *Plessy* ethics—that is, *separate and unequal* ways of being, knowing, and doing that guide our intradisciplinary function as the SCE and that propagate the further marginalization of already minoritized colleagues, who are subject to the structural facts and embodied consequences of racist-sexist-classist and cisheterosexist domination that continue to propel the field, notwithstanding benign intentions and/or oblivious neglect.

One example of this is found in the way in which the African/African American Working Group has been confined to the 8 pm hour of the SCE's annual meeting, with some exceptions, over the past nine years.[10] Based on a recent review of the SCE *Operations Manual* and call for proposals dating back to 2009, society leadership has claimed not to have "found any troublesome inconsistencies in what has been written and published," even while admitting that "our rules in this area are quite complex."[11]

The "quite complex" documentation that outlines current working group policies and practices was presented as long-standing policy to the working groups in February 2018. It clearly indicates that working groups are regularly eligible for daytime concurrent sessions without competitive review. This finding, however, obfuscates what has actually happened with the African/African American Working Group over the past seven years, the length of service of its current co-conveners. Data indicate that over the past seven years, the African/African American Working Group offered three independent concurrent sessions in 2011, 2013, and 2017, respectively. This means that over the past seven years of our tenure as co-conveners, the working group has had three independent daytime sessions and eleven evening sessions after 8 pm. The intellectual terrain has been unevenly structured for African American members of the SCE in ways that mirror the historical experience of minoritized people in the United States more generally.

Here it must be emphasized that though the SCE's policy may in fact state fairly democratic license for working group daytime participation, the practice of the SCE has verbally and actively deviated from its written policy, as noted below. The misalignment of policy and practices is not novel; in fact, the United States is a primary example of how such dissonance regularly occurs in ways that disproportionately and negatively affect minoritized groups. In other words, even as democratic policy, law, and musings can be written on parchment and placed in the Smithsonian next to the Liberty Bell, the fact of the matter is that the African/African American Working Group stands by its claim that what the SCE says it is on paper and what it has done in relation to black Christian ethicists are in fact two different things.

This past year, the practice of disproportionately scheduling working groups in the evening hours was identified as a primary mark of uneven intellectual geography in the SCE, insofar as it actively relegated blacks, Latinx, Asian, queer, and white antiracist colleagues to subaltern spaces on the margins of each conference day. It should be noted that this discriminating practice was highlighted by the African/African American Working Group about two years ago, in 2016.

In light of the challenge that the group presented to the SCE's board in 2016, the working group *was granted permission*, which would not have been necessary if adherence to policy had been actual, to schedule one of its 2017 sessions during daytime hours, alongside concurrent sessions. The working group's subsequent daytime panel, titled "If We Must Die: Christian Ethics and the Politics of Personal Responsibility," was constituted by Emilie M. Townes, the dean of Vanderbilt Divinity School, and Otis Moss III, senior pastor at Trinity United Church of Christ in Chicago, and engaged the problem of state-sanctioned antiblack violence in relationship to the idea that individuals are to be held morally responsible for their life conditions, in order to mine the interstices of personal responsibility and social justice that are often understood to be at odds with each other.

The working group's daytime panel attracted nearly one hundred attendees—relatively unheard-of attendance at a concurrent papers session—and provoked robust conversation on matters of race, violence, and community. In an effort to build on last year's success and the apparent desire of such a diverse contingent of the SCE to be in conversation with the African/African American Working Group, we endeavored to plan the 2017 session, "Chaos or Community? The Black Church Fifty Years after the Assassination of Martin Luther King Jr.," in like fashion. Regrettably, the group was verbally and electronically informed that it could not host a daytime panel as then configured because all the daytime sessions were subject to concurrent session rules. It should be noted that the rule in question had nothing to do with a baseline rejection of the working group from a daytime slot. Rather, it had to do with concurrent session presenters not being able to present two years in a row, because one of the confirmed speakers for the working group had presented in a concurrent papers session the year before.

The African/African American Working Group was faced with this challenge: Either withdraw its invitation from a confirmed panelist or maintain its panel as configured and convene in the evening hour with all the other interest groups. At face value, this might not seem like a major concern at all. The working group, however, is not a concurrent session. The formation of the working group was precipitated by the fact that concurrent sessions demographically favor the dominant group—a group in which numbers were sufficient to enforce a rule that would support representation of a range of voices across the years. Why, then, should the working group be subject to both working group policy and concurrent session policy in ways that representationally tax its constituents above and beyond other SCE members?

The African/African American Working Group is constituted by a small margin of the overall SCE membership. Although initially having been granted permission to break out of the after-hours lineup to more fully integrate into the life of the society and offer minoritized scholars whose scholarly concerns and personal commitments intersect with several interest groups an opportunity to engage in accordance with an assemblage of curiosities, the African/African American Working Group was penalized by rules that never considered the impact, import, and significance of racial minoritization within the society. Such a lack of consideration presumes that it is just and equitable for persons of color—and most especially, for the purposes of this essay, persons of black African descent—to regularly convene outside normal conference hours. During the 2018 annual meeting, vigorous discussion ensued among the executive board concerning these matters that the African/African American Working Group brought to its attention in 2016. Policy has heretofore been changed to reflect a "Working Group exception to the general rule that an SCE member may not present work in plenary and concurrent sessions two years in a row."12 Nevertheless, this one example is representative of the complexities of the tax on minoritized groups within the SCE.

Such displacement highlights the paradox of the African/African American Working Group in its function as both a retreat from the terror of uneven intellectual geography in the SCE—one that offers intellectual space for strategy and critique of the guild—as well as a marginal space.13 It further illumines the challenge of being invited and/or summoned from the garret/retreat to a presidential session to articulate the state of the question in African American Christian ethics. Katherine McKittrick helps to explain this complexity and the paradoxical realities of spatial boundaries and subject knowledge:

> That which is used to geographically displace and regulate black [people] . . . specifically patriarchal ways of seeing and white colonial [desire] for . . . racial-sexual domination, rest on a tight hierarchy of racial power and knowledge that is spatially organized. This organization assumes white masculine knowledge and the logic of visualization, which both work to objectify [minoritized communities] and negate their unique sense of place. For black [people], . . . the logic of visualization and patriarchal knowledge means that her place and body [on the margins] are seen to be and understood as naturally subordinate to whiteness and masculinity; it also means that her seeable presence is crucial to [a white] sense of place.[14]

Black feminist geography underscores, then, the ways in which spatial organization—that is, scheduling, room assignments, space, and the like—are continuous with the objectification of race-gender-sexual subordinates in ways that not only enhance the sense of place for the arbiters of power but also further amplify the dis/placement of others. The capacity to summon persons who have been relegated to the margins corresponds with a long-standing logic of visualization that resonates with the malevolence of the auction block and the stabilizing of an abstract, idealized human. The state of the question for a black womanist Christian ethic, therefore, has not vastly shifted from where the academic project began at the 1985 meeting of the American Academy of Religion—precisely because Cannon's guiding question then, "What makes them treat black people so terrible?" persists now with indubitable relevance.[15] Accordingly, black womanist ethics contends that the African/African American Working Group is not marginal because we want to be; it is marginal because we have to be.

Black womanist ethics presumes misery, suffering, and desolation as the starting point and the strange fruit of the problem of hegemonic anthropology that characterizes dominant branches of Christian ethics. Yet there is something more: a counterlogic of visualization, or what a black womanist ethical aesthetics (emerging from a womanist incarnation ethics) asserts as a *politics of visuality*. This way of seeing arises from the incarnate continuities between the spectacle of Saartjie Baartman, the attic of Linda Brent, the icon of the Memphis strikes, and the lynching of Michael Brown Jr., and contemporarily announces the critical intervention of black womanist ethics—namely, the capacity to see, hear, feel, and/or move in spaces historically designed for black concealment, captivity, and punishment.

In concert with McKittrick, black womanist incarnational ethics and aesthetics further underscores the capacity to resist within hidden spaces from multiple subject positions, even "after hours." The first position of resistance is as a *witness* to injustice, the second position is as an *intellectual activist* in critiquing and undoing oppressive intellectual geographies, and the third position is as a *fugitive* opposing injustice in ways that remain punishable but that "bring herself into being across uneven geographies" regardless.[16] Building on a black feminist analysis of the African/African American Working Group of the SCE as paradoxical space—one that is both a marginal space and a retreat that compels creativity, resistance, and survival amid oppressive institutional structures—a black womanist ethic of visuality asserts a reciprocal gaze that repositions the margin as not-margin, that is, as a concealed yet elevated position that looks outward through pain, freedom, and violence to tell a different story about *what is* and *what ought to be.* This counterperspective that asserts what is really going on, that is, what time of night it is for the African/African American Working Group, naturally antagonizes the fantastic hegemonic imagination of white power and male superiority. Marginalized though we are, the African/African American Working Group, and the SCE's working groups more generally, are the "beat and beating heart," that is, the center of any viable Christian ethical inquiry, even as they remain the last place of which most so-called Christian ethicists think.[17]

The issues to which the SCE's 21st-Century Committee called attention with respect to the needs of the African/African American Working Group persist in our society. We all must attend to the moral problem of whiteness that has historically been manifested within our guild as uneven intellectual geographies, and it is the task of the entire SCE to do so. As a working group, yet facing the stubbornness of marginalization, we press on toward a future for African/African American Christian ethics that prioritizes the development and cultivation of doctoral students and pretenure scholars of African descent in Christian ethics. To this end, in the years ahead the working group intends to formalize a mentoring network that will ensure the continuity of the field, as well as consistent representation on the SCE Board and annual program. The working group is also excited about its plans for an edited volume that definitively attends to the various strands African American Christian ethics—the first of its kind. This volume will serve as a documentary resource for teaching and research, and it will showcase the historical and methodological arcs of the field while gesturing toward the promising futurity of African American Christian ethical inquiry.

## Notes

1. Peter J. Paris, *The Social Teaching of the Black Churches* (Philadelphia: Fortress Press, 1985), xiii–xiv.

2. W. E. B. Du Bois, "The Souls of White Folks," in *Darkwater: Voices from within the Veil* (New York: Dover Thrift Editions, 1999), 18.

3. Katie G. Cannon, *Katie's Canon: Womanism and the Soul of the Black Community* (New York: Continuum, 2002), 56.

4. For the full definition of "womanist," see Alice Walker, *In Search of Our Mothers' Gardens: Womanist Prose* (New York: Harcourt, 1983).

5. Jacquelyn Grant discusses the multiple jeopardies that black women face are subject to in contradistinction to white women, on one hand, and black men, on the other hand. For further treatment of black women as "servants of servants" and/or the oppressed of the oppressed, see Jacquelyn Grant, "The Sin of Servanthood: And the Deliverance of Discipleship," in *A Troubling in My Soul: Womanist Perspectives on Evil and Suffering*, ed. Emilie M. Townes (New York: Orbis Books, 1993), 199–201.

6. In the second part of the "womanist" definition, Alice Walker discusses the significance of black women's occasional retreat—i.e., separation from the larger community—to support perseverance and healthy engagement in the struggle for justice. See Walker, *In Search of Our Mothers' Gardens*.

7. Katherine McKittrick, *Demonic Grounds: Black Women and the Cartographies of Struggle* (Minneapolis: University of Minnesota Press, 2006), 39–40.

8. Emilie M. Townes, "2008 Presidential Address: Walking on the Rimbones of Nothingness: Scholarship and Activism," *Journal of the American Academy of Religion* 3 (2009): 14–15.

9. Ibid.

10. A 2018 study of the society's *Operations Manual* and call for proposals surveyed data collected over a nine-year period, 2009–17, which corresponds to the annual meeting years 2010–18.

11. Society of Christian Ethics, personal e-mail attachment to all the conveners of the working groups, February 12, 2018, 2.

12. Ibid.

13. McKittrick, *Demonic Grounds*, 39.

14. Ibid., 40.

15. Katie G. Cannon, Society for the Study of Black Religion Study Tour video, Salvador de Bahia, Brazil, summer 2011.

16. McKittrick, *Demonic Grounds*, 44. See also the third part of the definition of "womanist" in Walker, *In Search of Our Mothers' Gardens*.

17. See Baby Suggs, "Holy, Sermon in the Clearing," in Toni Morrison *Beloved* (New York: Random House, 2004), 89.

# Asian American Christian Ethics:
# The State of the Discipline

## *Ki Joo (KC) Choi*

This essay provides a brief history of how Asian American Christian ethics came to be and sketches the main themes and questions with which this new theological-ethical discipline has grappled since its inception. It then provides an account of two interrelated issues that continue to shape the development of Asian American Christian ethics: (1) whether there is a distinctive Asian American perspective and (2) how the racial marginalization of Asian Americans in Christian ethics and society as a whole might inform this perspective. This essay proposes that as long as Asian Americans continue to be made invisible as model minorities, the goal of racial and social justice will fall short.

## History

No adequate understanding of where Asian American Christian ethics is today and where it is heading is possible without a brief history of the Asian American Working Group. The Asian American Working Group is the youngest of the three working groups in the Society of Christian Ethics, gaining recognition as an official working group in January 2008, due in large part to the visionary efforts of three members of the society: Christine Pae, Ilsup Ahn, and Grace Kao. They—along with Jonathan Tran, Sharon Tan, Irene Oh, and myself, and then Hoon Choi, Christina Astorga, and Hak Joon Lee—formed the core of the regular working group's membership, and we were all motivated by a desire to establish a supportive social space for Asian American members of the society. To make good on this desire for community, the working group has endeavored to form a distinctive working group culture by rotating leadership positions, being mindful of gender representation, and gathering for meals in order to network (a practice that reflects the central role that food plays in the ethnic communities and immigrant churches from which many of the working group members come from).

Ki Joo (KC) Choi, PhD, is associate professor and chair of the Department of Religion at Seton Hall University, Fahy Hall 326, 400 South Orange Avenue, South Orange, NJ 07079; kijoo.choi@shu.edu.

*Journal of the Society of Christian Ethics*, 38, 2 (2018): 33–44

This desire for community was coupled by a collective desire to assert ourselves as Asian American Christian ethicists (and not simply Christian ethicists who happen to be Asian American). But what it meant to do Asian American Christian ethics was hardly obvious. That was due in part to the fact that Asian American Christian ethics as a mode of theological-ethical inquiry did not really exist before the establishment of our working group in 2008. Although theological and biblical inquiry from Asian American perspectives gained increasing visibility through the works of noted scholars such as Peter Phan, SJ, Kwok Pui-Lan, Andrew Sung Park, Sang Hyun Lee, Rita Nakashima Brock, and Chung Hyun Kyung, theological ethics that is Asian American had hardly any forebears. Though we utilized the work of our colleagues in theology and biblical studies as points of departure, consensus on what it meant to do Asian American Christian ethics proved elusive other than a general agreement that our experiences as Asian Americans mattered and that we as a working group needed to play an essential part in the society's goal of supporting the work of ethicists of color.

The lack of consensus provided a great degree of freedom to explore and experiment. Our collective discernment of what the method and content of Asian American Christian ethics should be engendered a diversity of concurrent sessions and evening meetings, especially during our earlier years. We organized a panel on the relevance of Reinhold Niebuhr in Asian and Asian American contexts, and another panel on the prospects of Asian American public theology. At the annual meeting in Seattle, we critically engaged Brian Bantum's work on theology and race (the "new black theology"). In New Orleans in 2011, two of our working group colleagues, Christine Pae and James W. McCarthy III, explored the concept of Asian American hybridity. And on our working group's fifth anniversary in 2013, we organized a concurrent session on the future of Asian American Christian ethics from the perspective of various liberation theologies.

## The Birth of Asian American Christian Ethics

The question of what it might mean to do Asian American Christian ethics was not addressed in any sustained and systematic manner, at least not in writing, until Kao and Ahn led the charge to develop an edited volume titled *Asian American Christian Ethics: Voices, Methods, Issues* (Waco, TX: Baylor University Press, 2015). To facilitate the how and what of Asian American Christian ethics, Kao and Ahn proposed that all thirteen contributors to the edited volume begin by mapping the ways in which Christians ethics in general approaches a particular ethical question and then articulate how an Asian American perspective might inform that general Christian ethical approach. This way of proceeding proved highly valuable, producing Asian American perspectives on virtue ethics, racial solidarity, war and peace, gender and sexuality, the family, environment, health care, cosmetic surgery, immigration, economics, and education.

Although the publication of the edited volume was pivotal in mobilizing Asian American ethicists and inaugurating Asian American ethics as a formal discipline of theological-ethical inquiry, the edited volume also proved valuable in challenging the working group to address certain methodological and thematic issues that we as a group tended to tackle indirectly. For instance, though one aim of the edited volume was to underscore the immense plurality of Asian American perspectives on a number of theological-ethical issues, that plurality has raised the question of whether we can speak of only Asian American experiences or whether there is also such a thing as the Asian American experience. This question underscores the central challenge that the working group continues to discern: What does it mean to do ethics in a manner that is distinctively Asian American?

The question of whether there is a distinctive Asian American perspective is far from straightforward. Just surveying the wild cultural diversity and differences of Asian Americans underscores the complexity of this question. Although some of us have reflected on the import of Confucian virtues for mainstream Christian ethics, it is still an open question as to whether such "traditional" values cut across the diversity of Asian cultures.[1] It is worth noting that our working group's members, though identifying collectively as Asian Americans, are also by descent Korean, Japanese, Vietnamese, Taiwanese, Filipina, Chinese, and Sri Lankan, and some are also multiethnic and multiracial. As such, our members hail from nationalities and ethnic heritages that are not necessarily similar or complementary. For example, though many Hispanic Americans might be able to, at the very least, turn to Spanish as a common cultural base point, a similar recourse is not available to Asian Americans. This fact alone should disabuse pop culture assumptions that Asian Americans can be easily grouped together, even though many of us share common morphological features. As entertaining (or not) as the ABC sitcom *Fresh Off the Boat* or K-Dramas might be, let us be clear: Not all Asian Americans are Chinese, Taiwanese, or Korean.

But even if we were able to identify so-called traditional cultural practices and beliefs that Asian Americans share, whether those cultural base points are actually indicators of a common Asian American experience is complicated by *how* Asian Americans culturally appropriate ancestral heritages. For many Asian Americans, our cultural lives reflect deeply selective and re-creative appropriations of our ancestral heritages.[2] In other words, Asian Americans, rather than being wholly defined by our ancestral heritages, are, more accurately, in constant conversation with our ancestral heritages depending on our social location, influences, and interests. Thus, one cannot expect to find Asian Americans appropriating common, traditional cultural practices in the same manner, for the same purposes, and with the same meanings, if they are appropriating ancestral practices at all.

## Asian American Marginalization: Being Put in Our Place

The debate over what "Asian American" means in the midst of our cultural diversity is ongoing. There is, however, a growing consensus that wherever the discussion of our cultural selves goes, at the very least it must come to grips with the reality of our racial marginalization. I believe that our growing willingness to speak more intentionally and confidently about our social marginalization is long overdue.

That many Asian Americans actually experience marginalization may come as a surprise to non-Asians in light of the rapidly growing numbers of Asian Americans in the United States,[3] and the striking educational and economic affluence of Asian Americans.[4] Yet the so-called success of Asian Americans—that is, the assimilation and mainstreaming of Asian Americans—has a deeply insidious side. For instance, as a consequence of Asian American success (however it is defined), Asian Americans often find it difficult to escape the characterization of being "model minorities" by mainstream American society. Although such an ascription might be perceived as a compliment—look how hard working, industrious, and smart Asian Americans are!—that so-called honorific of being model minorities in fact serves to manipulate how Asian Americans are to perceive ourselves and "behave" in American society.

As model minorities, Asian Americans have not only made it but, in so doing, are more like "Americans," the subtext being that Asian Americans are, therefore, not like "them," namely, African Americans and Hispanics. To some extent, Asian Americans have not necessarily resisted this association. But whatever the reasons underlying that lack of resistance, and whatever benefits Asian Americans believe (or have been led to believe) are gained by assimilating into (and maybe even aspiring for) whiteness or the white ideal of American life, assimilation into whiteness (or, at the very least, buying into the myth that we are model minorities) has as a group rendered us deferential to our white benefactors, who deserve our gratitude for providing opportunities to pursue the American dream. As such, not only are Asian Americans expected to be held accountable to (that is, measured by) the prevailing mores and lifestyle standards of mainstream American life (both religious and secular), we are also to display a level of respect for these standards, whether they are just or unjust. (In fact, the question of whether American society is just or unjust is not something we have the right to raise as long as we are bestowed the privileges of white America by virtue of our model minority status.)

Thus, in working to map the cartography of our marginalization, especially the social effects of the model minority myth and its various permutations, a growing number of members within the Asian American Working Group are increasingly confronting the ways in which American racial discourse and racism play a surreptitious role in disciplining our embodied existence by, in a matter of speaking, putting us in our place. To put us in our place as model minorities—to be disciplined into a kind of quiet submission to the prevailing ideals and norms of race and personhood—preempts our capacity to determine our own agency and what it means to be full participants in American society. Instead, to be pegged as model minorities means that who we are as Asian Americans is always on someone else's terms.

## Being Invisible to Non-Asian Americans

But this role of disciplining Asian American bodies is not simply one of white racism subduing or domesticating Asian Americans. Rendering Asian Americans as model minorities (or, more precisely, as "almost" white) also functions to discipline African Americans and Hispanics by manipulating their perceptions of Asian Americans as "other"—as socially different from them.

The perceived social distances between African American and Latinx communities on the one side and Asian American communities on the other play out on at least a couple of levels. One level is overt conflict, for instance, in the tensions that boiled over into street protests between African Americans and Asian Americans before and after the February 11, 2016, conviction of a Chinese American New York City police officer, Peter Liang, for the accidental shooting death of Akai Gurley, an African American, in a Brooklyn housing project on November 20, 2014.[5] The 1991 Los Angeles riots also come to mind in this context. One worry is that such tensions and conflict provide fodder for white supremacist ideologies. Consider Dylan Roof, the white supremacist terrorist who killed nine African Americans in a Charleston, South Carolina, church, who looked to Asian Americans as potential allies in the hoped-for race war between white supremacists and African Americans.

Another level on which the perceived social distances between African Americans and Asian Americans plays out is in a kind of resentful idealization of Asian Americans. An anecdote from my own institution, Seton Hall University, is illustrative. In response to Ferguson, a student-driven town hall meeting was held to discuss the state of racial affairs in the United States. I found it interesting, if not troubling, that one of the African American students in attendance stood up and observed with some exasperation that Asian Americans, maybe because of our various social successes, have achieved safety, and thus are rarely the subject of racial discrimination. But this sort of perception—or mythologizing of Asian American inclusion and acceptance into mainstream American life—plays right into the hands of the divide-and-conquer dynamic of white racism: The regime of whiteness is more secure if social inequalities are regarded more as a function of personal failings rather than discriminatory practices and policies. Just look at Asian Americans, who have through their own efforts attained success and inclusion—if they can do it "on their own," then all persons of color can do it, and shame on those who have not worked to "earn it."

But the fact of the matter is that Asian Americans are not as secure, successful, and socially accepted as some non-Asians might be led to believe. Consider first that real economic adversity and inequality afflict Asian Americans, just as they do many non-Asian Americans. This reality is skewed by a myopic perception of Asian Americans through an East Asian lens. Although Asian Americans overall do well on many measures of economic well-being, when Asian Americans are viewed in their full ethnic diversity, many—especially Bangladeshi, Hmong, Nepalese, and Burmese Americans "have household incomes well below the median household incomes for all Americans" and "poverty rates higher than the US average."[6] But the realities of Asian American poverty and economic disadvantage are essentially unseen—nonexistent, really—in mainstream racial discourse by virtue of our collective status as so-called model minorities.

Also consider the issue of policing and Asian Americans. Although discriminatory policing in many black and Latinx communities is certainly an endemic problem and rightly receives sustained media attention, it is also the case that Asian Americans are not immune from policing biases if the cases of Kuanchang Kao, Cau Bich Tran, and Fong Lee are any indications.[7] These are hardly household names such as Michael Brown and Freddie Gray, but one wonders whether they would be if mainstream media paid more attention and approached racial injustice beyond a dogmatic black/white lens. Perhaps then, in addition to policing, there would be greater public outrage over the hundreds of documented cases of hate crimes against Asian Americans since January 2017.

Finally, though the concerns over the revocation of the Deferred Action for Childhood Arrivals (DACA) program typically center on those from Central and South America, the issue of deportations is also very much an Asian American issue, considering that 10 percent of DACA recipients are Asian American,[8] and 13 percent of the 1.1 million unauthorized immigrants who live in the United States are Asian Americans.[9]

Although it goes virtually unnoticed in mainstream public discourse, Asian Americans have been at the center of immigration debates since at least the Chinese Exclusion Act of 1882. To encourage the passage of that act, the Irish immigrant Denis Kearney, who founded the Workingmen's Party of California, described the Chinese as "cheap slaves," "contemptible," "docile and mean" people, who "hedge twenty in a room." Kearney called for an all "American" California, lest the US become totally Chinese.[10] Can we not in these words from Kearney hear resonance with how immigrants from Latin America are described in our current politics? These words continue to apply to Asian Americans as well.

For Asian Americans today, the legacy of Kearney's words—that call to exclude Asians from America's shores—finds both subtle and blatant expression in the persistent stereotyping of Asian Americans as chopstick-wielding, kung fu–fighting, ching-chong-speaking, slanted-eyed, curry-smelling foreigners. Also recall the internment of Japanese Americans during World War II. More recently, consider the case of the school board election for the town of Edison, New Jersey, where campaign postcards were found with the slogan "Make Edison Great Again," "The Chinese and Indians are taking over our town. . . . Enough is Enough!" And just in case the message of the postcard remained obscure, the word "DEPORT" was stamped on the pictures of the two Asian Americans running for the Edison school board.[11]

The persistent regard for Asian Americans as "other" cuts across Asian American demographics and underscores the paradox of being model minorities. Although Asian Americans are often touted as one of the more successfully integrated minority populations in the US, Asian Americans are at the same time hardly immune from economic and political marginalization. Add to that various modes of cultural marginalization, such as in the whitewashing of Asian American characters in Hollywood,[12] the sexual objectification and fetishization of Asian American women, or the emasculation of Asian American men.[13] It is that paradox of Asian American life that is invisible, reflecting the extent to which the model minority myth constitutes an effectively deceptive strategy of diluting, if not generally sequestering, the realities and harms of racial prejudice and stereotyping for Asian Americans from non–Asian American consciousness.

## Being Invisible and the Poverty of Contemporary Racial Discourse

The consequences of Asian Americans' collective invisibility—the invisibility of their racial marginalization—are significantly felt in contemporary racial discourse. Take the current concerns over diversity (or lack thereof) in the corporate workplace as a case in point. To be sure, recent calls for greater racial diversity in, for instance, the high-technology industry are appropriate. However, to observe that the tech industry is primarily white and, to a degree, Asian American as evidence for the racial biases and discrimination that pervades companies such as Google, Facebook, and Apple underscores the extent to which Asian Americans are regarded as either ancillary to the larger struggle for racial justice or, worse, part of the problem. Either way, by focusing on the underrepresentation of African Americans and Hispanics and the overrepresentation of Asian and white Americans, the call for diversity, though critically important, also becomes a hindrance to the goal of racial justice in the workplace.

If Asian Americans are indeed overrepresented, what is often avoided is the question of why so few Asian Americans hold executive-level positions.[14] Also avoided is the more difficult question of why Asian Americans feel compelled to gravitate toward the sciences and technology fields and find it necessary to achieve perfect GPAs and SAT scores. These decisions can hardly be explained by insisting that Asian Americans possess an extraordinary aptitude for mathematics and science, unless we want to accept as true the ridiculous notion that African Americans are "naturally" not good at math and science, which would explain why they are underrepresented in the tech sector and sciences. But tenacious perceptions of Asian Americans as intellectually gifted speaks directly to how Asian American life continues to be shaped and curtailed by larger racialized perceptions of Asian Americans as model minorities. Asian Americans are entitled to the privileges of American life only if we prove ourselves worthy by working harder than anyone else—black, brown, or white. Those racialized rules of the game not only engender a false sense of merited success and full societal inclusion but also mask the kind of racialized dynamic that seeks to (misleadingly) isolate Asian Americans from the plight of the racially afflicted.

If the model minority myth hides the realities of Asian American marginalization in our contemporary racial discourse, one growing worry among Asian American Christian ethicists is whether we are also in effect invisible within discussions on race in the Society of Christian Ethics, or the theological academy more generally. That is in part the reason why the Asian American Working Group formed in the first place, in response to the sentiment that the increasing presence of Asian American members of the Society of Christian Ethics was not being adequately acknowledged and represented in the larger push for racial diversity within the society. (Incidentally, this reminds me of the time when a non-Asian member of the society, after noticing a group of us from the Asian American Working Group gathering in the lobby as we prepared to go out to dinner, remarked to me in amazement that there were so many Asian Americans in the society. I guess we are noticed only when we gather en masse.)

This desire for greater visibility is not to suggest that we Asian American ethicists are looking to play victim, or to claim that our social situation is equal to the injustices experienced within non-Asian communities of color in the hope that non-Asian Americans will feel some modicum of guilt for perhaps not "noticing" how we are racially disciplined. And it is really not about wanting greater representation on governing boards, or a demand for our work to be cited more often (although that would be welcome). Rather, this desire for visibility—to make visible the extent to which Asian Americans are generally invisible—is the desire to call attention to a more complete picture of how white racism operates. In other words, it is when we pay attention to how the so-called honorific of model minorities marginalizes and essentially erases Asian Americans as Asian Americans that we are then afforded a larger window into the poverty of our current racial discourse, wherein the hyperfocus on black-white relations is perhaps the starkest symptom of that poverty.

That in no way should be taken to diminish the kinds of discrimination that afflict non-Asian communities of color at the expense of making Asian American struggles more visible. But our racial discourse, insofar as it is oftentimes singularly defined within black/white parameters, risks false or, at best, incomplete responses to the problem of racial injustice. If indeed the strategy of the model minority myth is to herd Asian Americans to the side of white America, then racial justice requires a profound recognition of how American racism serves not only to normalize the divides between white and black communities but also serves to normalize the divides (whether real or perceived) within communities of color (if not to create and maintain new divisions) as a means of bolstering the privilege of whiteness in society.

White racism, therefore, is not simply racism against black persons but, more insidiously, it seeks to isolate black persons from other persons of color. The model minority myth underscores that strategy of racial partition and subjugation. In this respect, it is simply inadequate to recognize the sin of white privilege and racism as predominantly a sin against black persons or the sin of antiblackness. Alternatively, it is simply inadequate to see racial justice as predominantly a call for reconciliation and solidarity between white and black communities, for such a narrow demand, in continuing to ignore the racial realities of Asian Americans, is in effect conceding (and, dare I say, enabling) the "territorial gains" over Asian bodies by the ideology of whiteness in its unchallenged rendering of Asian Americans as model minorities. In this case, racial justice is less about dismantling the white racial imagination in its totality than it is simply about limiting its colonizing reach.

## The Future of Asian American Christian Ethics

The increasing focus on Asian American racial marginalization and invisibility represents a critical trajectory in the ongoing study and development of Asian American Christian ethics. And confronting how the model minority myth continues to delimit Asian American agency and advance racial hierarchies will, for sure, be an important part of this trajectory. But excavating a fuller picture of how Asian Americans are racially disciplined, both within and outside our churches, will require more than focusing on Asian Americans as model minorities; additional racial concepts such as passing—the practice of nonwhite persons passing as white in a predominantly white society—may prove valuable.[15]

Asian American Christian ethics will also need to map strategies of resistance and empowerment. An important part of this task will be learning from the stories of Asian American civil rights activists such as Yuri Kochiyama.[16] It will also involve a more serious theological imagination, by which I mean the task of developing robust theological interpretations of our present situation as racially disciplined persons. Such theological interpretations are necessary if we hope to empower strategies of liberation that are distinctively Christian rather than simply veiled appropriations of the prevailing proposals of our deeply sorted and polarizing politics.[17]

Our work in excavating Asian American experiences of white racism and moving toward the construction of theological responses will be for naught, however, if this work is regarded as simply for the benefit of Asian Americans. That would be an unfortunate outcome, not only for Asian Americans but also for all non-Asian ethicists.

If the racial disciplining of Asian American life tells us anything, it is at least the proposition that white racism benefits, and maybe even flourishes, when Asian Americans are ignored. When Asian Americans are ignored (i.e., continue to be invisible because, after all, Asian Americans have made it; we are model minorities), white racism continues to succeed in dividing, isolating, and, ultimately, disempowering all persons of color. Less secure is the privilege of whiteness when all persons of color are able to identify with each other's experiences and stand in solidarity with one another; this is why it is beneficial when Asian Americans are made invisible, which effectively excludes or disqualifies Asian Americans from being relevant voices in contemporary discussions on race.

But if we are to move closer to dismantling white racism and privilege, we will then need to develop the capacity to identify with one another's experiences and learn from them. This will depend in part on whether we Asian American ethicists are able to confront our own racialization. It will also equally depend on whether non-Asian ethicists, whether African American or Latinx, as well as ethicists who are of white Anglo-European descent, are willing to undergo their own radical conversion of vision, a conversion that opens them up to a more truthful construal of Asian American life rather than the one that has been (successfully) peddled to non-Asians by the white racial imagination. If non-Asian ethicists are able to imagine us only as model minorities, then our racial discourse and struggle for racial justice will ultimately go nowhere.

## Notes

I thank the Asian American Working Group for entrusting me to represent our experiences, perspectives, and contributions. Special thanks to Grace Y. Kao for reading this essay at the annual meeting in Portland, Oregon.

1. E.g., see Ilsup Ahn, "Virtue Ethics," in *Asian American Christian Ethics: Voices, Methods, Issues*, ed. Grace Y. Kao and Ilsup Ahn (Waco, TX: Baylor University Press, 2015), 63–84.

2. See Ki Joo (KC) Choi, "After Authenticity: Clarifying the Relevance of Culture as a Source of Moral Reflection in Asian American Christian Ethics," *Journal of Race, Ethnicity, and Religion* 7, no. 2 (August 2016): 1–30.

3. Kate Linthicum, "Asians to Surpass Latinos as Largest Immigrant Group in US, Study Finds," *Los Angeles Times*, September 22, 2015.

4. Pew Research Center, "Key Facts about Asian Americans, a Diverse and Growing Population," September 8, 2017, www.pewresearch.org/fact-tank/2017/09/08/key-facts-about-asian-americans/.

5. See, e.g., David Swanson, "Thousands in Philadelphia Protest the Conviction of NYPD Officer Peter Liang," *Philadelphia Inquirer*, February 20, 2016, www.philly.com/philly/blogs/real-time/Thousands-in-Philadelphia-protest-conviction-of-NYPD-officer-Peter-Liang.html.

6. Pew Research Center, "Key Facts about Asian Americans." Cf. Irene Oh, "Education and Labor," in Kao and Ahn *Asian American Christian Ethics* (Waco, TX: Baylor University Press, 2015), 235; and Christina A. Astorga, "Wealth and Prosperity," in Kao and Ahn *Asian American Christian Ethics*, 121–22.

7. Jack Linshi, "Why Ferguson Should Matter to Asian Americans," *Time*, November 26, 2014, http://time.com/3606900/ferguson-asian-americans/.

8. Chris Lu, "What We Miss When We Ignore Asian Americans," *Time*, October 20, 2017, http://time.com/4992021/asian-americans-pacific-islanders-representation/.

9. Pew Research Center, "Key Facts about Asian Americans."

10. Dennis Kearney and H. L. Knight, "Appeal from California: The Chinese Invasion—Workingmen's Address," *Indianapolis Times*, February 28, 1878, cited in "'Our Misery and Despair': Kearney Blasts Chinese Immigration," History Matters, http://historymatters.gmu.edu/d/5046.

11. Jeff Goldman and Craig McCarthy, "Racist 'Make Edison Great Again' Mailer Targets Asian School Board Candidates," *NJ.com*, November 2, 2017, www.nj.com/middlesex/index.ssf/2017/11/racist_campaign_posctards_being_mailed_in_edison.html.

12. Christina B. Chin, Meera E. Deo, Faustina M. DuCros, Jenny Jong-Hwa Lee, Noriko Milman, and Nancy Wang Yuen, "Tokens on the Small Screen: Asian Americans and Pacific Islanders in Prime Time and Streaming Television," www.aapisontv.com/uploads/3/8/1/3/38136681/aapisontv.2017.pdf.

13. See Hoon Choi, "Sexuality and Gender," in Kao and Ahn *Asian American Christian Ethic*, 27–28.

14. This is especially so in the legal profession. See Tracy Jan, "Law Schools Are Filled with Asian Americans, So Why Aren't There More Asian Judges?," *Washington Post*, July 18, 2017, www.washingtonpost.com/news/wonk/wp/2017/07/18/there-are-94-united-states-attorneys-only-three-of-them-are-asian-american/?noredirect=on&utm_term=.66391255376b.

15. See Ki Joo (KC) Choi, "Passing While Asian: A Proposal for Asian American Theology and Ethics," paper presented at Colloquium on Asian American Theology: Promise and Challenge, Princeton Theological Seminary, Princeton, NJ, April 5, 2017.

16. See Grace Y. Kao, "The Life Witness of Yuri Kochiyama: Three Lessons for Asian American Christians," paper presented at Colloquium on Asian American Theology: Promise

and Challenge, Princeton Theological Seminary, Princeton, NJ, April 5, 2017. Also see Grace Y. Kao, "Setting the Captives Free: Yuri Kochiyama (1921–2014)," in *Can I Get a Witness? The Forgotten Tradition of Radical Christianity in America*, ed. Charles Marsh, Shea Tuttle, and Daniel Rhodes (Grand Rapids: Eerdmans, forthcoming in 2019).

17. See Jonathan Tran, "Moral Innovation and Ambiguity in Asian American Christianity," paper presented at Colloquium on Asian American Theology: Promise and Challenge, Princeton Theological Seminary, Princeton, NJ, April 5, 2017.

# US Latino/a Contributions to the Field: Retrospect and Prospect

*Rubén Rosario Rodríguez, María Teresa Dávila,*
*Victor Carmona, and Teresa Delgado*

The 2018 SCE meeting focused on the theme "Retrospect and Prospect" in order to build greater understanding of the discipline of Christian ethics in its varied cultural, methodological, and confessional forms. Latino/a ethics in the United States, by embodying a cooperative methodology (*teología en conjunto*) grounded in a liberative reading of the Christian Scriptures that employs a hermeneutics of suspicion, seeks to articulate an emancipatory and inclusive vision that yields distinctive forms of social and political action while working toward the common good. This essay provides a brief introduction to and history of Latino/a contributions to the field of Christian ethics, defines key themes that unite its various proponents, and identifies future trends.

## Introduction, *by Rubén Rosario Rodríguez*

David Gushee, president of the Society of Christian Ethics (SCE), has challenged our guild to take a long hard look back, assess the present, and then set an agenda for the future "in order to build greater mutual understanding of each other and of the history, current state, and potential future of our field, in all its complexity."[1] To this end, the Latino/a Working Group has been invited to provide a brief introduction to and history of Latino/a contributions to the field, define key themes that unite its various proponents, and identify future

Rubén Rosario Rodríguez is associate professor of theological studies, Saint Louis University, 300 Clion Lane, Saint Louis, MO 63141; ruben.rosariorodriguez@slu.edu.

María Teresa Dávila is a lecturer on theology and religious studies, Merrimack College, 17 Division Street, Malden, MA 02148; mariatdavila@gmail.com.

Victor Carmona is assistant professor of theology and religious studies, University of San Diego, Maher Hall #297, 5998 Alcalá Park, San Diego, CA 92110; vcarmona @sandiego.edu.

Teresa Delgado is department chair and associate professor of theology and ethics, Department of Religious Studies, Iona College, 715 North Avenue, New Rochelle, NY 10801; tdelgado@iona.edu.

*Journal of the Society of Christian Ethics*, 38, 2 (2018): 45–56

trends within our movement. Because Latino/a ethics embodies a cooperative methodology, four members of the working group present *en conjunto*—that is, we present as an ensemble—thereby reflecting a commitment to solidarity while also honoring the diversity within our community.

## Shared Themes of Latino/a Moral Reasoning

In the North American context, US Latino/a theology and ethics stand as a vibrant example of a contextual approach that engages the dominant modern (and postmodern) paradigms in critical discourse while articulating an alternative mode of Christian thought in which the particularities of culture are respected, yet no one manifestation of Christianity becomes normative. So, though the discipline of Christian ethics has done much to address the demographic shifts transforming North American Christianity, including efforts by the SCE to foster cultural and racial diversity, most Latino/a ethicists and scholars of religion still approach the discipline of Christian ethics with hermeneutical suspicion in great part because of the discipline's primarily white, male, and Eurocentric canon. Nowhere is this more evident than in the nominal presence of racial-ethnic faculty in theological education. In 1999, the percentage of Latino/a full-time faculty in Association of Theological Schools (ATS) member schools was about 4 percent. In 2011 that number hovered at under 4 percent. In 2017 the number of Latino/a faculty in ATS member schools has reached 5 percent.[2] An improvement? Perhaps, but given that Latino/as now constitute the single-largest ethnic minority population in the United States (58.6 million in 2017, or over 18 percent of the total population) while remaining the smallest racial/ethnic group among ATS faculty, maybe not.[3]

This stark reality is very noticeable within Christian ethics, where only a handful of Latino/a scholars—Ismael García (now retired), Ada María Isasi-Díaz (who passed away in 2012), Eldin Villafañe, Michael Manuel Mendiola (who passed away in 2008), and Miguel A. De La Torre (the 2012 SCE president)—have reached a level of national prominence in the field. Many factors account for the dearth of Latino/as in our guild, including documented patterns of discrimination that have historically excluded racial-ethnic minorities from the mainstream academy, the multidisciplinary approach employed by most Hispanic scholars of religion, and the relatively small body of literature articulating a distinctly Latino/a Christian ethics. Although there are few Latino/a scholars working within the field of Christian ethics (there is a growing but still small number of rising scholars and graduate students being mentored through the Latino/a Working Group of the SCE), almost *all* Hispanic scholars of religion, regardless of area of specialization, engage the ethical in their work. Accordingly, there is a forty-year history of Latino/a religious scholarship that can serve as a resource for constructing a distinctly Latino/a Christian ethics.

Our goal is to provide a brief overview of the existing literature in order to identify key figures, major themes, methodological contributions, and pressing moral concerns that distinguish Hispanic moral reasoning in the United States for the new millennium.

To facilitate a discussion of US Latino/a contributions to Christian ethics, it is useful to identify certain recurring themes within the work of Latino/a religion scholars that locate this movement at the margins—yet still within—the Western Christian tradition. First, US Latino/a theologians identify *revelation*—not scripture—as the primary source of Christian theology, affirming a liberative reading that "takes the Bible into its own hands and away from those in control of the present order, reading it from its own perspective rather than from the perspective of the powerful."[4] Second, US Latino/a religion scholars affirm the role of *culture* as an important source for theology: "All human reality is historical *and* cultural. All that is human and all who are human occur and live always within culture, and cannot ever be a-cultural. Culture, therefore, is a context we cannot avoid or even imagine to escape. We are only and always in culture."[5] A third locus of Latino/a theologizing centers on *popular religion*, the concrete religious practices of the people of God arising independently and often in resistance to the institutional church. Nevertheless, Latino/a theologians also affirm a fourth locus: *tradition* as a normative source in Christian theology. However, as a corrective against the tendency to universalize particular points of view, Latino/a theology remains methodologically committed to intercultural dialogue for attaining maximal understanding between different peoples. A fifth and final concern uniting most Latino/a scholars of religion is a commitment to *liberative social ethics*.

The implications for ethical methodology are clear. Christian ethics from a Latino/a perspective begins with an intentional act of solidarity with, by, and for the poor, marginalized, and disenfranchised. Not only does this faith commitment entail a critique of the dominant political and economic structures, but it also involves questioning the dominant Eurocentric paradigms that govern the academic study of ethics. Quite simply, the Eurocentric narrative that establishes supposedly color-blind, universal, and objective ethical norms reflects a hermeneutical naïveté that fails to account for the interestedness of its own point of view. When the dominant point of view is racist, sexist, and classist, fine-tuning existing models of ethical analysis cannot overcome prevailing structural inequities. Some form of revolutionary praxis is called for.

## Forebears in Latino/a Ethical Thought, *by María Teresa Dávila*

"Latino/a theology is interdisciplinary in its methodology as well as justice seeking in its epistemology."[6] Grounded on the preferential option for the poor, Latino/a ethics arises from the shared experiences of immigration, social and cultural invisibility, economic dislocation, legal persecution, and political vulnerability. At the same time, religious celebration and sustenance, strong family and community bonds, a profound sense of justice that is intergenerational and expansive to other groups, activism, ingenuity, a strong work ethic, and an indefatigable spirit shape the Latino/a experience and theological imagination. "Key themes such as *mestizaje*, *la lucha*, *teología en conjunto*, *acompañamiento*, and *dignidad*, became the pioneering expressions of theologians and ethicists daringly proposing to the theological academy that the Latino/a experience is a valid, important, and fruitful context for theological reflection and production."[7] Early on, Latino/a ethics crossed denominational boundaries, engaging conversations inclusive of people's concrete experiences of hope, justice, and holiness amid the challenges of ethnic, racial, economic, and legal marginalization, undertaking the theological project as an ongoing conversation among scholars of religion with the communities we serve.

In the 1983 groundbreaking volume *Galilean Journey: The Mexican American Promise*, Virgilio Elizondo challenged the theological world to consider Jesus' own identity as characterized by *mestizaje* and otherness.[8] Not only were we to consider Jesus' Galilean context as one that negotiated otherness, in many forms, but this interplay of margins and centers in Galilee also is representative of Jesus' very journey of salvation. Elizondo presents *mestizaje*—in its complicated and violent origin through conquest, colonization, and the encounter of Spanish, native American, and African peoples—as a mark of Divine being, one that considers the margins of being other, invisible, insignificant, and rejected as the very places where salvation and liberation are worked out. In Elizondo's work, the peoples, cultures, and religious experiences that the builders of the church rejected become the cornerstone of hope and liberation.

The missiologist Orlando Costas challenged evangelical Christianity to come to terms with the insights of liberation theology for the task of building the church. Communication of the Gospel entails living with the incarnate Christ, already on the margins, becoming Jesus outside the gates with the Lazaruses of the world.[9] These insights, Costas claimed, were to be fostered in *en conjunto* conversations between Latino/a and other minority scholars of the church. Embracing his Puerto Rican identity as integral to his own theological development, he asked that engagement with the church of the margins be at the heart of any missiological effort. This included the self-critical task of understanding why the margins exist—at all! A key task of Christian mission is prophesying against the structures that victimize so much of the world for profit and political and military power.[10]

Ismael García, professor emeritus of Christian ethics at Austin Presbyterian Theological Seminary, balanced the communitarian ethics of liberation theology and the Latino/a experience, and the personalist ethics that shaped mid- to late-twentieth-century Protestant thought. In *Dignidad: Ethics through Hispanic Eyes*, García places the person and the community in right relationship, acknowledging that overemphasis on either dimension would result in indifferent individualism or stultifying parochialism. A Hispanic ethics of recognition and care grounded in *dignidad* prioritizes relationality and the values that various communities build for themselves, especially communities that have been historically marginalized.[11] It is within this context that García explores human rights—language that he warns can tend to overemphasize the autonomy of individuals as distinct from their roles and relationships in communities of care. He emphasizes the dignity of a person as intimately tied to the communities (plural) that form the person and to which he or she belongs. Belonging to multiple communities means that people must constantly negotiate permeable boundaries, not just comparing values but also transforming them according to the needs of persons inside the group *and* those left outside, for whatever reasons. García challenges the notion that individual rights are determined independent of community, but community ought to be understood in ways that guard against communal prescriptions that stand in the way of human flourishing.

The Pentecostal ethicist Eldín Villafañe brings the wisdom and theology of the barrios and storefront churches to Latino/a ethics, where "the movement of the Spirit of God is the central lens through which to understand life in the family, community and the greater society."[12] Villafañe argues for a "social spirituality," one that challenges a hyperindividualized interpretation of the work of the Spirit in the world. Eschatological in tone, Villafañe brings Pentecostalism's emphasis on ushering the Reign of God in history. Here, the Spirit empowers the faithful to transform structures toward fullness in the Kingdom of God, a task that joins both the prophetic and vocational natures of baptism in the Spirit.[13]

Shaped by her Cuban heritage and transformed by the theology of the incarcerated men and women whom she taught as part of a prison education program, Ada María Isasi-Díaz understood that among Latinos and Latinas, *la lucha*, the struggle—for justice, for love, for dignity, for voice, for sustenance, for Spirit—was as much an understanding of who God is as it is a description of who humans are.[14] She brought to life the concept that we meet God's liberative agenda in the everyday struggle for life, *lo cotidiano*. These concepts represent acts of resistance, *la lucha*, against the forces that threaten life and dignity through cultural marginalization, detention, persecution, stolen wages and labor exploitation, and other forms of daily violence.[15] Justice, salvation, and liberation must also have meaning *en lo cotidiano*, on the daily, as communities join in solidarity, promoting life in their own context, defining what salvation looks like from within their own practices, rather than allowing it to be an externally imposed religious construct.

Miguel De La Torre, founder of the Latino/a Interest and Working Group of the SCE, and past SCE president, moved Latino/a ethics to new levels in constructive thought. His work engages mainstream ethical thought while confronting it with its complicity with the powers that have historically served to perpetuate marginalization, oppression, and racial and colonial violence. I highlight two of his many works, *Doing Christian Ethics from the Margins* and *Latina/o Social Ethics: Moving beyond Eurocentric Moral Thinking*.[16] In these two volumes, De La Torre addresses central concepts in Christian ethics through a Latino/a critical lens, questioning how these ought to be understood in light of the salvific story of Jesus Christ amid the poor and oppressed. Advocating a sort of blessed rage for disorder, De La Torre pushes Christian ethics to move beyond pontificating about liberation to empowering those who experience "civil order" as violence, genocide, and murder in order to create a new reality grounded on justice.

Latino/a ethics makes its mark by taking that which society, politics, and the economy chooses to discard, forget, or annihilate as central experiences for understanding Divine love and right relationship among us, and from the heart of our people. It promotes engagement with the religious, social, and political heritage and experiences of the groups that birth us, questioning the value of ethical thought that does not take their concrete liberation seriously. Believing in the redeeming power of close communal ties and the ways these shape us, even though we critically affirm personal dignity, especially that of women and sexual minorities, Latino/a ethics offers a caution to anthropologies that stress individual rights and autonomies isolated from the goods and the well-being of communities.

## Latino/a Contributions to Theological Ethical Reflections on Migration, by Victor Carmona

For nearly four decades, Latino/a biblical scholars, theologians, and Christian ethicists have published works that address immigration in one of two ways: either as a significant aspect of Latino/a experience, or as a significant experience in and of itself. Although there are outliers, as a general rule, Latino/a scholarship on immigration favored the first approach from the early 1980s until the early 2000s.[17] Since then, Latino/a scholars have also turned to the second approach, giving our community the ability to bridge the mature literature on Latino/a theology *and* the nascent literature on theologies of migration. In doing so, our community is contributing scholarship that possesses a unique ability to engage the breadth of the migratory process (which spans immigration, settlement, and minority formation).[18] Both approaches share a commitment to solidarity with immigrants—including undocumented ones—and refugees.

## Reflections on Immigration within Latino/a theologies and Christian Ethics

An article that Virgilio Elizondo wrote in 1972, titled "Educación religiosa para el México-Norteamericano," exemplifies the first approach.[19] In it, the *padre* of Latino theology argues that the sociocultural context of Mexican Americans calls for appropriate theological reflection and lifegiving pastoral care. To this end, Elizondo identifies immigration (the first phase of the migratory process) as an aspect of the Mexican American experience but presses the point that immigration *is not* the entirety of that experience. It would take another twenty years or so for an academically trained Christian ethicist, Ada María Isasi-Díaz, to engage immigration as an aspect of the Latino/a struggle. To this end, in the early 1990s she turned to ethnographic research—nearly twenty years before the method gained acceptance in the SCE.[20]

The struggle against discrimination that Latino/a communities confront across the United States has become fertile ground for theological-ethical reflections that are telling of settlement and minority formation (the second and third phases of the migratory process). As the missiologist Jorge Castillo Guerra notes, those phases are "an *inter*space, which is the space of struggle between the [immigrant's] culture and the resident culture."[21] Nestled in this interspace, Latino/a scholars have produced valuable texts on the meaning of hybridity as *mestizaje* and *mulatez*. In "Alternatively Documented Theologies: Mapping Border, Exile and Diaspora," Carmen Nanko catalogs these texts according to the social spaces and experiences that mark the identities of their authors: the border for Mexican Americans, exile for Cuban Americans, and diaspora for Puerto Ricans.[22] As Nanko acknowledges though, these categories have limits. They cannot account for the experiences of Central American refugees and asylum seekers—communities that continue to birth their first academically trained theologians and Christian ethicists.

*Apuntes*, which is published by the Perkins School of Theology at Southern Methodist University, is the oldest academic journal dedicated to Latino/a theology and ministry. This journal contains some of the earliest published theological reflections addressing immigration as a discrete topic rather than as an aspect of broader Latino/a experience. From 1981 to 1986, its authors reflected on the meaning of immigration, including the sanctuary movement, from within multiple disciplines. Early writers include the biblical scholar Francisco García-Treto, the theologians Hugo López and Jorge Lara-Braud, and the historian Justo González.[23] It would take another twenty years for this journal to publish a theological-ethical reflection on immigration. In 2003, *Apuntes* published Daniel Castelo's "Residents *and* Illegal Aliens," which critically engages Stanley Hauerwas's *Resident Aliens* in light of the witness of actual "illegal aliens."[24] It took another five years for the SCE's *Journal* to publish a Latino/a scholar's theological ethical reflection on migration. In 2008 it published Ana Bedard's "Us versus Them? US Immigration and the Common Good," a critical analysis of the US-Mexico Catholic bishops' pastoral letter on migration, "Strangers No Longer."[25]

During the last ten years, the community of Latino/a Christian ethicists has continued advancing research that is grounded in a commitment to solidarity with immigrants, refugees, and their mixed-status families.[26] It does so by authoring texts that bring the voices of immigrants themselves to bear on the conscience of US Christians, as Miguel De la Torre's books do;[27] through sustained reflection on the injustices that farmworkers suffer, many of them immigrants, as Jeremy Cruz's research does;[28] by turning our attention to the plight of the victims of human trafficking, as Nichole Flores's sustained inquiry does;[29] and by bridging the US academy with research taking place beyond the United States and the English-speaking world, as M. T. Dávila's work does.[30] Although our community is beginning to flourish, it is too early to tell if its growth within the Society will take.

### The Future of Our Field in Light of the History of Latino/a Scholarship on Migration

Immigration, Kristin Heyer reminds us, is bringing our society, and therefore our universities and churches, into closer contact with families, students, and Christians from the Global South.[31] The terrain in which our discipline pursues its social, academic, and ecclesial purposes is changing. This reality has influenced the discussion within the North America region of the Catholic Theological Ethics in the World Church network (CTEWC). During a three-year-long conversation at the Catholic Theological Society of America's annual meetings, we have asked how that changing terrain presents our teaching and scholarship with valuable opportunities and risks—the main one, I believe, being whether we engage, diminish, or outright ignore cross-cultural and global perspectives that are close to home.[32]

We need to ask similar questions at the SCE in a sustained way. At the CTEWC conversations, Bryan Massingale called Christian ethicists to "a kind of Copernican revolution" within the discipline.[33] The history of Latino/a Christian ethicists working on migration suggests why we need to echo his call here: Our academy seems to lag twenty years or so behind the religion, biblical, and theological academies in its ability to nurture and sustain Latino/a scholars and their research. There are multiple reasons why this may be so (including ongoing resistance among graduate programs to acknowledging Spanish as an academic language). And though we persist, the history I just shared, along with the conversation that the CTEWC has sparked, suggests this insight: Our discipline's future within an increasingly cross-cultural global academy and church—and the future of Latino/a scholars within it—are woven together.

## Considerations for the Future, *by Teresa Delgado*

I begin where the earlier panelists have directed, that is, with the future of Latinx ethics. I affirm completely Rubén Rosario's assessment that Christian ethics from a Latino/a perspective begins with an intentional act of solidarity with, by, and for the poor, marginalized, and disenfranchised. Who are the poor, marginalized, and disenfranchised within our community at this moment? Who are we called to accompany in solidarity? I would say that the future of Christian ethics *Latinidad* is black, queer, and (unapologetically) *en conjunto*.

### Afro-Latinx Possibilities

Race and racism continue to be a challenging subject within Latinx ethics. How do we begin to confront the binaries of black and white that have been the normative discourse of race in North America? How do we engage in an honest assessment of the racialized nature of our own *cultura*? I will never forget a conversation I had about fifteen years ago with a scholar of religion, a Latina, who proceeded to detail the variety of racial categories she encountered growing up in Puerto Rico: *morena, triqueña, india*—to name a few. Her naming of these was less about being descriptive and more about being dismissive of the need to engage in sustained interrogation about the reality and legacy of racial caste in Puerto Rico, indeed in all of Latin America, and how this has deeply informed our experience of Latinidad in the diaspora. The fact that Ruben Rosario-Rodríguez's volume on race and the Latino/a perspective is the only full-length treatment of the subject of race and Latinidad tells us something about our communities' unwillingness to examine our own racism and the racialized hierarchies we have perpetuated.[34] This will not change if we—as Latinx persons—continue to perpetuate the absence of Afro-Latinx voices and experiences from the content, context, and methodologies of Christian ethics. In this regard, we must draw from the rich womanist wisdom in the SCE and beyond, as well as from our Latin American *gente* in Brazil and Colombia, for example, as they confront the racial caste system persistent in their own theological and ethical discourse. This is not a new conversation.

### Queer Latinx Opportunities

The groundbreaking work of Marcella Althaus-Reid—from *Indecent Theology* (2001) to *The Queer God* (2003) to *Trans/Formations* (2009)—has provided fertile ground from which queer Latinx voices can articulate ways of being in relation that do not ascribe to the strict complementarity of our Latinidad and Roman Catholic inheritance. In addition to challenging the binaries of male and female, queer Latinidad presents opportunities for interrogating toxic masculinities, *machismo* and *marianismo*, and the puta/virgin complex, for example, in ways that expand beyond the feminist critique of structural patriarchy. The work of Robyn Henderson-Espinoza represents a growing edge of our necessary task to push against categories of either/or.[35] In many ways, this is familiar territory in that our challenge to the racial binary of black and white is based on our embodied disruption of these binaries. However, in the realm of gender and sexuality, we seem to forget the wisdom of our own embodied story: that we exist in the in-between, liminal spaces of borderlands, of undefined territories, of commonwealth status, of exile. These contested spaces are the geographies of queer Latinidad and, for many of us, can thrive only outside the boundaries of the church's institutional power and privilege. Walls have already been built and reinforced. Therefore, the future of Latinx ethics is multigenerational and communal, activist in solidarity, and expressed *en conjunto*.

## Conclusion

This brief overview of some major themes and innovations of US Latino/a theology provides markers for constructing a distinctly Latino/a Christian ethics. US Latino/a theologies tend toward a liberationist methodology and praxis; but even those that are not explicitly liberationist still nurture a liberative ethos committed to the interdisciplinary analysis of social reality in order to expose how existing social structures perpetuate racist, sexist, heterosexist, and classist agendas. This commitment to a "hermeneutics of suspicion" questions dominant power structures while privileging the perspective of the oppressed, yet it recognizes that many Latino/as are spiritually at home within the mainstream of the Western Christian tradition, even when subjected to marginalization, exclusion, and exploitation on the basis of their ethnicity and bicultural identity. Within these shared *loci communes* ("common places"), this burgeoning movement within Christian ethics reveals itself as a complex and varied mosaic.

## Notes

1. This is from the 2018 Society of Christian Ethics annual meeting's call for papers from the society's president, David Gushee.
2. See "2016–17 Annual Data Tables," compiled by Commission on Accrediting of the Association of Theological Schools, www.ats.edu/resources/institutional-data /annual-data-tables.
3. See Jens Manuel Krogstad, "US Hispanic Population Growth Has Leveled Off," Pew Research Center, August 3, 2017, www.pewresearch.org/fact-tank/2017/08/03 /u-s-hispanic-population-growth-has-leveled-off/.
4. Fernando F. Segovia, "Hispanic American Theology and the Bible: Effective Weapon and Faithful Ally," in *We Are a People! Initiatives in Hispanic American Theology*, ed. Roberto S. Goizueta (Minneapolis: Fortress Press, 1992), 43.

5. Orlando O. Espín, *Idol and Grace: On Traditioning and Subversive Hope* (Maryknoll, NY: Orbis Books, 2014), 44.

6. María Teresa Dávila, "Latino/a Ethics," in *The Wiley-Blackwell Companion to Latino/a Theology*, ed. Orlando Espín (London: Wiley-Blackwell, 2014), 249.

7. Ibid., 250.

8. Virgilio Elizondo, *Galilean Journey: The Mexican American Promise* (Maryknoll, NY: Orbis Books, 1983).

9. Orlando Costas, *Christ Outside the Gate: Mission Beyond Christendom* (Maryknoll, NY: 1982).

10. Orlando Costas, *Liberating News: A Theology of Contextual Evangelization* (Grand Rapids: Eerdmans, 1989).

11. Ismael García, *Dignidad: Ethics through Hispanic Eyes* (Nashville: Abingdon Press, 1997).

12. Dávila, "Latino/a Ethics," 251.

13. Eldín Villafañe, *The Liberating Spirit: Toward a Hispanic American Pentecostal Social Ethic* (Lanham, MD: University Press of America, 1992).

14. Ada María Isasi-Díaz, *Mujerista Theology: A Theology for the 21st Century* (Maryknoll, NY: Orbis Books, 1996).

15. Ada María Isasi-Díaz, *En La Lucha: Elaborating a Mujerista Theology*, 10th edition (Minneapolis: Fortress Press, 2004).

16. Miguel De La Torre, *Doing Christian Ethics from the Margins* (Maryknoll, NY: Orbis Books, 2004); Miguel De La Torre, *Latino/a Social Ethics: Moving Beyond Eurocentric Moral Thinking* (Waco, TX: Baylor University Press, 2010).

17. Allan Figueroa Deck, "A Christian Perspective on the Reality of Illegal Immigration: The 1978 O'Grady Award Winner," *Social Thought* 4, no. 4 (1978).

18. Stephen Castles and Mark J. Miller, *The Age of Migration: International Population Movements in the Modern World*, 4th edition (New York: Guilford Press, 2009).

19. Virgilio Elizondo, "Religious Education for Mexican Americans (1972)," in *Beyond Borders: Writings of Virgilio Elizondo and Friends*, ed. Timothy Matovina (Maryknoll, NY: Orbis Books, 2000).

20. Although she was among the earliest academically trained Latino/a Christian ethicists (if not the first), Isasi-Díaz did not join the Society of Christian Ethics. Ada María Isasi-Díaz, *En La Lucha / In the Struggle: A Hispanic Women's Liberation Theology* (Minneapolis: Fortress Press, 1993); Ada María Isasi-Díaz, "'By the Rivers of Babylon': Exile as a Way of Life," in *Reading from This Place*, ed. Fernando F. Segovia and Mary Ann Tolbert (Minneapolis: Fortress Press, 1995).

21. Jorge E. Castillo Guerra, "A Theology of Migration: Toward an Intercultural Methodology," in *A Promised Land, a Perilous Journey: Theological Perspective on Migration*, ed. Daniel Groody and Gioacchino Campese (Notre Dame, IN: University of Notre Dame Press, 2008).

22. Carmen Nanko-Fernández, "Alternately Documented Theologies: Mapping Border, Exile and Diaspora," in *Religion and Politics in America's Borderlands*, ed. Sarah Azaransky (Lanham, MD: Lexington Books, 2013).

23. Their texts break open four main veins of theological reflection on immigration, all of which still sustain scholarship. They assess the fundamental question of the meaning of "alien" in Hebrew Scripture, propose the need for "a Theology of Migration," challenge US Christians to be faithful to the Reign of God by practicing neighborly love toward our immigrant brothers and sisters, and discern the stance that our faith calls for in relation to US immigration laws. See Francisco O. García-Treto, "El Señor Guarda a Los Emigrantes (Salmo 146:3)," *Apuntes: Reflexiones Teológicas desde el Margen Hispano* 1, no. 4 (1981); Hugo

L. López, "Toward a Theology of Migration," *Apuntes: Reflexiones Teológicas desde el Margen Hispano* 2, no. 3 (1982); Jorge Lara-Braud, "Reflexiones Teológicas Sobre La Migración," *Apuntes: Reflexiones Teológicas desde el Margen Hispano* 2, no. 1 (1982); and Justo L. González, "Sanctuary: Historical, Legal, and Biblical Considerations," *Apuntes: Reflexiones Teológicas desde el Margen Hispano* 5, no. 2 (1985).

24. Daniel Castelo, "Resident and Illegal Aliens," *Apuntes: Reflexiones Teológicas desde el Margen Hispano* 23, no. 2 (2003).

25. Ana T. Bedard, "Us versus Them? US Immigration and the Common Good," *Journal of the Society of Christian Ethics* 28, no. 2 (2008); Conferencia del Episcopado Mexicano and United States Conference of Catholic Bishops, *Strangers No Longer: Together on the Journey of Hope* (Washington, DC: United States Conference of Catholic Bishops, 2003).

26. Mixed-status families include members who are citizens and permanent residents or undocumented immigrants (sometimes all three). In March 2010 the Pew Hispanic Center estimated that 16.6 million people lived in mixed-status families throughout the United States. It also reported that up to 54 percent of them, or 9 million people, lived in families "that include at least one unauthorized adult and at least one US-born child." Jeffrey S. Passel and D'Vera Cohn, *A Portrait of Unauthorized Immigrants in the United States* (Washington, DC: Pew Research Center, 2009), 6.

27. Miguel A. De La Torre, *Trails of Hope and Terror: Testimonies on Immigration* (Maryknoll, NY: Orbis Books, 2009); Miguel A. De La Torre, *The US Immigration Crisis: Toward an Ethics of Place* (Eugene, OR: Cascade Books, 2016).

28. Jeremy V. Cruz, "Traversing Merciless American Borders: Transnational Dialogue between Colonized and Diasporic Peoples," paper presented at Catholic Theological Society of America: Beyond Trento Interest Group, San Juan, June 2016.

29. Nichole M. Flores, "Looking beneath the Surface: Human Trafficking, Modern Day Slavery and Catholic Theological Ethics," paper presented at Catholic Theological Ethics in the World Church Conference "In the Currents of History: from Trent to the Future," Trento, Italy, July 2010; Nichole M. Flores, "Beyond Consumptive Solidarity: An Aesthetic Response to Human Trafficking," paper presented at Society of Christian Social Ethics, Toronto, 2016; "Human Trafficking and Modern Day Slavery: Interest Group," paper presented at Catholic Theological Society of America, San Juan, 2016.

30. Agnes M. Brazal and María Teresa Dávila, *Living with(out) Borders: Catholic Theological Ethics on the Migration of Peoples*, Catholic Theological Ethics in the World Church (Maryknoll, NY: Orbis Books, 2016); M. T. Dávila, "Who Is Still Missing? Economic Justice and Immigrant Justice," in *The Almighty and the Dollar: Reflections on Economic Justice for All*, ed. Mark Allman and National Conference of Catholic Bishops (Winona, MN: Anselm Academic, 2012).

31. Kristin E. Heyer, *Kinship across Borders: A Christian Ethic of Immigration* (Washington, DC: Georgetown University Press, 2012).

32. Victor Carmona, "A Response to Christine Firer Hinze," paper presented at Catholic Theological Society of America: Beyond Trento Interest Group, Milwaukee, June 2015.

33. Kristin E. Heyer and Bryan Massingale, "Beyond Trento: North American Moral Theology in a Global Church," *CTSA Proceedings* 69 (2014): 169.

34. Rubén Rosario-Rodríguez, *Racism and God-Talk: A Latino/a Perspective* (New York: New York University Press, 2008).

35. E.g., see R. Henderson-Espinoza, "Difference and Interrelatedness: A Material Resistance Becoming," *Cross Currents* 66, no. 2 (June 2016): 281–89; and N. Hoel and R. Henderson-Espinoza, "Approaching Islam Queerly," *Theology & Sexuality* 22, no. 2 (January 2016): 1–8.

# Medicine as Just War? The Legacy of James Childress in Christian Ethics

*Brett McCarty*

What do medicine and war have to do with each other? This question is explored through the writings of James Childress, whose early contributions to just war theory illuminate his work in bioethics. By considering the conceptual influences of just war theory on Childress's bioethics, the contributions and limits of his approach can be set in relief through normative engagement with certain areas of medicine. In particular, Childress's just-war-inspired bioethics befits the practice of surgery; but oncology, as a medical analogue to total warfare, requires significant transformation in order to be disciplined by Childress's approach. Childress offers a coherent schema for navigating moral conflict in a fallen world, but he does not provide a substantive account of the peaceable end toward which medicine as just war aims.

WHAT DO MEDICINE AND WAR HAVE TO DO WITH EACH other? This may seem like an odd question about fields of healing and killing. But significant figures in the field of Christian ethics have made major scholarly contributions by morally reflecting on these two arenas of human activity.[1] This essay considers the Christian ethicist whose work in bioethics has proven most influential: James Childress.[2] To do so, we must first specify our opening question: What kind of moral response is fitting in light of analogues between medicine and war? Childress's work on just war theory shows up in important ways in his writings on bioethics. To illustrate the influence of the former on the latter, this essay considers how Childress's just war paradigm responds to the moral schema and conflicts uncovered within the social imaginaries of the surgical ward and the oncology ward.[3] The surgical ward and the oncology ward are two paradigmatic medical sites within the modern hospital, with the term "site" referring to a set of practices, discourses, and practitioners that are deeply connected to recognizably distinct modes of imagining and engaging the human body within modern health care.

Brett McCarty, ThD, is the St. Andrews Fellow in Theology and Science at Duke Divinity School, Duke University, 407 Chapel Dr., Box #90968, Durham, NC 27708; brett.mccarty@duke.edu.

In what follows, then, I argue that Childress's approach to bioethics can be understood as a just war theory for health care. I also argue that Childress's just-war-inspired bioethics is a fitting moral response to the surgical ward's social imaginary, but it needs extending in order to provide an adequate moral response to the imaginary found within modern oncology. Within the surgical ward, the body is engaged with what the ethnographer Rachel Prentice calls "controlled violence."[4] The limited and controlled nature of surgical interventions seem to comport with the Hippocratic injunction "to help, or at least to do no harm." Childress's approach to bioethics likewise aligns in many ways with this stream of moral reasoning.[5] In contrast, the social imaginary historically found within the oncology ward requires substantial transformation if it is to be ordered by a just-war-inspired bioethics. I end by emphasizing the limits of just-war-inspired bioethics in light of the ultimate aim of bodily peace.

## Childress in Context: Theological and Philosophical Foundations

Over the past fifty years, James Childress has deeply shaped the field of bioethics as one of its earliest and most preeminent contributors. Trained at Yale in religious ethics, Childress was consulted in the writing of *The Belmont Report*, the landmark federal government document on research ethics, and he collaborated with Tom Beauchamp as coauthor of *Principles of Biomedical Ethics*. Originally published in 1979, it is now in its seventh edition and is by far the most influential bioethics textbook of the past generation.[6]

Although best known as a bioethicist, Childress began his academic career working in political ethics. His dissertation, published as *Civil Disobedience and Political Obligation: A Study in Christian Social Ethics*, offers a theological and moral "framework for the discussion and justification of civil disobedience."[7] After establishing early on that "nonviolence is an essential feature of disobedience," toward the end of the work Childress extends just war theory to analyze acts of civil disobedience.[8] He claims that "the 'just war doctrine' offers a set of considerations for determining when war is justified, and analogous criteria must be employed in determining when civil disobedience is justified, although perhaps it is more accurate to suggest that civil disobedience is subject to the same general demands of morality as any other action rather than that it is illuminated by just war criteria."[9]

In his first book, then, Childress extends just war theory into other areas of moral analysis. Childress also hints that "analogous criteria" to just war theory might serve as the "general demands of morality." As we shall see, Childress returns to analogues of just war criteria throughout his career, indicating that it serves as a fundamental framework for his evaluation of moral action.

In addition to this explicit point of connection with just war theory, Childress lays further foundations for extending it to other modes of moral reasoning. Childress argues that "a *pluralist* approach" to moral principles and values "is most consistent with an adequate, balanced interpretation of God's creative, ruling, and redeeming will."[10] When applied to theories of the state, this means that one single principle, such as order, cannot be valued to the exclusion of others, like justice. Childress notes that his pluralist perspective is influenced by the work of the philosopher W. D. Ross; and in particular, he develops Ross's concept of prima facie obligations and duties.[11] Prima facie duties often come into conflict and are assigned no priority. But such a duty "can be outweighed and overridden" by taking into consideration the totality of all relevant prima facie obligations.[12] Through this work of balancing, one's actual obligations in any particular situation emerge.

Through just war theory and the concept of prima facie duties, Childress developed conceptual resources for balancing competing moral commitments that he then extended into other areas of moral reflection. He first directly connects the logic of prima facie duties and just war theory in a 1974 essay attempting to clarify Reinhold Niebuhr's position on violence. In order for Niebuhr to consider violence as a "necessary evil" and "last resort," Childress argues that he must be committed to nonviolence as a prima facie duty, not a pragmatic choice. Even as a prima facie obligation like nonviolence is overridden, "residual effects of violated prima facie duties are very important," and this helps to explain why Niebuhr maintains that feelings of guilt accompany acts of violence.[13]

## Childress on Just War

Childress's 1982 book *Moral Responsibility in Conflicts* includes his essay on Niebuhr along with the essay "Just-War Criteria," which is an expanded version of a seminal paper that Childress first published in 1978.[14] Childress's just war essay has proven deeply influential, particularly in its claim that just war theorists and pacifists "reason from a common starting point. Both begin with the contention that nonviolence has moral priority over violence."[15] This "presumption against violence" is cited as the starting point for the just war work developed by both Lisa Cahill and Richard Miller.[16] It is particularly important to note that it is cited by the US Conference of Catholic Bishops in their 1983 pastoral letter *The Challenge of Peace*, in which they claim that "extraordinarily strong reasons" must be present to override "the presumption *in favor of peace* and *against* war."[17] This marked a significant shift in social teaching for the US Catholic Church,[18] and moreover stands as a key development in the modern tradition of just war reasoning.[19] Because of this, and because of the importance

Childress's work in just war theory has for his approach to bioethics, a summary of his just war position is merited.

Childress describes his approach to just war as a "rational reconstruction" of the "historical deposit of just war criteria." In crafting his theory, Childress sets out to "show how the traditional just war criteria can be reconstructed, explicated, and defended in relation to the prima facie duty of nonmaleficence—the duty not to harm or kill others."[20] By claiming that just war theory begins with nonmaleficence, Childress names this tradition of moral reasoning as deeply akin to that found in the Hippocratic tradition—which, as we saw above, is committed "to help, or at least to do no harm." Childress frames just war theory as an effort to understand the conditions necessary for overriding a prima facie duty not to injure or kill another, along with how one should act when overriding this obligation. These two considerations are the foundations of *jus ad bellum* and *jus in bello* criteria, which govern the morality of initiating and conducting a just war. Childress summarizes his rational reconstruction of just war theory as including the following criteria: "legitimate or competent authority, just cause, right intention, announcement of intention, last resort, reasonable hope of success, proportionality, and just conduct. All of these criteria taken together, with the exception of the last one, establish the *jus ad bellum*, the right to go to war, while the last criterion focuses on the *jus in bello*, right conduct within war, and includes both intention and proportionality, which are also part of the *jus ad bellum*."[21]

When these criteria are met, the prima facie duty of nonmaleficence can be overridden in the pursuit of other important prima facie duties, such as upholding justice and protecting the innocent.[22] Even as this occurs, the overridden prima facie duty is not erased but instead remains through "moral traces," a term that Childress draws from Robert Nozick and that connects with his earlier engagement with Reinhold Niebuhr. Through these "moral traces," the overridden prima facie duty "has 'residual effects' on the agent's attitudes and actions."[23] These moral traces lead to regret and perhaps even remorse over a choice of action, and this is manifest in the restraint displayed through *jus in bello*. Moreover, because for Childress "peace remains the ultimate aim of a just war," the conduct of the war should accord with this purpose, and so "the view that war is 'total' and without limits" is unacceptable.[24] We will return to the importance of "moral traces" and avoiding total warfare when we place Childress's theory in conversation with the social imaginaries found within the paradigmatic medical sites of the surgical and oncology wards.

Childress ends his essay on just war criteria by returning to his opening commitment to nonmaleficence, claiming, "If we accept this prima facie duty of nonmaleficence and if we accept the responsibility to think morally about the use of force in a sinful world, we should be committed to a framework and procedure of reasoning that is at least analogous to just war criteria."[25] Here we see Childress hint again at the wider implications of his work in just war theory. We now turn to the distinct presence and influence of just war reasoning found throughout his bioethical writings.

## Childress's Just-War-Inspired Bioethics

In 1981, Childress published his first book-length treatment of bioethics, *Priorities in Biomedical Ethics*, and in it he adopts just war reasoning to engage questions regarding the ethics of human subjects in research. He again refers to his approach as a "pluralist" model of ethics, and in pursuing it he argues that analogous criteria to those in just war theory "are used whenever we encounter situations that involve conflicting values, duties, or obligations."[26] Once again, he begins with the commitment to do no harm, and he proceeds to use just war criteria to argue for when this commitment can be overridden. Childress gives these criteria for human subject research:

> First, there should be a *morally important reason* for the research. . . . Second, there should be a *reasonable prospect* that the research will generate the knowledge that is sought. . . . Third, the use of human subjects in this research should be a matter of *last resort*; their use should be *necessary*. . . . Fourth, the research should meet the principle of *proportionality*. . . . Fifth, the research must have the subject's *voluntary* and *informed consent* to participate. . . . It is important to identify a sixth standard: Are the benefits and burdens of research fairly and equitably distributed among the population? . . . Finally, we need to establish and maintain procedures to ensure that these criteria are met.[27]

These criteria for human subject research align almost exactly with the just war criteria that Childress developed a few years earlier. Most are self-evidently the same, and only a few needing clarifying. In an important move, voluntary and informed consent takes the place of "legitimate or competent authority," and procedures ensuring that the criteria are met become "just conduct" for medical research. The just war criterion of announcement of intention becomes a part of voluntary and informed consent. Out of the seven criteria for human subject research, the only one that may not have a direct analogue in Childress's just war theory is the fair and equitable distribution of the benefits and burdens of research, and even it has strong parallels with the just war criterion of "right intention."

A year after Childress published this connection between just war criteria and human subject research, he extended the use of just war reasoning into clinical medicine in his 1982 book *Who Should Decide? Paternalism in Health Care*. Following the Hippocratic tradition, Childress differentiates between beneficence and nonmaleficence, and he quotes the Hippocratic axiom that medical practitioners should seek "to help, or at least to do no harm."[28] Childress sets the Hippocratic tradition of moral reasoning alongside the duty of respect for persons. Paternalism is a particularly pointed area in which these two duties, beneficence and respect for persons, come into tension. In response, Childress develops the principle of "limited paternalism," which requires these conditions to be met for paternalistic action in health care to be justified:

> It is essential, first, to rebut the presumption of an adult's competence to make his or her own decisions. The second condition for justified paternalism is the probability of harm unless there is an intervention. The third condition is proportionality—the probable benefit of intervention should outweigh the probable harm of nonintervention. Fourth, it is necessary to assess modes of paternalistic action, such as deception and coercion. Effectiveness is not sufficient. In general, the least restrictive, least humiliating, and least insulting means should be employed.[29]

These four conditions are a slightly shortened and condensed appropriation of just war criteria. Legitimate authority in a just war becomes a question of decision-making competence in medicine. Just cause, right intention, and last resort are all potentially carried within the condition of "the probability of harm unless there is an intervention." Proportionality is a direct parallel between the two approaches, with the just war criterion of a reasonable hope of success possibly collapsed within it. Finally, proper "modes of paternalistic action" in medicine match the just war criterion of just conduct and may also include the need for announcement of intent.[30]

By examining Childress's development of just war criteria into the concerns of bioethics, we are now better prepared to recognize the influence of just war theory on *the* most important book in bioethics, Childress and Beauchamp's *Principles of Biomedical Ethics*. The book sets out the position known as principlism, in which the four principles of autonomy (changed in later editions to "respect for autonomy"), nonmaleficence, beneficence, and justice are set forth as normative for modern biomedical practice. From its first edition, the book has described its four principles using language that strongly echoes passages from Childress's influential essay on just war theory, drawing from W. D. Ross's understanding of prima facie duties and referencing Robert Nozick's notion of "moral traces" to explicate the abiding nature of an overridden prima facie obligation.[31] Beginning with the third edition in 1989, the notion of balancing the four principles is introduced, using criteria drawn directly from Childress's work on just war theory.[32] In the book's most recent edition, the conditions that constrain balancing the four principles are

1. Good reasons can be offered to act on the overriding norm rather than on the infringed norm.

2. The moral objective justifying the infringement has a realistic prospect of achievement.

3. No morally preferable alternative actions are available.

4. The lowest level of infringement, commensurate with achieving the primary goal of action, has been selected.

5. All negative effects of the infringement have been minimized.

6. All affected parties have been treated impartially.[33]

These conditions align with most, though not all, of Childress's just war criteria. Condition 1 can be read as just cause, condition 2 as reasonable hope of success, condition 3 as last resort, and conditions 4 through 6 as combining elements of proportionality, right intention, and just conduct. Despite these parallels, Beauchamp and Childress make no mention of just war theory in the text or notes of *Principles of Biomedical Ethics*. In an essay reflecting on the book, however, Childress acknowledges the connection: "In short, the criteria for assessing wars and several other actions are similar because war and these other actions infringe upon some prima facie duties or obligations—an infringement that requires justification and can be justified along the lines suggested by the criteria."[34]

Interestingly enough, Childress's just war criteria of legitimate authority and announcement of intention are not included among the conditions that constrain balancing the four principles. Recall that in his 1981 *Priorities of Biomedical Ethics*, Childress makes "voluntary and informed consent" a research ethics analogue for legitimate authority and announcement of intention. This important criterion may be left out of the conditions that constrain balancing in *Principles of Biomedical Ethics* because the prima facie duty of respect for autonomy is one of the four principles whose conflict is supposed to be mediated by these balancing conditions. In other words, the conceptual framework Childress and Beauchamp use to balance the four principles is structurally predisposed to favor something like informed consent in medicine. Given that *Principles of Biomedical Ethics* has been criticized by many for privileging respect for autonomy above all other principles, this is a crucial point.

In his original just war article, Childress names "legitimate or competent authority" as the just war criterion that is "really a presupposition for the rest of the criteria," for it "determines *who* is primarily responsible for judging whether the other criteria are met."[35] So even though this criterion is not explicitly named as part of the conditions that constrain balancing in *Principles of Biomedical Ethics*, its absence in a conceptual schema meant to privilege it as a criterion before all others means that the prima facie duty of respect for autonomy may be favored from the start over the other three core principles. We see this playing out in modern bioethics, where, as in just war criteria, the question of who is the legitimate or competent authority often functions as a "presupposition" for all other moral considerations. Therefore, by attending to the way that Childress's work in just war theory illuminates his work in bioethics, we can now better understand why Childress and Beauchamp's principle of respect for autonomy may be conceptually privileged within their bioethical theory. We now turn to a final connection between just war theory and bioethics in Childress's work.

In a lecture delivered at the US Air Force Academy in 1992, later published as *War as Reality and Metaphor: Some Moral Reflections*, Childress explores how the language of warfare has suffused our public discourse in a variety of areas. His fundamental point is that we are prone to ignore the importance of "moral limits in war," and he explores the ramifications of this oversight when we understand medicine as warfare.[36] In this lecture, he briefly considers the central question of this essay: What kind of moral response is fitting in light of analogues between medicine and war? To understand the prevalence of the metaphor of medicine as warfare and its problems, he details the argument of Susan Sontag's influential work *Illness as Metaphor*, which describes how "the controlling metaphors in the descriptions of cancer [and its treatments] are drawn from the language of warfare."[37] In particular, Childress recognizes the problem of overtreatment as one that often arises when "death is the ultimate enemy." For medical practitioners, patients, and families, "death signals defeat and forgoing treatment signals surrender."

In understanding medicine as warfare, Childress claims we have lost "the sense of limits." He briefly calls for reclaiming a few such limits in the practice of medicine, including the importance of "the limits of discrimination—distinguishing combatant from noncombatant—and the limits of proportionality," along with "a reasonable prospect of success."[38] By making these brief connections between just war criteria and a fitting moral framework for modern medicine, Childress positions us to turn to the second major section of this essay. Here, we judge the fittingness of Childress's just-war-inspired bioethics as a moral response to the social imaginaries in the surgical and oncology wards.

## Just-War-Inspired Bioethics and the Surgical Ward

As surgery was incorporated into the wider practice of health care, surgeons learned to discipline their practices in order to adhere to the Hippocratic tradition's commitment "to help, or at least to do no harm."[39] Both surgery and Childress's just war theory begin with a presumption against violence. Childress connects nonmaleficence to the Hippocratic tradition, saying that the "Hippocratic principle *primum non nocere* (first of all, or at least, do no harm) presupposes the distinction between not harming and doing good and gives the former priority over the latter."[40] This emphasis on nonmaleficence places moral boundaries around the proper practice of medicine. If violence is to occur, it must be justified, controlled, limited, and devoted to the restoration of true peace.

Analogues of just war criteria are also at work in the practice of surgery.[41] According to the ethnographer Rachel Prentice, surgeons view their craft as "controlled violence," and so they "must balance the physical forces used to invade and alter patients' bodies against the possibilities of doing harm."[42] If violence is to be done, disciplined control is necessary to avoid harm and maintain devotion to the goal of healing. Childress's just-war-inspired bioethics is a fitting moral response to the social imaginary within the surgical ward and the moral problems that arise from the practice of "controlled violence."

Childress's emphasis on the importance of "moral traces" remaining after prima facie duties are overridden also has strong parallels in the practices of the surgical ward.[43] Childress references Augustine, whose work was foundational for just war theory, when he draws attention to the "residual effects" on attitudes and actions that remain from the duty to do no harm, even as violence occurs in a just war.[44] Evidence of these mournful "moral traces" is found in the reflections of surgeons on their practice. The British surgeon John Hunter claimed that every operation should be accompanied by "a sacred dread and reluctance," and the neurosurgeon Henry Marsh began his recent memoir with the line, "I often have to cut into the brain and it is something I hate doing."[45] These exemplary surgeons lament their necessities and so display the "moral traces" Childress emphasized in his just war theory, thereby highlighting how a just-war-inspired bioethics is fitting for the modern surgical ward.

In a recent essay, Richard Miller further develops this Augustinian notion of "moral traces," arguing that "just war morality involves a spiritual exercise—an ascesis—demanding political elites and ordinary citizens to discipline their attitudes, practices, and representations of the other."[46] Miller draws from the importance of confession in Augustine's thought to argue that the practice is a crucial part of the ascesis necessary for modern just war. For Augustine, confession was not simply a private affair, and Miller expands on this, saying of confession: "Such personal reports are part of a more general practice of rendering oneself accountable to standards that one does not wishfully create (or project), objective norms by which to measure one's subjective leanings and desires. Confession, in short, is a matter of making oneself accountable to standards and purposes beyond one's immediate interests."[47]

The formation of character involved with confession is deeply linked to the formation of the memory of a people. And here one finds a deep connection between Miller's just war argument for confession and surgery's weekly Mortality and Morbidity Conference, in which attending surgeons stand before their peers and subordinates, recounting their mistakes and failures for all to hear and learn from. In this analogue to confession, surgeons practice remembering rightly as they hold themselves and their community accountable to the standards of their craft. This work is described in Charles Bosk's ethnography of surgical training, aptly titled *Forgive and Remember*. When senior surgeons "put on the hair shirt" and confess their mistakes, they recommit themselves and all who work with and under them to the moral standards and limits of a tradition that pursues healing within a framework of doing no harm.[48]

In several ways, then, the just-war-inspired moral framework offered by Childress can describe the moral commitments and practices of surgery. Through informed consent, patients authorize the use of surgery's controlled violence. The members of the surgical team reassure the patient by announcing their intent to intervene for the patient's good. Surgeons are trained to operate only when they have a just cause and a reasonable hope of success, and surgery is often treated as a last resort. The common parlance of "minimally invasive" surgery indicates the continual concern for proportionality, and attending surgeons work to form trainees capable of differentiating between the targets of their intervention and the nearby flesh that deserves the protection of innocent civilians.

Indeed, much of surgical training instills the norms of just conduct. Preoperative checklists, sterilization practices, and further rituals of the operating theater ensure that the requirements of *jus ad bellum* and *jus in bello* have been met. Members of the surgical team often remind one another of this moral tradition. Nurses and anesthesiologists monitor the operating theater and the patient's body, functioning like UN military observers, but with real authority to halt a surgery if norms are transgressed. In this way, the surgical ward's moral framework is not simply reinforced post hoc during mortality and morbidity conferences but is actively instilled and policed throughout the practice and site of surgery.

Further connections could be made between just war criteria and the practice of surgery. In fact, it may be necessary for surgery to begin more explicitly making these moral connections, not least because some elective procedures may not meet the criteria of a just-war-inspired bioethics. Setting this task aside, however, we now turn to the oncology ward to set in relief a social imaginary that requires deep transformations in order to be placed within the moral limits of just war criteria.

## Just-War-Inspired Bioethics and the Oncology Ward

After connecting just war criteria and the morality of medicine in his lecture *War as Reality and Metaphor*, Childress briefly notes that modern medicine has deep similarities with modern total warfare.[49] In doing so, he references

William May's *The Physician's Covenant*, in which May claims, "Modern medicine has tended to interpret itself not only through the prism of war but through the medium of its modern practice, that is, unlimited, unconditional war. . . . Just so, hospitals and the physician-fighter wage unconditional battle against death."[50]

May describes how this "unconditional battle against death" conscripts patients into research trials that provide them with no benefit and also pushes them to fight on with no reasonable hope of success. Historically, such a social imaginary has often been found within the oncology ward as a paradigmatic medical site of the modern hospital.

In response to medicine construed as total warfare, Childress asserts that we must make medicine as total warfare "accountable to the moral tradition of just war."[51] However, he does not explicate what such accountability would require. The principles of just war cannot be applied simply in the midst of a total war as it rages, and so wherever medicine is analogous to total warfare, a profound transformation of its discourses, practices, and practitioners is necessary in order for the craft to become accountable to a just-war-inspired bioethics. As we saw above, Childress's moral schema befits the social imaginary of the surgical ward. In contrast, a substantive transformation of the social imaginary historically found within the oncology ward is necessary for this site to be governed by a just-war-inspired bioethics. As we shall see, some changes in this direction can be discerned since Susan Sontag and William May first described total warfare within modern medicine.

To understand how oncology is prone to a total warfare approach to medicine, the oncology ward's social imaginary can be examined using a set of categories for "how war becomes/became total."[52] According to one account, there are four distinct "varieties of ways in which war, by becoming total, can break out of the restraints of the just war tradition": first, what is claimed as just cause for war may become total; second, the means of war may become total; third, combatant status may become total; and fourth, last resort may become a hollow criterion when the military becomes so incorporated into a society that it "renders null the notion of any transition from peace to war."[53] All too often, all four of these conditions are present in the oncology ward's social imaginary. Death as the ultimate enemy can be a total cause for war in the oncology ward; the unrelenting assault of chemotherapy and radiation can totalize the means of oncology's fight; combatant status can be totalized when all body cells are seen as potentially cancerous; and the rise of a medical-industrial complex conflating research and therapy in an all-out effort to prevent and manage cancer can make it difficult to distinguish between peace and war.

For oncology to be governed within the bounds of a just-war-inspired bioethics, these four areas demand transformations of its social imaginary. We can trace the contours of a fitting response following Allen Verhey and William

May's claim that life is not an ultimate good and that death is not an ultimate evil.[54] If this is true, then in response to the first area of war becoming totalizing, the cause of oncology's fight can be just—but it is not a total one. There are other goods for the patient to pursue than simply the defeat of death. Recognizing that treating a patient's cancer is not an all-out assault on death itself requires medical practitioners in the oncology ward to discern and pursue the limited but real goods available to each patient throughout their illness, with shrinking and eliminating tumors being but one good among many. Such a recognition also has implications for the second category of ways in which war becomes total, as totalizing modes of treatment in chemotherapy and radiation may need to be rejected at times in favor of therapy more fitting for the pursuit of a particular patient's holistic and finite flourishing. The final two aspects of how war becomes total war may be the hardest to confront in the modern oncology ward. To reestablish noncombatant status and distinguish between peaceable and combative therapeutic engagements with the body, a change is required in the ways that cancer has historically been understood and how its treatment has been pursued.

The confusion between combatant and noncombatant in the modern oncology ward points to a long-standing difficulty in just war theory. As we saw above, Richard Miller argues that those attempting to adhere to just war morality must undergo a form of "ascesis" in order to "discipline their attitudes, practices, and representation of the other."[55] In describing the difficulty of properly understanding and relating to the other, Miller follows Augustine, who says, "In the miserable condition of this life, we often believe that someone who is an enemy is a friend, or that someone who is a friend is an enemy."[56] In response, Augustine offers no easy words of comfort, for he admits that this life is marked by both the betrayal and death of friends.[57] We must learn to properly grieve the bodily betrayal and death that mark the current life in light of the final hope of resurrection. This ascesis is particularly fitting for the oncology ward, which instead of promising the defeat of death may be a site where we might painfully learn to grieve bodily betrayal and the claims of death. Resistance may be necessary, but it ought to always be done in the hope of securing a bodily peace, however provisional. The ascesis that marks the oncology ward's incorporation into a just war morality trains us to discern and celebrate the proleptic inbreaking of life wherever it is found, learning to see our bodily peace in light of eternal peace, even as we recognize that it is fully realized only on the other side of death.[58] This rightly ordered grief and celebration enables the formation of medical practitioners and patients capable of adhering to a just-war-inspired bioethics in the oncology ward.

Finally, Augustine's understanding of peace and sacrifice provides a response to the final category of ways that war becomes total, and we can see how this applies to the oncology ward. In *The City of God*, Augustine argues that peace with the body and peace with the soul are bound up with social peace, which is itself a fraught category during the saeculum, this present age when we live within the earthly city's peace as we journey toward the heavenly city's true and final peace. For Augustine, pilgrims in this life should value and make use of this earthly peace as long as doing so "does not impede the religion by which we are taught that the one supreme and true God is to be worshipped."[59] Augustine turns to the notion of sacrifice to distinguish between acceptable and unacceptable forms of earthly peace. For Augustine, the true city of God "sacrifices to none" but God, so any effort to order a people around alternate sacrifices must be resisted. Stanley Hauerwas connects this notion of sacrifice with warfare, and especially the modern reality of total warfare, saying, "For in spite of the horror of war, I think war, particularly in our times, is a sacrificial system that is crucial for the renewal of the moral commitments that constitute our lives."[60]

Hauerwas's description of the modern sacrifices of war can also be fitting for the oncology ward. Here we often find that those lives sacrificed in the war against cancer, especially those enrolled in medical research, renew our commitment to fight on against death itself. To resist the claims of a medical-industrial complex devoted to total warfare against death and its emissary, cancer, we can draw from Augustine's notion of true sacrifice, in which the heavenly city participates in Christ's sacrifice and no others.[61] Founded by, existing in, and ordered to Christ, the heavenly city makes use of the peace offered by the earthly city while rejecting disordered notions of justice and sacrifice. Within the oncology ward, the goods of bodily peace can be celebrated as they are attained while also understanding them in light of more fundamental goods. This approach also offers a lens through which to discern and reject the notion of sacrifice offered by a medical-industrial complex that often knows no difference between peace and war in the body.[62]

In these four broad areas, we can see how the oncology ward's social imaginary could be transformed and thus made governable within the bounds of a just-war-inspired bioethics. There have been ways that the work of oncology has moved in this direction, from the development of more targeted therapies, including immunotherapies, to an increasing willingness to turn to hospice care. These changes make it more possible for the work of oncology to be governed by just war criteria like proportionality, discrimination, and just conduct, even in situations when cancer has metastasized.[63] But insofar as the social imaginary of the oncology ward, the surgical ward, or any other sector of modern medicine transgresses the bounds of just war morality and moves toward a total warfare approach, the above responses are also fitting for that site. In short, these transformations detail what is required to make, as Childress said, a medicine engrossed in total warfare "accountable to the moral tradition of just war."[64] Such accountability is a necessary prerequisite to Childress's just-war-inspired bioethics governing a medicine that engages the body as an enemy. When such a moral discipline is in place, the real goods offered by medicine as just war can be appreciated without becoming disordered. By focusing on the moral boundaries necessary in conflict, this moral response can be a fitting approach to bioethics in the modern hospital, but this does not necessarily make it fundamental to the moral work of health care.

## Conclusion: Prioritizing Peace with the Body

Although medicine construed as just war offers real goods to both patients and practitioners, what might it mean for peace with the body to be prioritized over conflict in health care? Although Childress does not explore this question, he does recognize that just war theorists and pacifists need one another. In his influential essay on just war, he states, "In conclusion, pacifists and just war theorists are actually closer to and more dependent on each other than they often suppose. Just war theorists sometimes overlook the fact that they and the pacifists reason from a common starting point. Both begin with the contention that nonviolence has moral priority over violence. . . . While pacifists can remind just war theorists of this presumption against violence, pacifists also need just war theorists."[65]

Childress's just-war-inspired bioethics offers the considerable resources of just war theory to the moral conflicts that pervade modern medicine, particularly when the body is engaged as an enemy. As such, it is a great gift. But it also needs to be reminded what peace of the body actually entails when, in Childress's own words, "peace remains the ultimate aim of a just war."[66] A thorough account of bodily peaceableness is beyond the scope of this essay, but pursuing it as the ultimate aim of health care may mean revaluing the importance placed on the wars waged in surgery and oncology.

A theological account of health care devoted to peace with the body might begin with a careful consideration of ordinary practices of bodily care that carry little of the promise or peril of battle against disease and death. Practices of bodily peaceableness—like cleaning wounds, giving baths, and attending with caring bedside manners—all serve to remind patients and practitioners of the goodness of the body even as it may be riddled by the emissaries of death. A significant challenge here, of course, is how the division of labor in the modern hospital makes it structurally difficult for some medical practitioners to practice bodily care in these ways. Nevertheless, wherever they are found, these slow and often uncelebrated practices of bodily care should be cherished; for in their work we can begin to discern the peace that remains the ultimate aim of a just-war-inspired bioethics. In his efforts to discipline both war and medicine, James Childress offers a moral schema for navigating conflicts in a broken

world, and this gift can be gratefully received even as we must look elsewhere
for accounts of the peace toward which we aim.

## Notes

I would like to thank Luke Bretherton, James Childress, Farr Curlin, Stanley Hauerwas, Ryan
Juskus, Matt Puffer, Greg Williams, and Tobias Winright for their generous feedback on
drafts of this argument. I also am grateful for the insightful comments offered by the editors
and anonymous reviewers of the *Journal of the Society of Christian Ethics*, along with those in
attendance at the annual meeting of the Society of Christian Ethics.

1. For example, Paul Ramsey, one of the foundational figures in the guild, wrote numerous
   works in just war theory and bioethics. Among others, see his *War and the Christian Conscience: How Shall Modern War Be Conducted Justly?* (Durham, NC: Duke University Press,
   1961) and *The Just War: Force and Moral Responsibility* (New York: Charles Scribner's Sons,
   1968), alongside his *Patient as Person: Explorations in Medical Ethics* (New Haven, CT: Yale
   University Press, 1973).

2. I am grateful to Tobias Winright for an early conversation about the connections between
   Childress's just war theory and his bioethics, and for sharing with me his conference paper,
   "Bioethics and Just War Ethics Will Meet," presentation for the panel on "Justice and
   Peace Have Kissed: The Inclusive Posture of Just War Theory" at the Annual Meeting of
   the American Society for Bioethics and Humanities, San Diego, October 18, 2014. For
   more of Winright's work on just war theory, see, e.g., Tobias Winright, "The Liturgy
   as a Basis for Catholic Identity, Just War Theory, and the Presumption against War," in
   *Catholic Identity and the Laity*, College Theology Society Annual Vol. 54, ed. Tim Muldoon
   (Maryknoll, NY: Orbis Books, 2009), 134–51; and Tobias Winright, "Introduction," in
   *Can War Be Just in the 21st Century?* ed. Tobias Winright and Laurie Johnston (Maryknoll,
   NY: Orbis Books, 2015), xiii–xxvii.

3. This conception of "social imaginaries" is drawn from the work of Charles Taylor, who
   defines the term as "the ways people imagine their social existence, how they fit together
   with others, how things go on between them and their fellows, the expectations that are
   normally met, and the deeper normative notions and images that underlie these expectations." Charles Taylor, *Modern Social Imaginaries* (Durham, NC: Duke University Press,
   2004), 23.

4. Rachel Prentice, *Bodies in Formation: An Ethnography of Anatomy and Surgical Education*
   (Durham, NC: Duke University Press, 2013), 137.

5. Hippocrates, *Epidemics* 1:11, in *Hippocrates*, ed. W. H. S. Jones (Cambridge, MA: Harvard
   University Press, 1923), vol. 1, 165.

6. Albert Jonsen, *The Birth of Bioethics* (New York: Oxford University Press, 1998), 102, 333.

7. James F. Childress, *Civil Disobedience and Political Obligation: A Study in Christian Social
   Ethics* (New Haven, CT: Yale University Press, 1971), x.

8. Ibid., 9.

9. Ibid., 204.

10. Ibid., 103. See Courtney Campbell, "On James F. Childress: Answering That of God
    in Every Person," in *Theological Voices in Medical Ethics*, ed. Stephen Lammers and Allen
    Verhey (Grand Rapids: Eerdmans, 1993), 127–56.

11. Childress, *Civil Disobedience*, 103n112.

12. Ibid., 163.

13. James F. Childress, "Reinhold Niebuhr's Critique of Pacifism," *Review of Politics* 36, no. 4 (1974): 467–91, esp. 488–90.

14. James F. Childress, "Just-War Theories: The Bases, Interrelations, Priorities, and Functions of Their Criteria," *Theological Studies* 39, no. 3 (1978): 427–45.

15. James F. Childress, *Moral Responsibility in Conflicts: Essays on Nonviolence, War, and Conscience* (Baton Rouge: Louisiana State University Press, 1982), 93.

16. Lisa Cahill, *Love Your Enemies: Discipleship, Pacifism, and Just War Theory* (Minneapolis: Fortress Press, 1994), 13; Richard B. Miller, *Interpretations of Conflict: Ethics, Pacifism, and the Just-War Tradition* (Chicago: University of Chicago Press, 1991), 7.

17. National Conference of Catholic Bishops, *The Challenge of Peace: God's Promise and Our Response* (Washington, DC: United States Catholic Conference, 1983), §83; Childress and Ralph Potter are cited at §84, n. 35.

18. As such, it has not been uncontested. In particular, James Turner Johnson has argued that this shift does not comport with the Catholic tradition of just war reasoning. For more on the dispute between Childress and Johnson, see James F. Childress, "'Nonviolent Resistance: Trust and Risk-Taking' Twenty-Five Years Later," *Journal of Religious Ethics* 25, no. 2 (1997): 213–20; James Turner Johnson, "Comment on James F. Childress's 'Nonviolent Resistance, Trust and Risk-Taking' Twenty-Five Years Later," *Journal of Religious Ethics* 26, no. 1 (1998): 219–22.

19. For a detailed bibliography of this tradition, see Richard Miller, "Just War, Civic Virtue, and Democratic Social Criticism: Augustinian Reflections," in *Friends and Other Strangers: Studies in Religion, Ethics, and Culture* (New York: Columbia University Press, 2016), 374–75n1.

20. Childress, *Moral Responsibility*, 64.

21. Ibid., 64–65.

22. Ibid., 71.

23. Ibid., 69.

24. Ibid., 72.

25. Ibid., 92.

26. James F. Childress, *Priorities in Biomedical Ethics* (Philadelphia: Westminster Press, 1981), 54.

27. Ibid., 55–58.

28. Hippocrates, *Epidemics* 1:11; quoted by James F. Childress, *Who Should Decide? Paternalism in Health Care* (New York: Oxford University Press, 1982), 40.

29. Ibid., ix.

30. A few years later, Childress lists proportionality, effectiveness, last resort, and least infringement as conditions for overriding "the prima facie principle of respect for autonomy." See James F. Childress, "The Place of Autonomy in Bioethics," *Hastings Center Report* 20, no. 1 (1990): 12–17.

31. Tom L. Beauchamp and James F. Childress, *Principles of Biomedical Ethics*, 1st edition (New York: Oxford University Press, 1979), 45–47.

32. Tom L. Beauchamp and James F. Childress, *Principles of Biomedical Ethics*, 3rd edition (New York: Oxford University Press, 1989), 51–54.

33. Tom L. Beauchamp and James F. Childress, *Principles of Biomedical Ethics*, 7th edition (New York: Oxford University Press, 2013), 23.

34. James F. Childress, *"Principles of Biomedical Ethics*: Reflections on a Work in Progress," in *Belmont Revisited*, ed. James F. Childress, Eric M. Meslin, and Harold Shapiro (Washington, DC: Georgetown University Press, 2005), 47–66, at 62. Recently, Childress has extended this approach to public health ethics, in which he considers a presumption against infringing liberty. See, e.g., James F. Childress, "Public Health and Civil Liberties: Resolving Conflicts," in *Routledge Companion to Bioethics*, ed. John Arras, Elizabeth Fenton, and Rebecca Kukla (New York: Routledge, 2015), 325–38.

35. Childress, *Moral Responsibility*, 74.

36. James F. Childress, *War as Reality and Metaphor: Some Moral Reflections*, Joseph A. Reich Sr. Distinguished Lecture on War, Morality, and the Military Profession, November 18, 1992 (Colorado Springs: US Air Force Academy, 1993), 5. Much of this lecture is incorporated in the chapter "Metaphor and Analogy in Bioethics," in *Practical Reasoning in Bioethics*, by James F. Childress (Bloomington: Indiana University Press, 199).

37. Childress, *War as Reality and Metaphor*, 11; cf. Susan Sontag, *Illness as Metaphor and AIDS and Its Metaphors* (New York: Picador, 2001), esp. 64–65.

38. Childress, *War as Reality and Metaphor*, 11.

39. For simplicity's sake, the term "surgical ward" refers collectively to sites of preoperative preparation, the operating room, and postoperative recovery.

40. Childress, *Who Should Decide?* 29.

41. For an example from the end of the eighteenth century, see John Hunter, *Lectures on the Principles of Surgery*, in *The Works of John Hunter*, vol. 1, ed. James F. Palmer (London: Longman, Rees, Orme, Brown, Green, and Longman, 1835), 210. Contemporary ethnographies of surgery range from the early work by Charles Bosk, *Forgive and Remember: Managing Medical Failure*, 2nd edition (Chicago: University of Chicago Press, 1979; 2003), to the recent book by Prentice, *Bodies in Formation*.

42. Prentice, *Bodies in Formation*, 137. For Childress's account of violence and nonviolence, see Childress, *Moral Responsibility*, 46–57.

43. For more on the importance of "moral traces" in Childress's thought and contemporary bioethics, see Aline H. Kalbian, "Moral Traces and Relational Autonomy," *Soundings: An Interdisciplinary Journal* 96, no. 2 (2013): 280–96.

44. Childress refers to Augustine to argue that regret and perhaps even remorse may be a fitting response. Childress, *Moral Responsibility*, 69–70. When Augustine argues in *The City of God* that "the wise man" compelled to serve as a public official has the duty to "wage just wars," he emphasizes the mournfulness that ought to accompany such actions. Augustine, *The City of God against the Pagans*, trans. R. W. Dyson (Cambridge: Cambridge University Press, 1998), 19.6–7.

45. Hunter, *Lectures on the Principles of Surgery*, 210; Henry Marsh, *Do No Harm: Stories of Life, Death, and Brain Surgery* (New York: Picador, 2016), 1.

46. Miller, "Just War, Civic Virtue, and Democratic Social Criticism," 205.

47. Ibid., 224.

48. Bosk, *Forgive and Remember*, 139. Daniel Hall notes that the Mortality and Morbidity Conference is a routine practice only for surgeons. Daniel E. Hall, "The Guild of Surgeons as a Tradition of Moral Enquiry," *Journal of Medicine and Philosophy* 36 (2011): 114–32, at 127.

49. Childress, *War as Reality and Metaphor*, 13–14.

50. William F. May, *The Physician's Covenant: Images of the Healer in Medical Ethics*, 2nd edition (Louisville: Westminster John Knox Press, 2000), 66.

51. Childress, *War as Reality and Metaphor*, 14. In this way, Childress indicates that the metaphor of total warfare has been tried and found wanting according to his criteria for all metaphors in health care, which "can be assessed by how well they illuminate rather than distort both what is going on and what should be done." Childress, *Practical Reasoning in Bioethics*, x.

52. John Howard Yoder, "Appendix II," in *When War Is Unjust: Being Honest in Just-War Thinking*, 2nd edition (Maryknoll, NY: Orbis Books, 1996).

53. Ibid., 130–35.

54. Allen Verhey, *The Christian Art of Dying: Learning from Jesus* (Grand Rapids: Eerdmans, 2011), 392; May, *Physician's Covenant*, 70.

55. Miller, "Just War, Civic Virtue, and Democratic Social Criticism," 224.

56. Augustine, *City of God*, 19.8.

57. Ibid.

58. Ibid., 19.17.

59. Ibid.

60. Stanley Hauerwas, *War and the American Difference: Theological Reflections on Nonviolence and National Identity* (Grand Rapids: Baker Academic, 2011), xv.

61. Hauerwas develops Augustine's thought by setting the "undeniable" sacrifices of war alongside the person of Jesus, in whom God "has forever ended our attempts to sacrifice to God in terms set by the city of man." Ibid., 69. For Augustine, the heavenly city belongs to Christ and becomes God's "most wonderful and blessed sacrifice." The body of Christ, broken for the blessing of the world, offers a different notion of sacrifice than the broken bodies that fill the data sets of medical research. Augustine, *City of God*, 19.23.

62. These connections between political theology and bioethics are indebted to recent work in Augustinian political theology. See especially Luke Bretherton, *Christianity and Contemporary Politics: The Conditions and Possibilities of Faithful Witness* (Malden, MA: Wiley-Blackwell, 2010); and Luke Bretherton, *Resurrecting Democracy: Faith, Citizenship, and the Politics of a Common Life* (Cambridge: Cambridge University Press, 2015). Among many others, see also Charles Mathewes, *A Theology of Public Life* (Cambridge: Cambridge University Press, 2008); and Eric Gregory, *Politics and the Order of Love: An Augustinian Ethic of Democratic Citizenship* (Chicago: University of Chicago Press, 2010).

63. I am grateful to Brian Quaranta for helping me appreciate these changes in modern oncology.

64. Childress, *War as Reality and Metaphor*, 14.

65. Childress, *Moral Responsibility*, 93.

66. Ibid., 72. In their own ways, Lisa Cahill's *Love Your Enemies* and Daniel Bell's *Just War as Christian Discipleship* both address this concern as it relates to just war theory. It is worth noting that Childress's later work embraces a more thoroughgoing pluralism of prima facie duties. Childress himself admits that he was "tempted" to rank or scale prima facie duties at one point but that he later settled on the position that "all principles and rules are equally prima facie binding." Childress, "*Principles of Biomedical Ethics*: Reflections," 59.

# Nature Elicits Piety: James Gustafson among the Wolves

*Nathaniel Van Yperen*

This essay explores James Gustafson's theocentric ethics for the work of constructing an adequate Protestant Christian ethic of the wild. Two critical questions arise in conversation with his ethics: (1) When the category of natural evil is rendered incoherent, what are the significant consequences for piety in Christian ecological ethics? (2) How does Gustafson's theocentric ethics, which emphasizes experience, help us to refigure gratitude in ecological ethics? The essay explores these questions in the context of the debate over the reintroduction and conservation of wolves in the American West.

TEN DAYS BEFORE THE PRESIDENTIAL ELECTION OF 2004, THE Bush-Cheney camp released a television attack ad titled "Wolves." The video opens with a wide angle shot that pans over a thick forest. Then, suddenly, we find ourselves in the midst of that dark wood, with rays of light streaming in from small gaps in the forest canopy. A woman's voice gravely warns that we live in "an increasingly dangerous world." John Kerry and the liberals in Congress, she continues, voted to "slash" the intelligence operations budget after the "first" terrorist attack on America. Precisely as the word "terrorist" is uttered, a wolf appears. The narrator continues: With "cuts so deep," America is in a "weakened state." Wolves flash through shaky, handheld camera shots. The lens finally settles on a pack of wolves resting, but alert, on a near hillside, and we hear a bold warning: "Weakness attracts those who are waiting to do America harm." As the narration concludes, the wolves suddenly leap up in unison and run toward the camera. The shot fades to a still photograph of George W. Bush at work in the Oval Office.

This attack ad capitalizes on a deeply rooted aversion to wilderness and wildness in America and updates its logic of fear. America is alone in a dark and dangerous wilderness. Wolves are rapacious, vicious, and terrifying. Terrorists are wild like wolves. Nature elicits terror.

Nathaniel Van Yperen, PhD, is visiting assistant professor at Gustavus Adolphus College, 800 West College Avenue, Saint Peter, MN 56082; nathaniel.vanyperen@gmail.com.

*Journal of the Society of Christian Ethics*, 38, 2 (2018): 75–91

The association of wolves and terrorists is troubling for a host of reasons. The predatory wolf is exaggerated as antihuman and antisocial—a creature that threatens safety, domestic stability, and economy. Figuring the terrorist as wolf mobilizes an unnatural view of the wolf—as a menace or outlaw—in a way that reduces the foreign terrorist to the status of a brute while simultaneously reinforcing the homocentric presupposition of humankind's singular status as the intrinsically valuable. Both the terrorist and the wolf trouble the borders of our domestic ideals, and both have been subjected to campaigns of torture. The ad reveals our misunderstanding of nature as much as it reveals our misunderstanding of what drives some to acts of terror.

Just as the arbitrary boundaries of a national park are incapable of containing the wild wolves, so too are the current disciplinary boundaries between social and ecological ethics inadequate to confront or answer the problem of the wolf as terrorist and the terrorist as wolf. As Pope Francis argues in *Laudato Si'*, "We are faced not with two separate crises, one environmental and the other social, but rather with one complex crisis which is both social and environmental."[1] In other words, we can no longer afford to ignore the ecological consequences of our theological anthropologies. The premise of this essay is that an adequate Christian ethic of the wild is of vital necessity for naming and addressing the moral conditions of our time, and that the theological ethicist James Gustafson contributes important, but limited, resources to this present and future task of Christian ethics.[2]

In conversation with Gustafson's ethics, I explore two interrelated questions of adequacy for a Christian ethic of the wild: (1) When the category of natural evil is rendered incoherent, what are the significant consequences for piety in Christian ecological ethics? (2) How does Gustafson's theocentric ethics, which emphasizes experience, help us to refigure accountability in ecological challenges that exceed the limits of personal experience? In other words, how are we to assume responsibility to and respect for the more-than-human world that elicits human affections, without compromising the integrity of the beings or entities in question?[3] Success in addressing these questions will awaken a sense of gratitude for authentic encounters with the wild—a shift that counters the domesticating, consumptive appetites of our culture of commodification. James Gustafson can be a helpful guide in navigating the wilderness of values in which the wolf, as creature and symbol, is often figured prominently.

## Nature Elicits Piety

The wolves of the attack ad play on a long-standing cultural narrative that depicts the creature as depraved and bloodthirsty. The symbol of the wolf reinforces binary views of nature and culture, and of vice and virtue. In contrast to Native American views, European colonizers brought to North America myths of the demonic wolf, which evolved to moral categories of outlaw, villain, and murderer on the American frontier. Today, the debate over conservation, reintroduction, and wolf hunting in North America is a contested terrain. It is a debate in which Gustafson's theocentric ethics can evoke a sense of new possibilities. Over his long career, Gustafson's prolific writings crossed disciplinary boundaries, contributed to both church and academy, and spurred on the diverse work of many students who have shaped the tradition of Christian ethics.[4] Here, in this essay, I focus on the aspects of Gustafson's legacy that explicitly address, or are applicable to, the particular challenges of constructing a Protestant Christian ethic of the wild capable of navigating the wolf's contested terrain in America.[5]

Gustafson's theocentrism is both a framework and an "attitudinal, dispositional, affective stance," and both aspects are significant for the development of a Christian ethic of the wild.[6] Gustafson's legacy vis-à-vis the natural world might be summarized thus: He gives us mystery without sentimentality, responsibility without harmony. It is, on Lisa Sideris's thoroughgoing interpretation, a "comprehensive naturalized ethic."[7] Gustafson's work is useful in the service of a Christian ethic of the wild because he offers a consistent and rigorous immanent critique of Christianity's negligence of the more-than-human world. Theocentrism knocks down the hierarchy of the Great Chain of Being and reconfigures values across an ambiguous and often mysterious nature. According to Gustafson, "God is the source of human good but does not guarantee it."[8]

Gustafson's theocentrism comes through clearly in his reformulation of the categorical imperative as a corrective to anthropocentrism: "Act so that you consider all things never *only* as a means to your ends, or even to collective human ends."[9] Responsibility is participating in what God is empowering one to do in a world that is bigger than the self or society.[10] Individualism is anthropocentrism magnified, and Gustafson rightly judges both to be idolatrous. Anthropocentrism displaces God as the subject of worship and replaces humanity as the central concern, which gets the first question of the Westminster Shorter Catechism wrong. The chief end of humankind, according to the catechism, is to glorify God and enjoy God forever, and anthropocentrism fails this basic requirement of Christian piety. Gustafson's theocentrism, instead, is nonanthropocentric: "The salvation of man is not the chief end of God; certainly it is not the exclusive end of God."[11] When the good and right are confined to the anthropocentric, our moral vision is distorted to see the human being as "the measurer of all things and the measure of all things—at humankind's own peril . . . and to the peril of the relation of which humankind is a miniscule part."[12] Such confusion muddies up the waters of theological anthropology because it inverts the proper relationship between Creator and creature.[13] We must admit that our knowledge of God is, at the end of the day, human knowledge of God in a world in which God will be God to all of creation.[14]

Gustafson argues that most theological ethicists hold incomplete views of the natural world. Nature is a source of multidimensional values, and it does not exist for the flourishing of human beings exclusively. Although Gustafson frequently states his "preference" for the Reformed tradition, he argues against the Protestant "preoccupation" with history at the expense of the reality of nature. When theologians are preoccupied with revelation in history, they bury their heads in the sand, oblivious to their self-styled contradictory stance relative to other humanistic and scientific disciplines. This is the path to isolation, irrelevance, and, significantly, indifference to our dependence on the world that God has created. If Protestants are historically deficient in developing a theology of nature, the Roman Catholic natural law tradition simply presumes too much.[15] First, Gustafson argues that the anthropocentrism of the natural law cannot be defended. Second, "nature" is not a static or unchanging order from which we can reliably draw inferences. Instead, humans are participants who must recognize that there is much more ambiguity and complexity than the natural law tradition allows. Third, there is often a "tragedy of human choices," which is a reality that troubles assumptions about the promise of human flourishing in the Kingdom of God.[16] A more rigorous engagement with advancements in science would, on Gustafson's account, lead away from the centrality of human flourishing in the story of God's purposes.

Gustafson's theocentrism opens up the scope of what is good in the sight of God, shifting our focus from the merely human. Gustafson's sentence, "Activity will have to be ordered by understanding our place in the universe as part of and participant of it," rings of Aldo Leopold's land ethic, in which people are participants, or citizens, instead of conquerors.[17] Such a shift matters for the appreciation of an apex predator that does not offer immediate instrumental value to human society. The project of wolf reintroduction in Yellowstone, for example, depended on at least a portion of our citizenry opening up to the possibility that we might have obligations to and affections for parts of the world that do not result in a profit. This is not to say that theocentric ethics has thus far played much of a part in the successes of reintroduction, but rather to suggest that theocentrism can give intelligible reasons for such commitments and that it can play a role in future democratic deliberations in conservation.

With regard to wolves in particular, the shift from anthropocentrism to theocentrism is not easy. The difficulties begin in the scriptures. In the Hebrew Bible, wolves are a symbol of corruption and savagery: dishonest officials are like "wolves tearing into prey" (Ez 22:27), the enemy's horsemen are "more menacing than wolves at dusk" (Hab 1:8), and corrupt judges are like "evening wolves that leave nothing until the morning" (Zep 3:3). In the New Testament, wolves symbolize threats to the Gospel: False prophets are "ravenous wolves" in sheep's clothing (Mt 7:15) and "savage wolves" that will invade the community (Acts 20:29). Matthew and Luke compare Christian believers to sheep in the midst of wolves (Mt 10:16, Lk 10:3), and John warns of a wolf that will "scatter the flock" (Jn 10:12).

The story of how the wolf became the demonic other is masterfully presented in Barry Lopez's classic *Of Wolves and Men*. Lopez invites the reader into the ambiguities that flow through the porous boundaries separating the wild from the domestic.[18] Lopez is a writer who ruminates in prose. His works fuse history, geography, and personal experience in a way that prompts reflection on the dynamics of mystery, humility, and gratitude. He writes beautifully about the dispositions that animate Gustafson's theological ethics. In this essay, I am intent to open up new space for the role of metaphor, art, and imagination in ethics by pairing Gustafson with an environmental writer such as Barry Lopez, and through a personal narrative at the end.[19] It is an attempt, in the words of John Elder, "to ventilate and invigorate the merely academic world."[20]

Lopez tells the story of the wolf's journey to villainy. In the Middle Ages, wolves threatened beliefs about the spiritual world when they exhumed the dead or were seen eating human carrion on a battlefield. The wolf is a symbol of greed and fraud in Dante's *Inferno*; and in Chaucer's *Canterbury Tales*, the "Parson's Tale" includes imagery of wolves devouring the sheep of Jesus Christ. From the biblical and literary imageries, traditions of werewolfery morphed into fears of demonic possession and became a focal target of the Inquisition. Similarly, in their many incarnations, fables and tales such as "The Boy Who Cried Wolf" and "Little Red Riding Hood" play with the themes of threat and treachery in the figure of the wolf.[21]

European colonists brought with them the literary and cultural associations of the wolf as savage beast. Puritans needed only to look out the window to the "howling wilderness" to see Satan at work on the boundary. The existential misfortunes that constituted life in the early colonies, or later on the frontier, cultivated a moral sense of good striving against evil, of taming wilderness and eradicating predators. This spiritual imagery gradually took on an economic dimension as anxieties and hardships were redirected and projected outward as character-forming purpose. Lopez shows how the wolf became the enemy in the American West by way of a confluence of American ideals that included "taming wilderness, the law of vengeance, protection of property, an inalienable right to decide the fate of all animals without incurring moral responsibility, and the strongly American conception of man as the protector of defenseless creatures."[22] The wolf, therefore, has long occupied the position of villain or other to the centrality of human virtue and industry. The shift from anthropocentrism to theocentrism is no mere shift of gaze. It requires a conversion. Conversions come through experience.

We do not experience the whole, but we experience the reality of the Divine in the details of creaturely life.[23] For Gustafson, it is our "capacities to intervene or to forbear" that are the "grounds of our accountability."[24] The marks of theocentrism are concern for the common good, the inevitability of moral ambiguity, and genuinely tragic choices.[25] Theocentrism relates all things as they relate to God, "insofar as this can be discerned. But God will be God."[26] Our finitude limits our capacities, which chastens too much confidence in traditional authorities.[27] The natural world is not a comfortable home nor only a site of beauty and connection. It is home, but one with hazards, trials, and tragedies. Consenting to our dependence with gratitude requires that the heart and will be "reordered; the values that guide human activity must be transvalued."[28] The possibilities of transvaluation are evoked in experience. Theocentrism "probably evokes better than it explains";[29] it "evokes in us a sense of the sublime, or more religiously, a sense of the divine calls for *respect* for nature."[30] Its promise is the "enlargement" of the soul and our interests against the narrow turn inward.[31]

Gustafson opens his lectures in *A Sense of the Divine* with an exploration of his own experiences of the natural world from his youth. This personal account offers a point of connection to readers who similarly have come to love nature by way of experiences and encounters rather than by theories or ideas. He notes that his consciousness of nature was formed "pre-reflexively" and free from any "scientific or aesthetic theories to explain and justify how nature and we were mutually engaged."[32] But this innocence is unsettled when the "reflexive consciousness" arrives with scientific knowledge animated by technology, politics, economics, and ecology.[33] He writes, "The sweet innocence, the joy of consenting to the given, is disturbed, and those moments of deep awe and overwhelming delight require a bracketing of the sophistication that has accrued."[34] Thus, amid experiences of dependence and gratitude spring questions of description and explanation. Early in his *Ethics*, Gustafson poses a question that drives at this tension: "How does one, in a prudent effort not to say too much too specifically and with excessive certitude, say enough about God to develop a theological ethics?"[35] I turn now to this question of piety.

Gustafson defines the term "piety" as a "basic disposition and attitude," a "settled disposition," and a "persistent attitude."[36] Piety can be natural or religious.[37] Christian piety is a theological construal of the world that offers no clear resolutions of ambiguity.[38] To say something theological, for Gustafson, is to religiously construe the meaning of powers that are known in various senses—gratitude, obligation, remorse, the form of hope, and a sense of direction.[39] The theological construal should never be confused with the power that induces piety in the first place. Religious affections are responses that participate in the symbols of a tradition that affect perception and interpretation.[40] The religious affections, expressed in the symbols of tradition, "appropriately point to the reality of the divine powers, but never exhaust them."[41] By piety, Gustafson does not mean faith. Rather, he is intent on making a sharp distinction between the two terms: Piety "is a response to the powers, objective to ourselves, that bring life into being and sustain it, that bear down upon us, and threaten us."[42] As opposed to faith, piety is never in conflict with reason.[43]

Modern science shows that humans are but a "miniscule" part of nature, and we cannot continue to insist that a "warm and friendly deity" will make our difficulties and tragedies right.[44] To put it bluntly, God does not have a preferential option for humanity.[45] Piety orients us through awe and respect for our dependence on nature as God, though our experiences of the conditions of our existence may range from gratitude to fear to mourning.[46]

On Stanley Hauerwas's assessment, Gustafson's piety is an "attempt to be a theologian who is only secondarily a Christian theologian" and represents something akin to Stoicism.[47] Hauerwas is wary of Gustafson's appeal to the ahistorical variety of "senses" that can be shared across pieties, ranging from natural to Christian. Hauerwas worries that "the church seems merely to confirm experience that can be known in other, quite different ways."[48] The trouble is that the "particular is only the illustration," such that the church is merely a symbol of the universal.[49]

Hauerwas's objections are echoed and expanded in new directions by Jeffrey Stout. Stout, like Hauerwas, admires Gustafson but, in the end, argues that Gustafson is not theological enough. Though his "is not a theocentric vision," Stout's definition of piety resembles Gustafson's account of natural piety.[50] In the end, the modest pragmatist, Gustafson, and the Barthian can surely share similar senses of dependence, gratitude, and awe. For Stout, Gustafson's problem is that he falls between the poles of pragmatism and revelation, such that his position lacks the distinctiveness that a Christian theology *should* provide. Stout's criticism is characteristically efficient and incisive: "Conversation partners must remain distinctive enough to be identified, to be needed. They must be able to clarify the difference their outlook makes and to say why they differ from the rest of us at the most crucial points."[51] I take this criticism to be a serious one, for not only Gustafson but also for my broader interest in constructing an adequate Christian ethic of the wild. If the modest pragmatist already has control of natural piety, what does Gustafson's account add if it eschews the confidence in revelation of a Barthian position? Is Gustafson, at the end of the day, a modest pragmatist with theological baggage? It would seem so when he writes: "No claims need to be made for exclusivity or for sufficiency as a basis for ecological ethics while indicating the value of its contributions. One judgment would be on that value, rather than the authority of the tradition from which the value comes."[52] Still, if it is true that Gustafson is not theological enough, the Barthian option is perhaps still *too* theological for the Christian ethic of the wild that I am interested in thinking with Gustafson to define and defend—namely, one that is not reducible to anthropocentric bias and does not easily fall prey to the temptation to explain away, or promise to redeem, the features of the natural world that do not mirror Christic ideals or themes of reconciliation, peace, or harmony (whether in the present or in the eschatological future). Common confusions regarding natural evil highlight the challenge and opportunity of a Christian ethic of the wild.

## Gustafson on Natural Evil

Lisa Cahill observes that the problem of evil "is a key concern" for Gustafson in his *Ethics* but that he does not address it with a "directness commensurate with its importance."[53] Cahill works out this observation in relation to Gustafson's method and his doctrine of God, demonstrating that the two categories are restructured from their traditional anthropocentric formulations. Gustafson's approach to the problem of evil is not to refuse the world God has created, as in the case of Ivan Karamazov's antitheodic rebellion; nor does he offer a theodicy that accounts for moral or natural evil.[54] I am not as troubled by Gustafson's lack of direct engagement on the problem of evil. I am inclined to think that Gustafson ceases to think about evil, or sin, or suffering as a problem that needs to be answered. To be sure, we still suffer losses. We transgress our limits, of justice and of nature. We articulate such losses and transgressions in the language of evil or suffering, or of tragedy; but even as we do so, the theocentric position does not suggest that such experiences are scandalous, *especially* with regard to natural processes.

The process of natural selection depends on adaptations that occur in relationship to a given environment, a natural community, and through competition and struggle that often produces suffering. If struggle also produces the goods that we can come to love in the more-than-human world, then it is improper to consider the processes evil or wicked, for to do so would be to implicate God in a process of creativity that depends on evil to achieve the good. Our own species, of course, is impossible without the competition and struggle of the evolutionary story. This is where the theological difficulties arise.

Is the natural world in need, properly speaking, of redemption in a way that is related to how humans are in need of transformation? Does the natural world require an evolutionary theodicy, as some process theologians, feminists, and animal theologians have suggested?[55] Gustafson's theocentrism, it seems to me, suggests that the theodic, evolutionary theodic, and antitheodic responses are all predicated on the same confusion—namely, the idea that God is (or should be) uniquely interested in human flourishing. Instead, Gustafson argues that the expectation that God exists for our salvation, or even that God intends or sustains the good of an individual, is the height of anthropocentrism. The question

"Where was God?" in response to tragedy or evil (natural or moral) is simply out of place for Gustafson. Theocentrism does not promise or "guarantee happiness," though Gustafson also believes it does not consign us to discontent."[56] In the end, his is an atheodic natural theology,[57] summarized in the following: "Silence before mystery: this, with deep religious power, expresses the human experience of God."[58] Silence before the mystery requires an acceptance of the realities of creaturely life—realities that sometimes threaten the order and stability of human society. A wolf who lies down with a lamb is a wolf who has gone wrong on a fairly deep level.

Humans are not exempt from the consequences of the natural world, of which we are only a part.[59] Thus, for Gustafson, there is both an attraction and aversion to the conditions of our dependence; yet they deserve our awe and respect, even when they are detrimental, or even tragic, to human experience. We are dependent, and we can be grateful. We might also become prey. To call the conditions or features of this interdependence evil is to deny the mysterious power and order of God's creativity.

Gustafson's theocentrism thus renders the category of natural evil incoherent; but his preference for the Reformed tradition cannot ignore the role of sin in Christian theology. Sin, on Gustafson's theocentric view, is not understood in the narrow individualistic way but as the overstepping of appropriate limits. We have too long assumed that God had to be moral as defined by humankind: "The problem of theodicy itself assumes this principle. To interpret the justice of God differently does not make one indifferent to human suffering and flourishing, but it does set these concerns within a different and wider theological context."[60] Gustafson's readjustment of the relation of the human creature before God and Creation breaks down the fantasies of anthropocentrism. Gustafson's account of sin and evil, however, stops short of satisfactorily explaining the particular human capacity for wickedness, a capacity exemplified in the distorted intimacies of wolf torture.

## Gustafson among the Wolves

In the history of encounters between Euro-American people and North American wildlife, the villainous wolf confirmed presuppositions about the hierarchical role of the human in the landscape. The rhetoric of evil mapped the moral territory of colonization, and of the frontier, and of the distinctly American fetishization of private property. The predatory techniques of the wolf often fed human disgust regarding the "wastefulness" of the wolf. Wolves hunt by chasing their prey and, because they are undersized in relation to much of their prey, they target sensitive areas such as the nose, ears, flanks, and genitalia. Ranchers were horrified when they found surviving cows udderless and prized bulls castrated.[61] Wolves also sometimes kill more than they can eat. Wolves sometimes disembowel and begin consuming the organs of animals that have not yet died. In response to such disvalue—namely, the meaningless degree of suffering by the prey—humans searched for explanations and pronounced condemnation on moral subjects that cannot be moral agents. Natural laws were woven with human ideals of justice: Wolves became outlaws, criminals, killers, monsters, and thieves.[62] The wolf became the antirancher, laying waste to the goods of domestic society. The wolf inverted the ideals of Manifest Destiny and threatened the reversion to the primal. This rhetoric of evil reinforced senses of identity—the validation of one's role within natural and cultural worlds—and provided a rationality for the contextual animus toward wolves.

In North America, purging wolves was a practice that measured the scope of human modification of the landscape, and it often included vengeful acts of torture. Men poisoned wolves with strychnine, arsenic, and cyanide. They doused wolves in kerosene and set them on fire. There are reports of trappers wiring wolf jaws shut and leaving them to starve. Cowboys affixed ropes to upper and lower jaws and then ripped apart live wolves with the help of horses spurred in opposite directions. Farmers trapped wolves in pits, hamstrung them with knife or ax, and set their dogs on them.[63] Colonists hid mackerel hooks in balls of tallow. Branding irons pierced wolf eyes. Snares strangled necks. Men lynched wolves. Some staked bitches in heat to lure male wolves so as to bludgeon both to death during the copulatory tie. Wolfers shotgunned or dynamited wolf pups in their dens. Airborne sport hunters terrorize animals from above, a technique that rarely results in a "clean" shot. Such acts testify to the imaginative spectrum of human wickedness. No other nonhuman animal has endured such hatred and persecution, a fact that has led some to use the language of pogrom and holocaust to describe the human drive to torture and obliterate the population of wolves in North America.[64] Rick Bass laments, "May we all never be judged by anything so harshly or held to as strict a life or be as unremitting of borders as the ones we try to place on and around wolves."[65]

There is the temptation to simply condemn the animus toward wolves as a feature of a pre-Enlightened time. This progressive vision of human ethics is hard to square with the human capacity to do wicked acts, and it does little to safeguard against societal views that could easily shift again to threaten a species like the wolf. The history of wolf persecution can also be inverted such that the symbolism of evil is flipped from the wolf to the human. If the first option trusts humanity too much, the second disregards potentialities for human responsibility in the natural world. Further, merely switching the symbol of evil from the wolf to the human reinforces the pervasive sense of disconnection between human society and the wild, a move that Gustafson wants to avoid. If we want to see humankind as part of nature, how can we account for the evil, or wickedness, that shows forth in the hatred of the wolf? What of a man in the nineteenth century who jumps into a pit and slices the Achilles tendon of a wolf, then hauls the animal up with a rope and commands his dogs to tear it to pieces?

James Gustafson's theocentrism rightly chastens our desire to fold the unfavorable or distasteful elements of the natural world into an anthropocentric story of God's fixation on human happiness. His emphasis on silence before mystery, the role of human as participant who consents to our dependence, and the possibilities of the sense of gratitude all help to productively redirect the goals of a Protestant Christian ethic of the wild that may, one day, learn to tolerate both the graces and threats of a species like the wolf. This promise resonates with those of us who experience a profound sense of awe and respect for animals that cannot abide human society and elude our capacities to explain or reconcile with our hopes of our own redemption. Gustafson's theocentrism amplifies such possibilities. Yet, perhaps, Gustafson's emphasis on our silence before mystery silences too much in the end. He wants to return us to a nature that is not compromised by the consumptive drive to satisfy all our desires in the name of God's love, but Gustafson does not do enough with regard to our own exceptional nature.

We are *unnatural* as the only species that designs pogroms, and that delights in sensuous tortures that, in the words of Ivan Karamazov, are "so artfully, so artistically cruel."[66] The wolf does not torture. The wolf does not demonstrate the terrible meanness that uniquely manifests in the human spirit. The depravities of humankind are different in kind from the conditions that bear down on all creaturely life. Cannot we consent to the mysteries of our dependence, refusing the elements of tradition that run counter to our experience without silencing the cry for redemption and the story of God's answer to our uniquely human condition? Elizabeth Johnson encourages this line of thought: "Rather than a theodicy, what is needed is a theological inquiry that takes the evolutionary function of affliction at face value and seeks to reflect on its workings in view of the God of Love made known in revelation."[67] The Christian theological tradition testifies to our experience of God in Jesus Christ, which is more than Gustafson wants to say. But as Richard McCormick queries, "Is misuse a reason for abandonment?"[68] The Christian story of fall, covenant, incarnation, and resurrection destiny tells a true story about the particularity of our place in a nature of limits. It need not be abandoned, even as we trouble the confidence of theologies that say too much (or nothing much at all) about the fate or status of nature.

## Gustafson and Gratitude

Gustafson brings us to a productive crossroads in addressing the theological legacy of anthropocentrism. The central emphasis on mystery resonates with experiences of the natural world that escape easy reconciliation with the social-ethical commitments that organize our day-to-day endeavors, in that the mystery always exceeds our striving. Holmes Rolston III describes this tension well: "Humans can respect the alien in nature not only in its autonomous otherness but even in its stimulus, provocation, and opposition. This is ethics comprehensively extended once again: Love nature, the gift of grace. Love nature, even when beauty confronts us as enemy. Such gift with challenge is a more sophisticated form of creative beauty."[69] The more we explore the mysteries of creation, the more we come to see how the category of natural evil is rendered incoherent. Instead, we are part of a world that is good but may often not be good for us. To live into the mystery of a world that includes predators and prey is to accept a sense of dependence that can be known through a sense of gratitude for even the frailty of limited, vulnerable creatures. However, for Gustafson, to accept with gratitude conditions that include functions for pain and suffering seems to cancel out the possibility of a personal God.

A natural world of predators, viruses, and tornadoes evokes in us a sense of dependence on conditions and processes and directs us to gratitude for the contingencies that, for now, permit our survival. A sense of gratitude is evoked through the recognition of the fragile connections that attach us to a world that is indifferent to our suffering. Because this is our situation, Gustafson concludes, all talk of a personal God is romantic at best and delusional at worst. God has no preferential option for humanity. To pretend otherwise is the height of anthropocentric fantasy. Gratitude, then, is a personal response to impersonal conditions. In this way, the Stoicism charge sticks. Gustafson give us an intelligible but impoverished view of gratitude amid conditions that rightly destabilize anthropocentric theologies. Ironically, Gustafson's Stoicism has an anthropocentric quality: The human assumes the seat of judgment over what or who God is and how that God *must* relate to the world (or not). Yet Gustafson's theocentric conclusion is not the only one that his protest of anthropocentrism will permit. A different sense of gratitude can point us to more constructive theological possibilities.

In a brief aside, Lisa Cahill contrasts Gustafson's sense of gratitude with Abraham Joshua Heschel's "radiant gratitude."[70] Cahill shows that, like both Job and Gustafson, Heschel wrestled with the scope of suffering and death. He lost more than two dozen family members to the horrors of the Shoah. In his engagement with the fact of suffering—known especially through tremendous moral evil—he "seeks to illumine the meanings of service and piety, and refuses to take comfort in expectation of future reward."[71] In the face of suffering, he refuses the question "Where was God?"—choosing always instead to pursue the question, *Where was humanity?* Heschel's question follows from his thesis that God is in search of humankind. For Heschel, senses of dependence, gratitude, and the others index the beauty of the world to "the grandeur of God; His majesty towered beyond the breathtaking mystery of the universe." The biblical person, on Heschel's account, was not "crushed by the mystery" but "was inspired to praise the majesty."[72] The biblical example is instructive today even, perhaps especially, in our age of modern science.

For Heschel, mystery is an ontological category. He writes: "In using the term 'mystery' we do not mean any particular esoteric quality that may be revealed to the initiated, but the essential mystery of being as being, the nature of being as God's creation out of nothing, and therefore, something which stands beyond the scope of human comprehension."[73] We apprehend but do not comprehend the divine presence—"Trying to pierce the mystery with our categories is like trying to bite a wall."[74] Awe amid mystery lies not in passivity or ecstatic enjoyment; it is mystical only as it leads us in the pursuit of justice in the world. The experience of awe is the recognition that "something sacred is at stake in every event."[75] According to Heschel, "Awe, unlike fear, does not make us shrink from the awe-inspiring object, but, on the contrary, draws us near to it."[76] Awe is the beginning of wonder, and wonder is the beginning of faith. For Heschel, "There is no concern for God in the absence of awe, and it is only in moments of awe that God is sensed as an issue. In moments of indifference and self-assertion, He may be a concept, but not a concern, and it is only *a concern* that initiates religious thinking."[77] When we give in to moments of indifference and self-assertion, God does not concern us and relationship ceases. In the face of mystery, Gustafson's gratitude manifests in Stoic silence. Heschel's gratitude ends in praise.

By way of encounters with the wild, our senses of dependence and gratitude are elicited and refined. Although the wolf cannot be pulled into human society, its health as a species (as with the case of the grizzly or other charismatic megafauna) can and should return to the boundaries of our domestic lives. Encounters with them can inspire new understandings of commitment, responsibility, justice, and love that will reveal and then expand the horizons of our moral and theological traditions. Gustafson helpfully challenges us to accept the goods of creaturely life as products of a world that also includes these limits. Our loves and losses are bound up together, for though love does not depend on the experience of loss, it cannot escape its risks. In this consent to our dependence lies the possibility of gratitude. As I have suggested, Heschel's response of gratitude is a compelling alternative to Gustafson's vague tracking of divinity. For both Gustafson and Heschel, gratitude is issued through the appreciation of the fact that we are not the only story in God's Creation. God will be God. The Earth is the Lord's and all that is in it (Ps 24:1). Who can say how the wolf meets its Creator?

## An Encounter as Conclusion

Two adult red wolves flitted and flashed nervously against the back fence.[78] I followed the others into the enclosure, clutching a long pole with a fixed Y at one end. We formed a line and lowered the poles like spears. We were a prehistoric hunting party with a local TV cameraman. We advanced slowly, herding the wolves into the northeastern corner. When they were surrounded, they laid down with their ears back. We moved in and pinned them down, several poles on each wolf. The wolf's strength vibrated down the length of the pole. Peggy administered the sedatives and, after a few moments, the drugs took over and the powerful muscles relaxed. We lifted our poles and watched as she placed blindfolds on the wolves to protect their eyes during the sled ride out. Two brothers went to sleep. One would wake up to an imported stranger, a potential mate; the other would wake up in a metal crate on Route 169, hurtling down the highway toward a new home at the Great Plains Zoo in Sioux Falls.

Suddenly, one of the wolves began to convulse, and my mind flashed to an image of my son. I thought of the horror of the first febrile seizure—the way the world stopped spinning when he slipped away. Absence makes the heart grow fonder, they say. Peggy removed the blindfold and gently, intimately, stroked the wolf's face and neck until the seizure subsided. She asked me to lift the wolf onto the sled. I asked her if I could stick around for the afternoon feedings.

A few hours later, I found myself holding the rear hooves of an upside-down dead deer. A large gray wolf paced a few feet away. We watched the wolf, and the wolf watched us. Peggy turned and walked back to a truck piled high with roadkill. A dead calf, donated by a local farmer, peered out from among the tangle of wild limbs. A live rat terrier perched on top of the pile like a conquering queen. She licked at frozen blood. Peggy reached her arm in among the bodies. "You know," she called over her shoulder, "after all these years, we still prefer Chicago Cutlery." Her arm reappeared with a green-handled chef's knife.

Peggy's boots crunched on the frozen snowpack, and she gestured for me to step aside. "Let's give this one a treat," she said, waving the knife at the restless wolf on the other side of the chain-link fence. Pulling apart the rear legs of the deer, Peggy glanced up at me and said simply, "This one was pregnant." The incision opened a hole the size of a cantaloupe. Pushing up her coat sleeve, Peggy reached in with a bare hand and, after a moment, pulled out a bloody fetus. The wolf stopped pacing and stared intently at the flesh. She met the wolf at the fence and offered the fetus like the sacrament. Powerful jaws crushed the tiny skull, and the severed body dropped to the ground. Blood stained the snow. As the wolf was alone in the enclosure, her face registered that familiar look of distant thoughtfulness, not unlike the way my domesticated canine chews the toddler's toys underneath the coffee table. The wolf bent down and snatched up what remained. We picked up the deer and walked it to the next enclosure. It was as if a strong wind swept over the coals: the slow burn of yearning for connection to the wild suddenly aflame. Later that night, when sleep finally came, I dreamed of wild wolves.

## Notes

1. Pope Francis, *Laudato Si'*, chap. 4, §139.

2. Although it is beyond the scope of this essay, it is important to note that an adequate Christian ethic of the wild, when developed fully, will attend to the racial qualities of our ecological anthropologies. An adequate Christian ethic of the wild will attend to what Martin Luther King Jr. called the giant triplets of racism, militarism, and materialism. I have developed the ecological legacy of King elsewhere. See Nathaniel Van Yperen, "The Fierce Urgency of Now: The Ecological Legacy of King's Social Ethics," *Journal of the Society of Christian Ethics* 36, no. 2 (2016): 159–72.

3. Cf. David Abram, *The Spell of the Sensuous: Perception and Language in a More-Than-Human World* (New York: Vintage, 1997).

4. On this influence, see Childress and Hauerwas's introduction in the Focus edition on James Gustafson's thought, *Journal of Religious Ethics* 13, no. 1 (Spring 1985).

5. Douglas Ottati got it right when he quipped—in recognizing James Gustafson with the Lifetime Achievement Award of the Society of Christian Ethics in 2011—that an attempt to summarize Gustafson's contribution and influence was a "foolhardy" enterprise. This essay heeds Ottati's compliment as a warning.

6. James Gustafson, *A Sense of the Divine: The Natural Environment from a Theocentric Perspective* (Cleveland: Pilgrim Press, 1994), 73.

7. Lisa Sideris, *Environmental Ethics, Ecological Theology, and Natural Selection* (New York: Columbia University Press, 2003). Sideris borrows this phrase from Holmes Rolston III.

8. Gustafson, *Sense of the Divine*, 48.

9. Ibid., 106.

10. Cf. ibid., 149.

11. James Gustafson, *Ethics from a Theocentric Perspective*, Vol. 1, *Theology and Ethics* (Chicago: University of Chicago Press, 1981), 110.

12. James Gustafson, "A Theocentric Interpretation of Life," in *Moral Discernment in the Christian Life: Essays in Theological Ethics*, ed. Theo A. Boer and Paul Capetz (Louisville: Westminster John Knox Press, 2007), 77. See also Gustafson, *Ethics*, 1:96.

13. Gustafson, *Ethics*, 1:83.

14. Ibid., 1:115.

15. Gustafson, "Nature," in Boer and Capetz, *Moral Discernment*, 112.

16. Ibid., 125.

17. Gustafson, *Ethics from a Theocentric Perspective*, Vol. 2, *Ethics and Theology* (Chicago: University of Chicago Press, 1984), 124.

18. Barry Lopez, *Of Wolves and Men* (New York: Charles Scribner's Sons, 1978).

19. William C. French also, albeit briefly, connects the work of Lopez and Gustafson; William C. French, "Ecological Concern and the Anti-Foundationalist Debates: James Gustafson on Biospheric Constraints," *Annual of the Society of Christian Ethics* 9 (1989): 113–30, at 125.

20. John Elder, "Poetry as Experience," in *Beyond Nature Writing: Expanding the Boundaries of Ecocriticism*, ed. Karla Armbruster and Kathleen R. Wallace (Charlottesville: University of Virginia Press, 2001), 314.

21. The wolf pervades children's literature. For an excellent study, see Debra Mitts-Smith, *Picturing the Wolf in Children's Literature* (London: Routledge, 2010).

22. Lopez, *Of Wolves and Men*, 148.

23. Gustafson, *Sense of the Divine*, 14.

24. Ibid., 67.

25. Gustafson, *Ethics*, 2:18.

26. Gustafson, *Sense of the Divine*, 149.

27. Ibid., 135, 121.

28. Gustafson, *Ethics*, 1:311.

29. Gustafson, *Sense of the Divine*, 46.

30. Ibid., 55.

31. Gustafson, *Ethics*, 1:306.

32. Gustafson, *Sense of the Divine*, 5.

33. Ibid., 7.

34. Ibid.

35. Gustafson, *Ethics*, 1:37.

36. Ibid., 201.

37. Cf. Gustafson, "Say Something Theological," in Boer and Capetz, *Moral Discernment*, 87.

38. Gustafson, "Theocentric Interpretation," 82.

39. Gustafson, "Say Something Theological," 89.

40. Gustafson, *Ethics*, 1:229, 233.

41. Ibid., 1:279.

42. Gustafson, "Say Something Theological," 87.

43. Gustafson, *Ethics*, 1:203.

44. Ibid., 1:41, 112.

45. Cf. Gustafson, "Theocentric Interpretation," 83.

46. Cf. Gustafson, *Ethics*, 1:204.

47. Stanley Hauerwas, *Wilderness Wanderings: Probing Twentieth-Century Theology and Philosophy* (Boulder, CO: Westview Press, 1997), 64. See also Stanley Hauerwas, *With the Grain of the Universe: The Church's Witness and Natural Theology* (Grand Rapids: Brazos Press, 2001), 107n45.

48. Hauerwas, *Wilderness Wanderings*, 75.

49. Ibid., 78.

50. See Jeffery Stout, "The Voice of Theology," in *Ethics after Babel: The Languages of Morals and Their Discontents* (Princeton, NJ: Princeton University Press, 2001), 181.

51. Ibid., 184.

52. Gustafson, *Sense of the Divine*, 121.

53. Lisa Sowle Cahill, "Consent in Time of Affliction: The Ethics of a Circumspect Theist," *Journal of Religious Ethics* 13, no. 1 (Spring 1985): 22–36, at 24.

54. For an exploration of antitheodicy, see Zachary Braiterman, *(God) after Auschwitz: Tradition and Change in Post-Holocaust Thought* (Princeton, NJ: Princeton University Press, 1998).

55. See, for representative examples, Christopher Southgate, *The Groaning of Creation: God, Evolution, and the Problem of Evil* (Louisville: Westminster John Knox Press, 2008);

Elizabeth Johnson, *Ask the Beasts: Darwin and the God of Love* (New York: Oxford University Press, 2015); and Andrew Linzey, *Creatures of the Same God: Explorations in Animal Ethics* (Brooklyn: Lantern Books, 2005).

56. Gustafson, *Ethics*, 1:342.

57. Gustafson writes, "Theologically and ethically my work is a form of 'naturalism.'" *Intersections: Science, Theology, and Ethics* (Cleveland: Pilgrim Press, 1996), xvii.

58. Gustafson, *Ethics*, 1:35.

59. Cf. Gustafson, *Sense of the Divine*, 72.

60. Gustafson, *Ethics*, 1:112.

61. Bruce Hampton, *The Great American Wolf* (New York: Henry Holt, 1997), 9.

62. Ibid., 7.

63. Cf. Jon T. Coleman, *Vicious: Wolves and Men in America* (New Haven, CT: Yale University Press, 2004), 1–2; and Hampton, *Great American Wolf*, 92, on an unnerving passage from the famous naturalist and artist John James Audubon, in which he describes, with startling moral neutrality, observing a farmer torture three trapped wolves.

64. See "An American Pogrom," chap. 9 in Lopez *Of Wolves and Men*. Hampton, *Great American Wolf*, 127, borrows the term from Lopez and later employs the related term "ecological holocaust."

65. Rick Bass, *The Ninemile Wolves* (Boston: Mariner, 2003), xvii.

66. Fyodor Dostoevsky, *The Brothers Karamazov*, 232.

67. Johnson, *Ask the Beasts*, 187.

68. Richard A. McCormick, "Gustafson's God: Who? What? Where? (Etc.)," *Journal of Religious Ethics* 13, no. 1 (Spring 1985): 53–70, at 65.

69. Holmes Rolston III, "Loving Nature: Christian Environmental Ethics," in *Love and Christian Ethics: Tradition, Theory, and Society*, ed. Frederick V. Simmons and Brian C. Sorrells (Washington, DC: Georgetown University Press, 2016).

70. Cahill, "Consent in Time of Affliction," 22–36.

71. Ibid., 33.

72. Abraham Joshua Heschel, *God in Search of Man: A Philosophy of Judaism* (New York: Farrar, Straus & Giroux, 1955), 96.

73. Ibid., 57.

74. Abraham Joshua Heschel, *Man Is Not Alone: A Philosophy of Religion* (New York: Farrar, Straus & Giroux, 1951), 30.

75. Heschel, *God in Search of Man*, 74.

76. Ibid., 76.

77. Ibid., 111.

78. A version of this final section was originally published online as a piece of creative nonfiction, "Wolf," in *The Common: A Modern Sense of Place*, December 27, 2017, www.thecommononline.org/wolf/.

# Ethics in the Afterlife of Slavery: Race, Augustinian Politics, and the Problem of the Christian Master

*Matthew Elia*

The recent renaissance of Augustinian ethics remains mostly silent about the central place of slavery in Augustine's thought. Although Augustinians appear confident his insights can be excised from his legitimation of the institution of slavery, two facts challenge this assumption: First, slavery constitutes not simply one moral issue among others for Augustine but an organizing, conceptual metaphor; second, the contemporary scene to which Augustinians apply his thought *is itself the afterlife of a slave society*. Thus, to bear faithful witness in a racialized world, Augustinians must grapple with slavery as Augustine's key conceptual metaphor, one that animates his thought and subtly reproduces the moral vantage of the master.

> Masters always pretend that they are not masters, insisting that they are only doing what is best for society as a whole.
> —Dr. James Hal Cone (1938–2018)

## Introduction: Translating Augustine's God

In a recent issue of the *New York Review of Books*, Peter Brown credits a new translation of Augustine's *Confessions* with a startling feat.[1] While most translations give us "an ever-so-human Augustine," Brown notes, they tend to leave his God "an immense Baroque canvas, . . . suitably grand, of course, . . . but flat as the wall." So, in the eyes of the eminent scholar of late antiquity, what does this translator, Sarah Ruden, do differently? How does she bring Augustine's God back to life? "She renames Him," writes Brown. "He is not a 'Lord.' That is too grand a word. . . . Augustine's God was a *dominus*—a master. And a Roman *dominus* was a master of slaves." Augustine calls God *dominus* dozens of

Matthew Elia is a PhD candidate in Duke University's Religious Studies Program and a 2018–19 Mellon/ACLS Dissertation Completion Fellow, 15 Washington Street, #1, Valparaiso, IN 46383; matthew.elia@duke.edu.

*Journal of the Society of Christian Ethics*, 38, 2 (2018): 93–110

times in *Confessions*, and each one Ruden renders "Master," breaking with the long-standard "Lord." "Unlike 'Lord,'" writes Brown, "the Latin word *dominus* implied, in Augustine's time, no distant majesty, muffled in fur and velvet. It conjured up life in the raw—life lived face to face in a Roman household, lived to the sound of the crack of the whip and punctuated by bursts of rage." The image is a "rude shock," Brown continues, but it should not surprise us, given studies by historians like Kyle Harper, which establish that "slavery was alive and well in Roman Africa and elsewhere," shaping the social imaginary in Augustine's time. Of its central place in that world, Brown writes, there can be "no doubt."[2]

Nevertheless, a few days after Brown's review appeared online, one scholar objected to the "Master" language and Brown's praise of it. The philosopher James K. A. Smith took to his blog to make an apt if familiar point: Translation dilemmas like this one cannot always be settled lexically, nor by reference to the translated culture alone. "Words in either language are not static," Smith writes, "they have a life of their own."[3] His point is that movement from the translated culture to the translator's is a journey, "an adventure in sailing from one language to another, and often from one time to another." Sometimes, passengers jump ship: Upon reading "Master" in the first line, Smith recalls, "I quite literally closed up the Ruden translation in a kind of literary disgust."

What matters for my purposes is that Smith goes on to make explicit what usually remains unsaid: His disgust had everything to do with his having just read Colson Whitehead's recent novel *The Underground Railroad*, in which he encountered white Christian plantation owners called "Master." In other words, Smith makes explicit that the way we read *Augustine's* slave language today has everything to do with *our own* slave-haunted imagination—everything to do with inhabiting a social world that is, as Saidiya Hartman writes, "the afterlife of slavery."[4] *That* is what made the Ruden translation "jarring and offensive" to Smith, and *that* is what made Brown's praise of it feel like "willfully ignor[ing] all the connotations that have attached themselves to the word 'Master.'"[5] Smith does not mention that Ruden herself notes she had to "govern her distaste" toward the imagery with "its reminders of American plantation slavery."[6] The "disgust" Smith feels toward these connotations of New World racial slavery drives him (and us) to the critical point: "In some ways," he writes, "this is a question of who 'owns' Augustine, . . . which *afterlife* of words is most germane to the project that Augustine himself is engaged in? Which history of connotation overlaps with Augustine's endeavor?" Based on this set of questions, one might expect the connotations of "master" language to press Smith to examine Augustine's slavery talk more closely, to explore its moral significance in view of both the differences and continuities between Roman and New World systems. Instead, turned away by "disgust" for the connotation itself, Smith proposes "digging in and sticking with" the "Lord" translation of *dominus* in the name of "Christian piety," and in this way, he finds himself not only turning away from Brown's point about the social realities of Augustine's day but also turning away from the helpful, if disturbing, questions he himself has raised about what it means to read Augustine's slavery discourse within the modern world as we have it.

This essay lingers inside these questions a little longer. I aim, in short, to develop an approach to reading the moral and theological significance of Augustine's slavery discourse for contemporary Augustinian thought. This task matters because Smith's question about how to properly translate Augustine's slavemaster God emerges within the larger context of political Augustinianism, which is itself a translation project in a broader sense.

In the last two decades, scholars of religion and politics have made a striking return to Augustine's writings—not as "pure" historical study but rather in search of constructive, normative resources to theorize citizenship, virtue, and the place of religion in contemporary public life.[7] Distinctive to the current moment in political Augustinianism is a particular kind of interpretive task, which Eric Gregory and Joseph Clair recently called "democratic translation": the thorny problem of "translating" Augustine's counsel to the elite statesmen of antiquity into guidance for the citizens of modern liberal democracies.[8]

The first section of this essay contends that this modern Augustinian translation project has not yet reckoned with the challenges posed by the central place of slavery in Augustine's thought. Instead, Augustine's slavery discourse often generates an affective response—Smith's "disgust," Brown's "rude shock," Ruden's "distaste"—which results in the gesture Smith performs: the recognition of a problem, then a turning away from it toward other concerns—a simultaneous acknowledgment and denial. I show how several key modern Augustinian texts display this double movement of disavowal in concert with a general assumption that Augustine's legitimation of slavery, however unfortunate, may be easily excised from those political insights to be "translated" into modern democratic life. The second and third sections identify two challenges to this assumption, which, I suggest, must be examined if Augustinians wish to enrich their capacity to bear faithful witness amid ongoing racial injustice in the era of Black Lives Matter.

The second section argues that excising slavery from Augustine's thought is not as easy as it may first appear, because as we have seen already from the opening conflict over "Master" in the *Confessions* translation, slavery is not simply one moral "issue" among others but an abiding presence in Augustine's thought, providing a metaphor that animates his treatment of God, sin, Christology, order, desire, virtue, and freedom. This section surveys what I term "the master's house" as shorthand for this set of metaphors, by which the Roman *domus* (household) ruled by a *dominus* (owner, slavemaster) provides Augustine a generative symbolic space that animates his treatment of the same normative concepts Augustinians wish to recover for today. What emerges is that the line between "actual" and "symbolic" slavery is not as easy to disentangle as has been previously assumed. Instead, both show Augustine's subtle alignment with the moral and intellectual standpoint of the master class, even as he criticizes, reworks, and Christianizes this standpoint. The third section argues that this alignment—what I term the problem of the Christian master—has certain parallels with the present, given that the contemporary scene to which Augustinians apply his thought is *itself the afterlife of a slave society*. Our imprecise name for this afterlife of slaves and masters—*race*—indexes the long shadows slavery casts into the present. As the opening example illustrates, this is not a question I am inserting into Augustinianism by some "ideological" reading. It is already internal to the question of Augustinian politics insofar as it forms a crucial part of the situation into which Augustinian concepts are to be "translated." Why then has it not been dealt with by modern political Augustinianism? The answer lies, in part, in modern Augustinians' neglect of the immense resources of the African American intellectual tradition, one which—across overlapping inquiries in politics, literature, and religion—has excavated the myriad ways in which the order of slavery outlives its formal abolition, persisting up to the present day. Drawing from this tradition, the third section thus argues that race, especially whiteness as long-standing modern claim to mastery, marks out a set of normative dilemmas for theorizing citizenship, virtue, and moral agency that contemporary Augustinian political thinkers must address. They can best begin this task not by applying preformed Augustinian perspectives to "race issues" but by reexamining the challenges, limits, and blind spots that arise from Augustine's own ambivalent entanglements with the position of the Christian master.

It should be noted at the outset that the difficulties raised by positing parallels between ancient and modern slave systems are considerable but not unique to this project.[9] Moving from one context to another demands intense labors of translation, but translation itself is not anachronism. Internal to all constructive political thought is the challenge of letting an ancient figure be not only an object to scrutinize but a voice to translate, and thus a subject with whom to converse. If political Augustinians are right to insist Augustine's resources are "translatable," mutatis mutandis, into modernity, so too, I argue, are the distinct moral challenges that arise from inhabiting the master's position—or inheriting its legacies in the present. The point is not to vilify Augustine's ambivalent entanglements with the position of the master. Rather, in reading him with care, we learn better to confront our own. Black thought provides a privileged "conceptual precipice," to borrow Alexander Weheliye's term, from which to recognize the problem with these Christian slavery metaphors: the problem of the master—that is, that these metaphors index nothing about the slave so much as the master's own self-deceptions.[10] If the concepts of citizen or city or public/private can travel, so too do the moral risks of entanglements in the master's position. From this reckoning, a stronger picture emerges of how to build a constructive vision of religious ethics for moral agency and political citizenship in our world—marked by the afterlife of slavery—by eschewing neither "traditionalist" nor "liberationist" strands of Christian thought but instead posing an encounter, at once timely and long overdue, between an ancient figure of Christian tradition and the distinct moral challenges of ongoing racial violence in the Black Lives Matter era.

## Augustinian Disavowals

This section sets the scene for the present political conversation in Augustinianism. The argument is simple: Augustinians have not simply been "silent" about modern racial slavery or ignored the slavery in Augustine's own thought. Rather, there has been what Neil Roberts terms a "disavowal" of both. To sketch how this works, I begin with a story.

In a 1988 interview with Paul Gilroy, Toni Morrison gave us an adage that now appears everywhere: "Modern life begins with slavery."[11] This adage first gained prominence in 1993, when Gilroy himself quoted it in the final chapter of *The Black Atlantic: Modernity and Double Consciousness*.[12] For Gilroy, Morrison's adage offers a dense restatement of a founding argument of black thought, found in canonical works like W. E. B. Du Bois's *Black Reconstruction* and C. L. R. James's *Black Jacobins*. Put simply, this argument contends that Western modernity is unintelligible apart from grasping slavery as a phenomenon of world-making significance—not only for enslaved persons but also for everyone else. Nearly thirty years later, it seems that every week a new book confirms this argument, showing slavery's key role in the making of capitalist economy, property law, the insurance industry, the university, or medical science. With each new example, Morrison's adage gets weightier: Modern life begins with slavery.[13]

In the year after Gilroy's book emerged, just up the road from where Gilroy was teaching in London, Oliver O'Donovan delivered the prestigious Hulsean Lectures at Cambridge, which became *The Desire of the Nations*, wherein O'Donovan writes: "'Slavery' has existed, for most of the last millennium, only on the fringes of civilization, as a colonial indulgence or as a subpolitical pathology. To the ancient world, on the other hand, it was central to any imaginable economic organization."[14] The book is a major work of Christian ethics, and O'Donovan is a crucial figure in the political Augustinian renaissance of the last few decades.[15] Twenty years have passed since the book's publication, and it has attracted many pages of scholarly engagement; but as best I can tell, this take on the "fringe" importance of modern racial slavery has not yet elicited a single line of criticism. No trace of Morrison's adage emerges, nor the founding texts of black thought, and this absence invites us to consider another line from Morrison's interview: Of the centrality of slavery to modern life, Morrison says, there is a "struggle to forget which was important in order to survive."[16] In this section, I am interested not simply in pointing out that O'Donovan's claim reflects a serious neglect of the available historical evidence but also in asking what this wider struggle to forget slavery's centrality to modern life, a forgetting implicit in the absence of interest in contesting O'Donovan's claim, might imply about the broader state of the Augustinian conversation concerning matters of race.

It may be objected that O'Donovan's claim occurs in a context in which he is not primarily talking about modern racial slavery at all. Or at least, he is *trying* not to talk about it but finds he cannot avoid doing so while discussing what he *wants* to discuss, namely, slavery in the ancient household codes of the early churches. Our own slave-haunted imagination intervenes. O'Donovan finds he cannot discuss one context without dealing with the other. And so, quite reasonably, he wants to ensure that ancient Christianity's entanglements with slavery are not dealt with in an anachronistic, presentist manner. There are good reasons for avoiding using the word "slavery" in too univocal a way.[17] But for this very reason, it is all the more striking that O'Donovan's desire to avoid conflating ancient slavery with modern slavery winds up distorting both:

> The misunderstanding arises in part from the word "slave" itself, which to us denotes a social institution altogether apart from the normal structures of economic organization and exceptionally oppressive in the terms on which it governs the exchange of labor for livelihood. "Slavery" has existed, for most of the last millennium, only on the fringes of civilization, as a colonial indulgence or as a subpolitical pathology. To the ancient world, on the other hand, it was central to any imaginable economic organization, providing the only skilled labor market for the chief unit of production, which was the household business. So the word *douleia* appears in contexts where we might speak not of "slavery" but of "domestic service," or quite simply of "employment."[18]

O'Donovan's worries about anachronism lead him to overcorrect for, and thus reinscribe, the problem of anachronism, as he presses a series of contrasts between what "slavery" indexes in modernity versus antiquity far sharper than what evidence can support: To us, he says, slavery is an institution "altogether apart from the normal structures of economic organization." But to them, slavery was so normal we should "speak not of 'slavery' but of 'domestic service,' or quite simply of 'employment.'"[19] This claim raises questions: If I mentioned an "employee," would that bring to mind a person whose body is his or her employer's legal property? Do we picture a person subject to being whipped by his or her manager, tortured without legal recourse, regarded with shame and dishonor, and made available as a sexual outlet with no right to say no? These conditions were utterly normal for most enslaved persons in antiquity, *and* they are precisely those connoted to modern ears by the word "slave"—not despite but precisely because this word conjures disturbing images from New World plantations. "Employment" is the misplaced, anachronistic term, not "slavery."

My purpose is not simply to supplement neglected historical facts but to consider how the neglect occurred in the first place and explore why it matters for political Augustinianism. For this, we need to recognize that the simplistic contrast O'Donovan draws in the claim above—between the "fringe" importance of slavery in modernity and its "central" importance in antiquity—does not emerge from nowhere but is rather a solution designed for a particular aim: to shield Christianity from what he variously refers to as "discomfort," "disappointment," and the "quarrels" which emerge for moderns upon encountering early Christian acceptance of slavery.[20]

This affective register, leading to a double movement—acknowledgment and denial—recalls Smith's gesture above. O'Donovan's extended engagement with slavery suggests that what Morrison has termed "the struggle to forget" does not only take the form of "silence" about slavery. The problem is not simply that Augustinians have ignored or failed to mention the history of slavery and matters of race more broadly. Instead, the problem we see in O'Donovan's statement marks an instance of what the black political theorist Neil Roberts calls "disavowal:" "Disavowal," he writes, "centrally requires what I take to be a simultaneous *double movement*: an acknowledgment *and* a denial. By simultaneously acknowledging and denying an event, one does not silence its existence. Rather, one strategically locates an event and then rejects its relevance, knowing full well that it occurred."[21] Strategically locating something in order to reject its relevance. *Forgetting in order to survive*. In the case of this Augustinian disavowal, who and what are meant to survive?

Where Smith's denial simply turned away from the questions he raised, O'Donovan wants to confront the discomfort directly and reveal it as a "misunderstanding" resulting from what the word "slave" denotes "to us." I am interested in the composition of this "us." Who is included in it? What questions matter to this "us," and what questions does this "us" preclude? The "us" O'Donovan invokes is evidently a group of people who consider slavery "*exceptionally* oppressive," that is, consider slavery an exception to, or a departure from, the normal course of European modernity. For O'Donovan's "us," the words "colonial indulgence" suggest a matter of marginal, rather than central, importance. But as we have already seen, the founding works of black thought saw things rather differently: Modern life begins with slavery. It is central. What this suggests, perhaps uncomfortably, is that O'Donovan's "us" is unintentionally, but inescapably, an unmarked *white* "us," one with liability to certain blind spots. And if there is an unnamed whiteness to the political

Augustinian conversation itself, it is perhaps best seen as not merely about the skin color of the bodies in the room, but as involving deep epistemic assumptions that govern what counts as "central" and what counts as "fringe."

Disavowals of slavery, then, aim to protect both the moral priorities of an implied white readership and their investment in the authority of ancient texts in which slavery appears. Through this juxtaposition of ancient and modern settings, O'Donovan believes he has fended off any critique of Christianity's entanglements with *both*: In antiquity, slavery was so central that its embrace by Christians cannot be faulted; in modernity, it was so minor that its perpetuation by Christians may be safely left aside. Any seeming challenge that slavery might pose to Christian self-understanding is misplaced—its existence in society was always either *too* central or not central enough: "One strategically locates an event and then rejects its relevance, knowing full well that it occurred." Forgetting to survive. But as we have seen, the disavowal necessary to secure this survival risks creating distortions not only of modern slavery but also of ancient slavery, which in turn leads to impoverished understandings of ancient thinkers, including, I suggest below, Augustine himself.

The limited nature of this "us" can resurface in subtler ways than O'Donovan's here, often when issues around slavery appear among political Augustinian writers who, elsewhere in their work, show serious interest in the differences internal to any claim to "we." Eric Gregory writes, "It would be ironically prideful to blame Augustine or any other premodern author for limited historical horizons of social and economic reform, most especially in relation to his often neglected moral criticisms of slavery. Augustine was no abolitionist."[22] Gregory rightly cautions modern readers to avoid placing themselves in a superior moral position to premodern authors like Augustine on slavery. He also models a response to the implicit problem of slavery in Augustine that has become a standard formulation: Augustine was no abolitionist, but facts x, y, and z complicate any portrayal of him as a villain.[23] This formulation, I suggest, does not at all imply that Gregory is mitigating the sinfulness of ancient slaveholders so much as reveal that he—and we—find ourselves already aligned with *their* position in society. His statement juxtaposes our modern response to that of Augustine, slaveholders, and those who failed to criticize ancient slavery. But the silence of the statement is our position vis-à-vis the ancient slaves. Did they also fail to resist ancient slavery? This question never arises. There is no slave agency to contend with. So it is the moral vantage of the masters that we find ourselves contending with, whether we criticize it or empathize with it, and this unstated condition—our shared moral horizon with the master class—is a deeper aspect of the unmarked "us," a condition of moral reflection we may wish to bring more clearly into view.

Another aspect of the unmarked "us" occurs in the work of Charles Mathewes. "In the Middle Ages," writes Mathewes, "scholars wrote guidebooks for kings,

. . . wherein the contours of a virtuous ruler were displayed. . . . Today we may use the virtues analogously, to detail a mirror of Christian citizenship . . . where there is no king, where 'the sovereign' is *us*—you and I and our neighbors."[24] As with O'Donovan, some readers may not find it straightforward to locate themselves within that "us" of sovereign citizens, because of intersecting histories of oppression, and therefore may not share Mathewes's confidence that "we need not be victims of the rulers anymore. We are not subjects of kings, we are citizens of republics, sharing in our common sovereignty; *genuine participation in the governance of our world is possible*."[25] The afterlives of racial slavery make this possibility uncertain, but these histories surface nowhere in the account of the present Mathewes offers, the present into which Augustinians wish to translate Augustine's best insights. A kind of selective ahistoricism results, whereby ancient concepts like "citizens," "city," and "republic" are presumed to be translatable, mutatis mutandis, into modern political life, while the moral problems of mastery and slavery are left safely in the ancient past, unfortunate relics of a different age.[26] In this way, by reinscribing patterns of disavowal, even the strongest accounts of Augustinian politics risk standing at a remove from the social world revealed in Morrison's adage—modern life begins with slavery. The way forward begins, I now turn to suggest, with reconsidering the specific ways slavery animates Augustine's own texts.

## The Master's House: Augustine's Slave Metaphors

This section argues that the first key fact challenging the habit of disavowal discussed above is that "slavery" is best understood not as one isolatable moral "issue" in Augustine's texts. Rather, slavery forms an abiding presence in Augustine's writings, not only as a social institution he occasionally defends but also as a pervasive series of interrelated metaphors. And indeed, literal and metaphorical slavery are not as easy to separate in Augustine's thought as is often assumed. Instead, we find what I call "the master's house," a symbolic structure whereby Augustine both uses slavery metaphorically to clarify theological matters *and* speaks theologically about "actual" masters and slaves in tightly interconnected ways. As a *domus* owned and ordered by a *dominus*, the master's house is both a material space, an "actually existing" locus of social life in which Augustine is negotiating how Christ shapes relationships between masters and slaves *and* it is a symbolic space, the imaginative realm in which Augustine raises, clarifies, and answers major political and theological questions.[27]

Take the Ruden controversy above, wherein Peter Brown notes that whenever Augustine calls on God as slavemaster, he is "conjuring up the life of the Roman household." Throughout the *Confessions*, this household image "brings Augustine to life. In relation to God, Augustine experiences all the ups and downs of a household slave in relation to his master. He jumps to the whip. He tries out the life of a runaway."[28] It is as though Augustine looks upon the body of the fugitive slave and finds his own restless soul staring back. Reflecting his aimless wandering and his stubborn pride, his illusory freedom and his will to flight, the fugitive also signified for him the final impossibility of escape. In book 2, he renarrates his famous theft as a "perverse imitation of my Lord (*dominum*)," one which, like all sin, turned out to be self-defeating: "you are the creator of all nature and so, . . . there is no place where one can entirely escape from you. . . . Here is a runaway slave fleeing his master (*dominum*) and pursuing a shadow (Job 7:2). . . . What a monstrous life and what an abyss of death!"[29]

The fugitive image forms one subset of Augustine's larger metaphorical use of slavery, which plays flexibly with the appearance of actual enslaved persons. In a memorable passage in *Confessions*, Augustine displays his mother Monica's virtue by recounting her teaching other women that, in marriage, wives "become slaves" to their husbands; they must not, she says, "proudly withstand their masters." The very next paragraph finds her virtuous reputation threatened by the "interfering tongues of the slavegirls," then restored by her husband "subjecting the girls to a whipping." The wife-as-slave bit is straightforwardly "metaphorical," but the significance of the "actual" slaves of the second event serves as a kind of metaphor as well—the enslaved body's radical vulnerability to violence—in order to illustrate a larger point about the restoration of "domestic harmony." Monica's "patience and gentleness" work in tandem with her husband's whip to restore "peace in the household" and a "memorably gentle benevolence" (*Conf.* 9.9.19–20).

Indeed, the image of the bad slave punished—for gossip, theft, running away—does wide-ranging conceptual and symbolic work across Augustine's corpus. In *De libero arbitrio*, the slave "caught in a sin" is forced to clean the sewer; by this "detestable" punishment, "the slave's disgrace" and the sewer's cleaning are "woven into an orderly household . . . with the most orderly beauty" (*Lib arb.* 3.9.27.96–97).[30] In Letter 185, Augustine frames the Donatists as a band of runaway thieves who must be "recalled to their [Master] by the stripes of temporal scourging, like evil slaves, and in some degree like good-for-nothing fugitives" (*Ep.* 185.21). In *In Johannis Evangelium tractatus*, Augustine likens schismatic groups to the fugitive slave Hagar: "God stirs [heretics] up," he writes, "that Hagar may be beaten by Sarah. Let Hagar . . . yield her neck" for punishment; after all, the angel sends the slave girl back to her masters (*Jo. ev. tr.* 11.13). In these anti-Donatist examples, the line between metaphorical and literal slaves is again blurred by the discursive context, his well-known complaint about the Donatists' actual practices (*Ep.* 185.15): "What master was not forced to live in fear of his slave, if the slave fled to the patronage of the Donatists?"

Indeed, part of the difficulty of interpreting these slave images is that Augustine routinely traverses a would-be boundary between slavery-as-metaphor and slavery-as-institution, regarding the latter by no means more "real" than the former. Indeed, slavery to sin, particularly to the *libido dominandi*, is the truest slavery of all.[31] As historian Susanna Elm argues, "Augustine . . . in nearly all his writings, moves seamlessly between actual and metaphorical slavery because these are the metaphors he and his audience *lived by*."[32] In forms "metaphorical" and "literal," the slave's body appears at key junctures in major works following Augustine's 391 ordination, like *De utilitate credendi* (c. 391), *De doctrina Christiana* (c. 395), and *De bono conjugali* (c. 401).[33]

In *De civitate Dei* 18, Augustine confronts the slave logic of civilization itself: "Human society is generally divided against itself," such that "the conquered part" chooses "peace and survival at any price—so much so that it has always provoked astonishment when men have preferred death to slavery." Existing relations among various empires and peoples obtain when, guided by the "voice of nature" (*vox naturae*), the conquered choose enslavement over death.[34] Here, Augustine sees in the slave's body civilization writ small—the secret truth of the body politic, made visible in her chains.

When slavery in Augustine's thought receives attention in modern Augustinianism at all, it overwhelmingly centers on *De civitate Dei* 19's treatment of the nature of political authority in relation to sin. Book 19 has been rightly considered a "microcosm of Augustine's social thought," to use O'Donovan's phrase, yet recent years have seen Augustinians helpfully expanding our sense of Augustine's politics beyond it.[35] It is worth mentioning in this context that it is often presumed that any qualms one may have about Augustine's acceptance of slavery can be mitigated, if not resolved, by pointing to book 19's explanation of slavery as caused by sin rather than nature: "By nature," Augustine writes, "as God first created man, no one is a slave either to man or to sin."[36] This resolution is premature just to the extent that Augustine immediately clarifies: "But it is also true that the punishment of slavery is ordained by precisely the same law which commands that the natural order is to be preserved and forbids it to be disturbed."[37] Thus, although slavery is punishment for sin, it is indeed *divinely ordained* punishment, blessed by God for preserving that order of limited temporal peace that is itself among the most important goods the heavenly city shares with the earthly during the saeculum. Thus, it should not surprise us that when it comes to slavery in everyday life, Augustine's basic concern is most often the containment of disorder, both social and moral. Practically, that looks like denouncing the fugitive option to enslaved persons and encouraging a "loving spirit" among masters, while acknowledging that if a master asks, "Shall discipline sleep?" he would clarify: "That's not what I'm saying. . . . If you see your slave living badly, what other punishment will you curb him with, if not the lash? Use it: do. God allows it. In fact he is angered if you don't."[38]

It is perhaps best to say that Augustine, while genuinely troubled over the question of slavery, seeks not to challenge the institution but to Christianize it, which is to say, to recalibrate it within the terms of an emerging Christian conception of political order, and thus, to stabilize it. Interpretations that wish to find in him the contrary, while intending to be "charitable" toward intellectuals of a different time, are often themselves anachronistic, imputing to ancient Christians the presence of subversive inclinations that available evidence cannot support.[39] Instead, we find that Augustine explicitly defends the justice of slavery for the way he believes it provides a modicum of order to a fallen world, denounces slaves who run away from or resist their masters, supports the use of the whip to prevent this, and marshals theological reasons for it all.

My aim is not to use this assessment as reason to stop reading Augustine, but on the contrary, to shift the terms of the debate by grasping how areas that Augustinians wish to recover—concepts of pilgrimage, the virtues, Christology— are so often articulated precisely through slavery's metaphorical resources. The point is not to generate one more reductive caricature of Augustine's politics as mere slaveholding "ideology," or to advance an easy critique through moral anachronism or uncritical valorization of modern secular sensibilities (which, after all, often accompanied modern racial slavery). Nor still can we afford to resort to gut-level offense at Augustine's slavery discourse—shock, discomfort, distaste—which, as I have argued above, leads to disavowal rather than reckoning. To move beyond this, it is important to note that heretofore, I have advanced no argument to suggest why the slavery metaphors themselves are problematic, only shown in the first section how they have not yet attracted significant attention among political Augustinians, and in the second section that they provide an organizing structure for Augustine's thought, inside which slavery metaphors cannot be neatly separated from practical statements about life under slavery.

## Black Thought and the Problem of the Master

This final section turns to several resources from black thought's analysis of slavery and its afterlives to illumine the nature of slavery metaphors further and to specify with precision what sort of problem they present to Augustinian moral and theological thought. The problem cannot be simply *that* Augustine liberally uses slavery metaphors. In the world he inhabited, how could he not? The problem requiring further analysis for those applying Augustinian concepts in the present, especially those who hope an encounter with his thought has something to offer in the era of Black Lives Matter, lies in examining *how* these slave metaphors do their work.

Returning to Ruden's translation, it is worth noting that she does not suggest that Augustine is reflecting the experiences of enslaved persons with his slave metaphors. Instead, "Augustine's humorously self-deprecating, submissive, but boldly hopeful portrait of himself in relation to God echoes the rogue slaves of the Roman stage."[40] Augustine's slave metaphors reflect not the perspective of enslaved persons—about which the sources tell us little—but rather the culture of the masters themselves. Ruden has her finger on something more significant than she acknowledges, given what black thought, especially black feminist scholarship, unveils about the dynamics in play when the captive body functions as a "playground for the imagination," as Toni Morrison says.[41] Similarly, Hortense Spillers notes that when the dominant culture proposes to elaborate the figure of the slave, these elaborations, metaphors, and signs "tells us little or nothing about the subject buried beneath the epithets, but *quite a great deal more concerning the psychic and cultural reflexes that invent and invoke them*" (emphasis added).[42] These reflexes interest me, which come into view when, as Saidiya Hartman writes, the symbolic activity of the dominant "[makes] the captive body speak the master's truth."[43] To acknowledge this is to acknowledge that the figure of "the slave" here is fundamentally an index of the mind of the master. Its referent is to the master's own desires, wishes, reflections, and meditations, *not those of the enslaved person*. What is the moral significance of such significations being built into the grammar of Christian thought and practice?

The answer lies, in part, in recognizing that because the relation between an enslaved person and her master is always premised on force, domination, and antagonism, to accept such metaphors is, subtly but unmistakably, to adopt the perspective of the master and thus to *take the master's side against the slave*. Here I want to be careful to avoid misunderstanding: I am not exporting the problem of race back to the fifth century, in which there is no modern conception of race. What I am tracking is a set of parallel moral dynamics in the present that race indexes and that can be specified with precision by way of returning to the examples of slavery language in Augustine.

From the second section's overview, with numerous metaphors of disobedient slaves punished and restored into good order, one might get the impression that the enslaved body works as a signifier of evil or disorder for Augustine. But this is misleading. For Augustine, it is not that *slaves* are univocally bad, only that *bad* slaves are bad. The fugitive slaves punished in the images above are contrasted not only against the figure of the faithful pilgrim throughout Augustine's writings (i.e., *Conf.* 7.27) but also the figure of the *good* slave. And "good slave" images also permeate Augustine's work, whether in his use of the apostolic self-designation "slaves of God" or his articulation of Christ himself as one who took the form of the slave—a crucial term in *Confessiones* 7.9 and his mature Christology in *De Trinitate* 1–2. This slave Christology, as we should expect, also traverses any neat border between actual and figurative slavery, as seen in the guidance given to masters and slaves in his sermons. To the Christian who finds herself enslaved, Augustine writes, "That is as it should be . . . [Christ] has not made slaves free, but turned bad slaves into good slaves."[44]

As we assess the moral significance of the master's house, then, here is the crucial point: Augustine's slave metaphors function as a moral-symbolic contrast between "good" and "bad" slaves, which is not a neutral description of facts but a particular way of encoding social reality, one that serves to perpetuate that reality and preserve its stability. In this way, it displays what Willie Jennings calls a "fabricated moral universe," in which "good" and "evil" are calibrated to the aims of masters regarding their slaves' conduct. By this evaluative measure, "evil," in the context of slave behavior, means fugitivity and disobedience, and "goodness" means humility and obedience.[45] In short, then, the problem with these slavery metaphors is that they presume a moral-symbolic contrast that attains coherence only from the vantage of the master's side of the master/slave conflict—not the vantage of the enslaved. In an arresting footnote, James Wetzel hints at this dynamic: "[Augustine] measures the success of different definitions at least partly in terms of their facility to identify as evil what the consensus of his society identified as evil (for example, slaves killing their masters) and to leave as permissible what the consensus left as permissible."[46] So when what is permissible includes the master's lash but not the slave's resistance to it, it is evident that the public consensus of that society, on the matter of moral "goodness" in master–slave relations, was not built to reflect the vantage of the enslaved but that of their masters. This suggests that responsible historians must remain skeptical regarding whether enslaved persons internalized this view of the moral life as their own. We do know they resisted—fled, stole, lied, stopped work, and, occasionally, physically confronted their masters, sometimes to the point of revolt.[47] We cannot know whether or how they described the moral significance of such actions, insofar as the evidence provides only the most fleeting points of access to enslaved viewpoints. Thus, even scholars whose interests are purely "historical," in the narrowly descriptive sense, increasingly turn to New World comparisons to illumine ancient enslaved life. How much more does such comparative work make sense for those who think constructively and normatively in conversation with ancient thinkers like Augustine?

## Conclusion

By way of a conclusion, I want to probe the limits of the "excising" language to which I have made recourse above in order to revisit an important question I was asked during SCE's annual meeting. When I speak of "excising" slavery, I draw on Alasdair MacIntyre's framing of certain "unfortunate" beliefs Aristotle held about enslaved persons and women. MacIntyre finds it "important to ask whether such assertions can be excised from Aristotle's thought without denying his central claims about the best kind of polis," then immediately proposes "it seems clear that they can."[48] The metaphor of "excision," conjuring the image of a body under the knife, helpfully presses the corresponding issue in my study of Augustine's corpus: If the slavery discourse were "cut out," would the body itself survive? Is slavery in Augustine's texts a tumor—a malignant growth in an otherwise healthy body—or its heart?

To ask this is to echo the question both John Bowlin and an anonymous reviewer invited me to clarify: "Is Augustine really all about domination?" It is difficult to answer with precision because the question is formulated, I assume by design, somewhat imprecisely. What does "all about" mean? What does "domination" mean?[49] If "all about" asks whether the slavery discourse—and with it the issues I have raised throughout—appears in *all* major areas of Augustine's thought, then the answer is, essentially, yes. But if "all about" implies a stronger claim, that in all his talk of humility or virtue or God, Augustine's "real" concern is simply domination, then the answer is no. Indeed, it has been precisely my purpose to insist that domination is not simple, that projects of mastery rarely announce themselves as such (as the Cone epigraph declares), and thus to examine how Augustine's best insights coexist with, operate through, and in this way *stabilize* rather than contest the violent order of slavery. What does this mean for ongoing Augustinian "translation" projects?

To answer this, it is helpful to identify a limitation of the "excision" metaphor: The scene it invokes presumes that whether tumor or heart, accidental or essential, the problem we confront is hidden safely inside the patient's body alone, over whom our bodies stand like surgeons, the environment controlled and sterile. But this is not the case. By centering Hartman's concept of slavery's afterlife as a framework for understanding our own world, I wish to block the possibility of continuing to retrieve Augustine as though his entanglements with slavery have nothing to do with us and, equally, to undermine any notion that by jettisoning Augustine—or slavery language itself—we will have escaped the enduring dilemma of Christian mastery. Its ghosts still haunt us. The end game cannot be to eradicate all traces of slavery metaphor from Christian thought, as though its ghosts could be banished by policing habits of speech long internal to Christian grammar. It is both too late and too early for this. Too late in that there's too much blood already on the ground, too many drowned in the sea, too many violated wombs. One more disavowal will not work. Too early in that we have not yet imagined a social order beyond the world slavery built. It remains to be seen whether Augustine—brought into encounter with black religious and political thought—can play a role in this imagining.

One possibility emerges if we shift from excision to the terms of reference set by my other metaphor: Augustine thinks from within the master's house, which is to say, from within a structure he neither chose nor built, but *inherited*. In this parallel, perhaps reading Augustine through the tradition of fugitive black thought shows some of us—those who yet profit from the white supremacist order racial slavery made—more clearly to ourselves *as* masters, with a set of troubling questions following close behind: What does it mean to inherit a structure of mastery, to come to defend it as one's own, to guard a position within it that has trained one's ears not to hear the voices of the very ones the structure devastates? How might such habits be unmade, abandoned, refused—and how to refuse what makes one's life possible, organizes one's identity, sustains one's safety and power? "By faith Moses, when he was come to years, *refused* to be called the son of Pharaoh's daughter. . . . By faith he forsook Egypt. . . . By faith the people passed through the Red Sea as if on dry land."[50] By faith, Moses refused to be at home in the master's house. Perhaps *fides* demands impossible Mosaic labors of refusal: to lose your kin;[51] to refuse to betray any longer the ones you have, for so long, betrayed; to forsake instead the house itself, in search of dry land where God may appear—a point of passage through the sea to another world.

## Notes

*Epigraph*: James Cone, *A Black Theology of Liberation* (Maryknoll, NY: Orbis Books, 2010), 12.

1. Peter Brown, "Dialogue with God," *New York Review of Books*, October 26, 2017, www.nybooks.com/articles/2017/10/26/sarah-ruden-augustine-dialogue-god.

2. Kyle Harper, *Slavery in the Late Roman World: 275–425 AD* (Cambridge: Cambridge University Press, 2011).

3. James K. A. Smith, "Translation and the Afterlife of Words: A Few Thoughts on Ruden's New Translation of the Confessions," October 10, 2017, http://forsclavigera.blogspot.com/2017/10/translation-and-afterlife-of-words-few.html.

4. Saidiya Hartman, *Lose Your Mother: A Journey along the Atlantic Slave Route* (New York: Farrar, Straus & Giroux, 2007), 6.

5. Smith, "Translation."

6. Sarah Ruden, "Introduction," in *Confessions: Augustine*, trans. Sarah Ruden (New York: Modern Library, 2017), xxxiii.

7. For a survey, see Michael S. Bruno, *Political Augustinianism: Modern Interpretations of Augustine's Political Thought* (Minneapolis: Fortress Press, 2014).

8. Eric Gregory and Joseph Clair, "Augustinianisms and Thomisms," in *The Cambridge Companion to Political Theology*, ed. Craig Hovey and Elizabeth Philips (Cambridge: Cambridge University Press, 2015), 191.

9. Keith Bradley advances a strong case for comparative work. Keith Bradley, "Resisting Slavery at Rome," chap. 17 of *Cambridge World History of Slavery, Volume 1* (Cambridge: Cambridge University Press, 2011), 369–70.

10. Alexander Weheliye, "After Man," *American Literary History* 20, nos. 1–2 (Spring–Summer 2008): 322. This argument is indebted to feedback from Eboni Marshall Turman on an earlier version of the essay and, broadly, to conversations with Jay Carter and Willie Jennings.

11. Paul Gilroy, "Living Memory: Meeting Toni Morrison," in *Small Acts*, by Paul Gilroy (London: Serpent's Tail, 1993), 175–82, at 178.

12. Paul Gilroy, *The Black Atlantic: Modernity and Double Consciousness* (Cambridge, MA: Harvard University Press, 1993), 221.

13. For an accessible introduction to this vast literature, see Greg Gandin, "Capitalism and Slavery," *The Nation*, May 1, 2015, www.thenation.com/article/capitalism-and-slavery/.

14. Oliver O'Donovan, *The Desire of the Nations: Rediscovering the Roots of Political Theology* (New York: Cambridge University Press, 1996), 184–85.

15. For a survey of O'Donovan's contributions, see Bruno, *Political Augustinianism*, 191–93.

16. Gilroy, "Living Memory," 179.

17. I thank Charles Mathewes for pressing my thought here.

18. O'Donovan, *Desire*, 184–85. Whatever differences exist between Greek and Roman terms, Myles Lavan rightly concludes that both "*douleia* and *seruitus* always retain the force of their connection within the domain of chattel slavery." See Myles Lavan, *Slaves to Rome: Paradigms of Empire in Roman Culture* (New York: Cambridge University Press, 2013), 75ff.

19. O'Donovan, *Desire*, 184–85.

20. Ibid., 183ff.

21. Neil Roberts, *Freedom as Marronage* (Chicago: University of Chicago Press, 2015), 28.

22. Eric Gregory, *Politics and the Order of Love: An Augustinian Ethic of Democratic Citizenship* (Chicago: University of Chicago Press, 2008), 54.

23. Rowan Williams writes, "[Augustine] may not give the answer we would like (he is never a straightforward abolitionist), but he concludes that slavery is a sign of something fundamentally wrong in human relations." See Rowan Williams, "Patriarchal Villains?," *New Statesman*, November 10, 2015, www.newstatesman.com/politics/religion/2015/11/patriarchal-villains-it-s-time-re-think-st-paul-and-st-augustine.

24. Charles Mathewes, *The Republic of Grace: Augustinian Thoughts for Dark Times* (Grand Rapids: Eerdmans, 2010), 8.

25. Ibid., 4.

26. I thank Amaryah Armstrong for this point.

27. Cf. Kate Cooper, *The Fall of the Roman Household* (New York: Cambridge University Press, 2007), 110.

28. Brown, "Dialogue."

29. *Conf.* 2.6.14, Chadwick translation.

30. Cf. *De civ.* 21.11.

31. *De civ.* 19.15 and throughout. Cf. *In Johannis Evangelium tractatus* 41.4.

32. Susanna Elm, "Sold to Sin through Origo: Augustine of Hippo on the Slave-Trade," Michael I. Rostovtzeff Lecture at Yale University, November 12, 2014 (video recording).

33. *De libero arbitrio* 1.4.9.25, on sin, order, and providence; *De utilitate credendi* 12.27, on epistemology, folly, and wisdom; *De doctrina Christiana* 3.4.8, on the metaphorical and literal senses of texts; and *De bono conjugali* 17.19, on order and marriage.

34. *De civ.* 18.2.

35. Oliver O'Donovan, "The Political Thought of *City of God 19*," in *Bonds of Imperfection: Christian Politics, Past and Present*, ed. Oliver O'Donovan and Joan Lockwood O'Donovan (Grand Rapids: Eerdmans, 2004), 72.

36. *De civ.* 19.15.

37. Ibid.

38. *En. Ps.* 102.14 (CC40:1464–5), as quoted by Harper, *Slavery*, 230.

39. By "subversive implications," I have in mind Williams, "Patriarchal Villains?," n. 28.

40. Ruden, *Confessions*, xxxiii.

41. Toni Morrison, *Playing in the Dark: Whiteness and the Literary Imagination* (New York: Vintage, 1993), 37.

42. Hortense Spillers, "Notes on an Alternative Model—Neither/Nor," in *Black, White, and in Color* (Chicago: University of Chicago Press, 2003), 302.

43. Saidiya Hartman, *Scenes of Subjection: Terror, Slavery, and Self-Making in Nineteenth-Century America* (New York: Oxford University Press, 1997), 38.

44. *En. Ps.* 124.7.

45. Willie James Jennings, *The Christian Imagination: Theology and the Origins of Race* (New Haven, CT: Yale University Press, 2010), 183–84.

46. James Wetzel, *Augustine and the Limits of Virtue* (Cambridge: Cambridge University Press, 1992), 65.

47. See Keith Bradley, "Resisting Slavery at Rome," in *Cambridge World History of Slavery, Volume 1* (Cambridge: Cambridge University Press, 2011), 362–84.

48. See *Whose Justice? Which Rationality?* (Notre Dame, IN: University of Notre Dame Press, 1988), 104–5.

49. It is not self-evident that the normative issues raised by black thought concerning the afterlife of slavery are intelligible within the framework of "domination" and "nondomination" in the work of Philip Petit, Quentin Skinner, and others.

50. Heb 11:24–29; I owe this line of thought to conversations with Willie Jennings.

51. Christina Sharpe, "Lose Your Kin," *New Inquiry*, November 16, 2016, https://thenewinquiry.com/lose-your-kin/.

# A Social Praxis for US Health Care: Revisioning Catholic Bioethics via Catholic Social Thought

*M. Therese Lysaught and Michael McCarthy*

Catholic health care has long been a key place where the Church embodies its social doctrine. However, the moral methodology that shapes Catholic bio-ethics relies on an act-based approach to decision making, which is rooted in the pre–Vatican II manualist tradition, focusing primarily on clinical issues related to the beginning and end of life. This essay argues that given the doc-trinal status of Catholic social thought (CST), Catholic bioethics must revisit its scope and methodology. It proceeds in three steps: (1) a meta-analysis of traditional Catholic bioethics, validating the claim made above; (2) an overview of the limited literature published since 1980 engaging Catholic bioethics and CST; and (3) a map of a Catholic bioethics informed by CST generated from a dual starting point. The essay concludes by focusing on both the places where marginalized persons encounter Catholic health care and the ethical issues presented, including race, health care disparities, immigration status, and gen-der inequality, as well as the interrelated perspective of the common good, expanding the array of issues to include environmental degradation, unions, health care financing, and more.

AN UNDOCUMENTED HONDURAN FIELD WORKER LAYS IN the intensive care unit in kidney failure. A gender-questioning middle schooler sits awkwardly in a pediatrician's office, alongside her frustrated mother. In Wisconsin and Kansas, public health experts grapple with an African Ameri-can infant mortality rate triple that of white infants,[1] while nurses, doctors, and students on a short-term mission trip take pap smears with no plan to follow up with women who test positive.[2] Such scenarios occur frequently in

M. Therese Lysaught, PhD, is a professor at the Neiswanger Institute for Bioethics, Loyola University Chicago, Stritch School of Medicine, and Institute of Pastoral Studies, Loyola University Chicago, 2160 South First Avenue, Building 120, Suite 292, Maywood, IL 60153; mlysaught@luc.edu.

Michael McCarthy, PhD, is an assistant professor at the Neiswanger Institute for Bioethics, Loyola University Chicago, Stritch School of Medicine, 2160 South First Avenue, Building 120, Suite 292, Maywood, IL 60153; mpmccarthy@luc.edu.

*Journal of the Society of Christian Ethics*, 38, 2 (2018): 111–130

Catholic health care, raising complex ethical challenges for physicians, nurses, billing liaisons, chaplains, social workers, and administrators. Yet via the lens of Catholic bioethics, they remain largely invisible. To peruse this literature, one might conclude that the only issues vexing health care practitioners are those at the beginning and end of life, with occasional dilemmas about access to health care and conscience.

The focus on issues at the beginning and end of life in Catholic bioethics derives from multiple sources. One is the field's engagement with secular bioethics over the past fifty years, which has emphasized clinical decision making without adequately considering injustices that mark health care's social context. Although Catholic bioethics has succeeded in shaping important questions about abortion, contraception, physician-assisted suicide, genetics, and more, it has remained virtually silent concerning social determinants, environmental effects, and broader questions in global health.

A second source of this narrow scope lies in the historical trajectories of moral theology and CST throughout the twentieth century, which proceeded on parallel tracks, as many have noted, but rarely conversed or intersected. Yet the silence of social issues in Catholic bioethics is puzzling, for two reasons. First, Catholic health care plays a significant role in the United States: roughly 15 percent of in-patient care per year and an outsized proportion of ancillary care delivery, especially long-term care and behavioral health. In this environment, it regularly encounters questions of justice, ranging from the infrastructure for health care delivery and finance in the United States to ways in which many patients bear effects of social injustices. In doing so, it has, second, been a key place where the Church embodies its social doctrine. From its inception, Catholic health care has brought to bear—in practice and proclamation—the Church's commitments to human dignity, the common good, the preferential option for the poor, subsidiarity, and more. In other words, although Catholic health care in the US and globally has long foregrounded the social tradition, fifty years after Vatican II, there is still little rapprochement between CST and Catholic bioethics.

Our essay seeks to address this practical and methodological fissure. We argue that given CST's doctrinal status, Catholic bioethics must revisit its scope and methodology within the praxis of Catholic health care. The word "praxis" is intentional. Catholic health care leads with the practice (action) of providing care, but this action is informed by Catholic faith, tradition, and teaching as they respond to needs precipitated by health care's ever-changing landscape. Thus, praxis provides a crucial epistemological framing for Catholic bioethics that redefines its starting point, illuminates a new range of issues, and provides new analytical tools. Praxis presses Catholic bioethics beyond the parameters of traditional methodology toward what we name *a Catholic social perspective for bioethics*.

This essay is a first step in a longer project of seeking to address more systematically the dialectics between Catholic bioethics and the social injustices that confront Catholic health care and between standard Catholic bioethics methodologies and CST. We begin with a selected review of the literature from the last forty years that brings the lens of CST to bear on questions in bioethics. On the basis of this review, we constructively reimagine a methodology for Catholic bioethics that integrates essential aspects of CST. We conclude by sketching four next steps for a scholarly and practical agenda for Catholic bioethics that begins with the concerns of those marginalized within health care and emphasizes the challenges they face when interfacing with Catholic health care.

## The Intersection of Catholic Bioethics and Catholic Social Thought, 1980–2017

Catholic bioethics is a vibrant subdiscipline within Catholic moral theology. A comprehensive search suggests that between 1980 and 2017, about forty titles, on average, were published in any given year.[3] This includes ninety-two books, almost half of which focused on specific issues, while the rest were positioned as comprehensive or textbooks.[4] Of these, approximately 85 percent could be characterized as taking (for lack of a better term) a traditional approach to Catholic bioethics.[5]

These books provide a representative sample for characterizing this majority discourse. First, volume after volume repeatedly engages a finite set of issues: the beginning of life (procreation/contraception, reproductive technologies, marriage, abortion), the end of life (withholding and withdrawing treatment, medically assisted nutrition and hydration, persistent vegetative state, euthanasia, physician-assisted suicide, futility, pain management), organ donation, research with human subjects, stem cells, culture wars, conscience, and genetics.[6] Only Benedict Ashley, Kevin O'Rourke, and Jean deBlois's classic text *Health Care Ethics: A Catholic Theological Analysis* expands significantly beyond this range to attend to reconstructing the human body, mental health, pastoral care, and uniquely, a chapter on social responsibility.[7]

Likewise, methodologies employed to examine these topics pivot within parameters defined by manualist, neo-Thomist categories. Some authors seek an unabashed return to manualist neo-Thomism.[8] Most incorporate some aspects of the manualist tradition (e.g., the notion of moral norms, the principle of double effect, conscience), but they seek to relocate these within frameworks that are philosophically or theologically more adequate. These frames include Christological personalism;[9] a scriptural/virtue frame informed by *Veritatis Splendor*, Servais Pinckaers, and/or other writings of John Paul II;[10]

natural law;[11] a deeper but selective return to Aquinas;[12] a phenomenological account of "the acting person";[13] or proportionalism.[14] Insofar as these new frames seek a more adequate account of the human person or human acts than is found in the manuals, they remain largely defined by neo-Thomist/ manualist methodologies.

In addition, this majority discourse has a significant blind spot—it pays scant attention to resources, categories, or concepts of CST, beyond an occasional reference to the common good or a focus on human dignity. Yet within this literature, a minority discourse has begun to emerge, one that brings the lens of CST to bear on questions in health care. Of the ninety-two titles mentioned above, only thirteen incorporated resources of CST. Most focused on a single issue, with only Lisa Cahill's *Theological Bioethics* providing an integrated, book-length treatment employing a methodology that draws on CST and attends to a spectrum of issues, albeit a traditional spectrum (genetics, access to health care, end of life, and reproductive technologies).

In other words, the scope of works integrating Catholic bioethics with CST remains small. To ascertain the contours of this subdiscourse, we ran a more textured search for the period 1980–2017.[15] This generated a bibliography of seventy-five publications—or about two a year. Most focused on a single issue—for example, most frequently access to health care and HIV/AIDS, with occasional attention to end-of-life issues, reproductive issues, genetics, global poverty, and, after the publication of *Laudato Si'*, the environment.

In what follows, we map the landscape of this emerging minority discourse. Contributions at this interface can be organized into six categories: those who (1) reject the integration of Catholic bioethics and CST; (2) argue for the connection between CST and Catholic bioethics; (3) attend to questions in global bioethics; (4) employ a rights-based framework; (5) reimagine justice via the principle of participation; and, finally, (6) address bioethics from a liberationist perspective. These categories are of course porous, and they overlap. Although many authors could be located under more than one heading, we categorized them based on their argument's central features and practical implications. Because of space constraints, in the following analysis, we have selected one or two authors or contributions to represent each category.

## *The Naysayers*

We begin with a minority opinion: those who are critical or suspicious of attempts to incorporate CST into the method/analyses of Catholic bioethics. Largely confined to the journal *Christian Bioethics*, these Kantian/libertarian critics—particularly David Denz and H. Tristram Engelhardt—raise concerns about CST's conceptual strength along with the risk that, when purveyed as a point of common ground with the secular sphere, appeals to CST will become disconnected from doctrinal foundations and elide with "post-Christian" activities.

Denz opens with a premise that is diametrically opposed to our thesis: "Health care," he avers "is a context that exposes some of the weaknesses of Catholic social teaching."[16] He voices four primary concerns with the "contemporary social ideology" of CST. First, he maintains that CST simply asserts human dignity and correlative rights, obscuring the conceptual foundations for posited rights. Second, as a set of principles or criteria, he suggests that CST functions at an ideal or abstract level, leaving its vision unclear and out of touch with reality. Third, he finds conceptual conflicts between subsidiarity (which he refers to as "vague and unfocused") and the preferential option for the poor, along with CST's "implicit 'statism.'"[17] Finally, privileging libertarianism—or perhaps capitalism—over a thick Christian theological vision, he challenges CST's cooperative portrayal of social life as flawed and inadequate to health care's competitive nature.

Not one to be outdone, H. Tristam Engelhardt offers a vocal and harsh critique, peppering several critical essays throughout *Christian Bioethics*.[18] Engelhardt argues that appeals to social justice, especially as points of common ground with secular interlocutors, will become decoupled from thick theological foundations, particularly Christian anthropology, serious doctrinal commitments, and the epistemological centrality of liturgy and worship. As such, privileging CST risks dampening authentic Christian health care and rendering bioethics or health care Catholic "in name only."[19]

Although we reject their general thesis, both Denz and Engelhardt raise two important critiques worth further consideration. First, principles of CST can be deployed too often in a conceptually thin manner. In many instances, careful theoretical and theological work is either unarticulated or presupposed, or remains to be done. Second, they remind us that CST is rooted in a faith tradition and cannot be uncoupled from our theological traditions. Engelhardt points consistently to the liturgical foundations of all Christian practices. Both reminders have potentially powerful ramifications for both method in Catholic bioethics and the practice of Catholic health care. However, to argue that Christian bioethics should not participate in critical conversations and instead should double down on doctrinal rebukes "against abortion, homosexual acts, and physician-assisted suicide, major battlegrounds in the culture wars," bifurcates Catholic doctrine and fails to provide guidance on critical moral issues facing the health and health care of patients.[20]

### Method, Europe, and the Magisterium

Contra the "naysayers," the authors in our second category tackle the bright line presumed to divide Catholic bioethics and CST. They can be subdivided into three groups. The first demonstrates how CST has been integrated into European bioethics.[21] The second group seeks to radically reimagine particular issues in Catholic bioethics via CST.[22] And the third group details the intersections between traditional moral methodologies and CST in papal teaching.[23]

Schotsmans and Pijnenburg and his colleagues outline how the Roman Catholic tradition influenced the development of European bioethics, resulting in an understanding of the human person, society, and their interrelationships that differs significantly (Schotsmans uses the term "essentially") from the US context. Personhood, for example, is reconfigured beyond "a minimalistic concept of the person, . . . not only [focusing] on autonomy but also [looking] at the concepts of integrity, dignity, and vulnerability."[24] This nuanced and realistic anthropology grounds a vision of society that understands the mutual dependence and responsibility between persons for the flourishing of all, summarized in the term "solidarity." The commitment to solidarity provides the foundation for national health care systems that recognize the social determinants of health—that is, that circumstances beyond one's control affect health outcomes—and prioritize meeting the health needs of all. For Pijnenburg and his colleagues, Catholic health care should embody an even more "radical commitment to solidarity" than its secular counterparts.[25] Although admitting that solidarity often functions as a secular concept, they provide an in-depth account of its practical and theological underpinnings from the beginnings of Catholic health care that is bolstered by Christian doctrine.

Dan Daly and others draw on CST to offer novel approaches to particular questions; Daly focuses on withholding and withdrawing treatment at the end of life. He traces "the presence of a robust notion of the common good in the Catholic end-of-life tradition" from Juan Cardinal de Lugo to Pope John Paul II, detailing how communal considerations factored into end-of-life decision making throughout this history.[26] He outlines how the theological virtue of charity or caritas catalyzes the connections between justice and the common good, drawing particularly on Benedict XVI's *Caritas in Veritate*, John XXIII, and Aquinas. Finally, he turns to what he names the "Global Structure of Vice in Health Care"—a more complex way of casting the preferential option for the poor—which includes "the globalization of health care and health care structures, and the scandalously high level of global suffering and premature death that is due to a lack of access to basic medical care."[27] Together, these threads enable Daly to radically reimagine the ordinary-versus-extraordinary distinction.

Whereas Pijnenburg and his colleagues and Daly refer to intersections between traditional moral methodologies and CST in papal teaching, a third subgroup focuses specifically on this question. Bishop James McHugh argues that Pope John Paul II's *Evangelium Vitae* should be understood as a social encyclical, incorporating both natural law and social methodologies. Others find similar points of contact in Benedict XVI's *Deus Caritas Est* and *Caritas in Veritate*.[28] For John Gallagher, Pope Francis's *Evangelii Gaudium* holds the potential to reframe questions of Catholic bioethics. Francis's theological vision, rooted in evangelization, provides "the basis for a theological ethics that is primarily a social ethics, more clearly related to Catholic social teaching than classical moral theology."[29]

These authors make two critical contributions. First, they have begun to map the points of contact between CST and traditional methodologies, be they Catholic or secular, demonstrating how the groundwork for this integrated methodology has been laid in magisterial teaching. Second, they have begun to illustrate how this integrated methodology can help creatively reimagine the ways Catholic bioethics approaches traditional issues. Yet with the exception of those in Daly's subgroup, many here offer very little by way of practical application. Although much more theoretical work remains to be done, more precision is also needed to demonstrate what a Catholic bioethics infused by CST will mean in the everyday practice of Catholic health care.

### The Global Scope of Bioethics

During the past two decades, some bioethics scholars have begun to address health care's global challenges. Again, questions of access to health care with regard to specific diseases loom large—particularly, the complex social, cultural, and ethical challenges raised by those living with HIV/AIDS.[30] In addition, the essays in this section make the important methodological move of including multiple theological voices grounded in various sociocultural locations. This commitment to diverse perspectives provides an important corrective to the white male perspective that tends to dominate discussions in bioethics. To illustrate this category, here we draw on essays from Mary Jo Iozzio, Elsie M. Miranda, and Mary M. Doyle Roche's *Calling for Justice throughout the World: Catholic Women Theologians on the HIV/AIDS Pandemic* and Linda Hogan's *Applied Ethics in a World Church*.[31]

Iozzio and her colleagues raise questions of solidarity and justice by speaking to sociohistoric contexts that contribute to the reality of those living with HIV/AIDS. However, only Shawnee Daniels-Sykes explicitly draws on CST to address the challenges presented by the pandemic, referencing human dignity, respect for life, the common good, social solidarity, and an option for the poor, vulnerable, and marginalized. Although Daniels-Sykes brings CST to bear on bioethics, the whole book might be read as a social bioethics that challenges the sexual ethics of the Catholic Church, incorporating the cultural dimensions that are needed to address the spread of HIV/AIDS.

Linda Hogan's volume devotes one section to HIV/AIDS and another to bioethical questions that need further exploration when viewed on a global scale. These latter essays in many ways embody what José Roque Junges describes as a "hermeneutical bioethics."[32] Junges, a Brazilian theologian and bioethicist, argues that hermeneutical bioethics allows theology to ask critical questions from a perspective outside the pragmatic and efficiency-oriented operations in health care and emphasizes the public role of theology in contributing to bioethical conversations. The public face of theological bioethics requires a move beyond traditional questions that surface with hospital ethics committees and with respect to ensuring responsible conduct of human subjects research. Theological bioethicists ought to bring awareness to new areas for ethical reflection. Darlene Weaver and Jorge José Ferrer exemplify such a hermeneutic. Weaver's essay on embryo adoption acknowledges teachings about embryo development and sexual ethics but urges further thinking on issues of responsibility, generosity, and the "increasing tendencies in medical and cultural attitudes toward genetic determinism."[33] Medical and cultural attitudes about genetics extend to biotechnology and research, an area to which Ferrer's essay brings much-needed theological attention.[34]

Each of these anthologies offers theological reflections that draw on CST and contribute to the ongoing discourse within bioethics. Moreover, they incorporate voices that are heard from too infrequently, highlighting the importance of drawing from broader perspectives to analyze emerging global questions. However, though they expand bioethics' geographical scope and bring new resources to bear on traditional topics, apart from Ferrer's essay, they—like their counterparts in the second category above—stop short of detailing how to incorporate their insights into the day-to-day practice of Catholic health care. Again, attention to practice in bioethics remains elusive.

## A Rights-Based Framework

The commitment to health as a human right is a key area in which the fourth group of contributors finds common ground with secular bioethics. Again, here contributors focus broadly on health care access and more specifically on HIV/AIDS, drawing on the notion of rights in connection to human dignity and the common good.[35] Beyond HIV/AIDS and access, Maura Ryan utilizes a rights-based analysis of public health as a necessary resource for addressing many global health challenges.[36]

Ryan utilizes the work of the physician and global health pioneer Paul Farmer, who, though hardly a Catholic bioethicist, has innovatively drawn on liberation theology's preferential option for the poor and pragmatic solidarity to highlight the neglected human rights that pertain to quality of life and health care services.[37] Ryan's human rights approach takes up public health by considering environmental risk factors—a lack of education, economic disempowerment, limited access to clean water, political and social unrest, and the like—as key factors that receive too little attention.[38] Both she and Farmer call on bioethics to reorient its focus to consider the needs of the marginalized in order to reform how we conceptualize the right to health care access and to help cultivate an environment that fosters positive health outcomes.[39]

Similarly, María del Carmen Massé García and Javier de la Torre Díaz adopt a human rights framework to critique how the benefits of biotechnological innovation and the skills to develop such biotech rarely engage with the Global South.[40] UNESCO's Universal Declaration on Bioethics and Human Rights provides their starting point by highlighting the importance of sharing biotech resources. Of greater urgency, they argue, is the need to develop research capacity in order to participate in the biotech industry. As a necessary tool for development, they characterize assistance in developing such a capacity as a right, not an act of helping or kindness. They argue that current models of technology transfer establish dependence rather than participation and capacitation, furthering the advance of high-income countries at the expense of others.[41]

For these scholars, a human rights framework enables bioethics to view questions from perspectives of those who are most often excluded from the ability to participate in advances that science and medicine have to offer; again, diverse and marginalized voices are brought into the discourse. One challenge, however, with a rights-based approach is the question of who ensures that these rights are available and who is responsible for the cost of delivering these rights. This question speaks to the complexity of the needed response and also to the "malaise in bioethics" that remains preoccupied with clinical and highly technological innovations and neglects the global reality of "stupid deaths."[42] Although the challenges of bioethics framed in a human rights context can seem daunting and may seem too far removed from the ethical questions facing health care providers in the United States, they provide important resources for illuminating the rights questions faced by those who are marginalized within our own health systems.

## *Participation, Justice, and Change*

The fifth category—participation, justice, and change—is our largest, an umbrella incorporating a diversity of approaches. As a window into this category, we focus on Lisa Cahill's important book *Theological Bioethics: Participation, Justice, Change*.[43] Here she outlines a trajectory for the theoretical and practical ways in which theology ought to engage bioethics. Her argument draws from a decade of work addressing questions about genetics, biotechnology, end-of-life care, and access to care. However, *Theological Bioethics* is more than an anthology of previous essays. Cahill incorporates most clearly the historical importance that theologians have played in developing the field of bioethics and framing its questions. She further illustrates how social dimensions of these questions have too long been neglected and that one of the most powerful contributions theological scholars and practitioners can now bring to the field is engagement with social theory and practice.

Cahill argues that "bioethics in the twenty-first century must in every case be social ethics, not just a theory of engagement."[44] Over against the tendency to reduce clinical decisions to individual, private choices, bioethics is a form of public moral discourse, one that she envisages as a practice of participatory democracy. In such a model, theology is not only permitted to participate—it is indeed compelled to do so, bringing unique and important resources to the conversation. She argues that participatory theological bioethics proves capable of critiquing and offering solutions to injustices pertaining to health and health care by drawing on commitments to human dignity, the common good, and the preferential option for the poor.[45]

Consider, for example, Cahill's two-chapter engagement with questions at the end of life. She first situates the issue within the social context of policy debates on physician-assisted suicide and decision making at the end of life. She then details traditional teaching on double-effect and the Church's opposition to euthanasia. This recap covers some well-trodden Catholic bioethical ground, but then explores how Christian bioethics has advocated for an increased role in palliative and hospice services and the role that various institutions—including local parishes—play in creating communities that better address questions of aging and dying.[46] Her argument develops by detailing the teaching—in both traditional and social forms—that bears on the issue being addressed and the practices of particular organizations that demonstrate alternative social structures that publicly resist the status quo and embody a Christian response.

Cahill's prophetic argument expands the array of resources that are brought to bear within the discipline of Catholic bioethics and demonstrates how a participatory bioethics—informed by the common good, the option for the poor, and human dignity—shapes policy and resists social injustices through social practices. Although making an important methodological shift, Cahill attends to a traditional set of issues—for example, end of life, genetics, and access to health care. And her framework of participatory democracy continues to locate the practice of bioethics largely within public moral discourse or public policy rather than at the more granular level of the day-to-day realities of Catholic health care institutions and Catholic health care practitioners.

### Liberating Bioethics

Our final category includes those who bring a liberationist lens to bioethics. This perspective, articulated as early as 1987 by Márcio Fabri dos Anjos, draws attention to bioethical questions as a "complexity of social relationships within which sickness and death occur" and "challenges bioethics to face up to one fact: The majority of viruses that the doctor scrutinizes under the microscope not only feed and develop on the biological body of the patient, but also nurture themselves in the body politic."[47] Dos Anjos's work, along with the more recent work of Alexandre Martins,[48] describes a Latin American approach to bioethics, whereas Marie Giblin offers a feminist perspective[49] and Shawnee Daniels-Sykes brings a black Catholic perspective.[50] These authors are unified in issuing a call for both the *liberation of* bioethics and for bioethics to be reenvisaged via a *liberationist method*.

First, they join forces in mounting an incisive critique of the practice of bioethics with respect to its focus, social location, and priorities, and its lack of a critique of neoliberal economics. For example, dos Anjos observes that bioethics as a discipline tends to focus on problems unique to first world contexts—high-cost, high-tech medicine and experimentation, issues that affect a small percentage of the world's population, while being blind to the problems faced by the poor[51]—what Paul Farmer has elsewhere referred to as "the quandaries of the fortunate."[52] This blindness to the full spectrum of bioethical issues derives in large part from the social location of most bioethicists, who often limit their scope to what occurs within the hospital walls.[53] As a rule, bioethics has been focused on protecting the interests of medical providers, including both physicians and institutions.[54] Moreover, there exists almost no critique of the hospital as a place that shapes and contributes to systemic injustices pertaining to economics, sexism (Giblin), and racism and white privilege (Sykes). From a liberationist perspective, bioethics often functions to simply legitimize and "serve the currently dominant social system without any capacity for criticizing it."[55]

Yet how can the liberation of bioethics occur? These authors press bioethics to shift its locus or starting point to those people who are impoverished, marginalized, disenfranchised, oppressed, and/or "at risk of disadvantage." For Giblin, these include "women, people of color, those who lack insurance, the 'subjugated,' those who will be affected by the outcome of a decision, especially those who will be disadvantaged or bear its burden."[56] This epistemological shift reshapes how bioethics is understood; it calls for inclusion, and it incorporates a wider spectrum of voices into deliberation about questions in bioethics.[57] Akin to Cahill's approach, doing so helps create a dialogical process that empowers the excluded to participate in the social and political arena.[58]

Martins takes the challenge even further—for him, it is not sufficient to simply invite the poor to the table; the table itself must be moved. It requires bioethicists "to join with the poor and marginalized to share their lives and see reality from their perspective."[59] Thus, priorities are established from the "place of the poor," shifting the way we think about health care. The reprioritization requires a physical shift in "our network of social relationships, the people to whom we attribute importance, the necessities or problems to which we give priority."[60] In doing so, it roots bioethics "in a community of persons who develop a preferential solidarity."[61] Thus, a Catholic social bioethics not only is cognizant of social relationships but also privileges relationships with those individuals and communities that are overlooked in the provision and organization of Catholic health care.

## Toward a Catholic Social Bioethics

From the naysayers to the liberationists, each of the foregoing perspectives engages Catholic social thought. Some reject CST outright; others incorporate components of the tradition—sometimes singularly, sometimes in conjunction with tools from secular philosophical or political frameworks. Each of these perspectives merits much greater attention than we have been able to give them here. Yet this overview suggests that the groundwork has been laid for the development of an approach to Catholic bioethics that draws on theological, social, liturgical, and theoretical resources that address health care practitioners and marginalized communities. In this final section, we collate their method-ological challenges and outline next steps. As a heuristic for gathering the meth-odological insights of this literature, we utilize Anne Carr's succinct overview of key methodological loci—social location, audience, starting point, sources, norms, theoretical assumptions, and interpretive strategies for method—that opens Catherine LaCugna's *Freeing Theology*.[62]

### *Social Location*

The social location of the Catholic bioethicist significantly shapes the method and content of his or her work. To date, those doing Catholic bioethics have been located primarily in the academy, the policy arena, or the management structure of contemporary health care. These domains of privilege and power are distant from the realities that shape morbidity and mortality and are largely shaped by the same structures that push people to the margins. The forego-ing authors challenge those doing Catholic bioethics to augment their social location in two ways: to have regular experience of joining with the poor and sharing aspects of their reality and to acknowledge the importance of being practitioners in the clinical and institutional setting and allowing this setting to inform the realities and questions with which they engage.

### *Audience*

For the most part, those practicing Catholic bioethics—both traditional and social—have taken as their primary audience the fields of theological ethics or secular bioethics. Even when successfully raising the consciousness of fellow scholars, such a narrow audience risks devolving the field into increasingly esoteric conversations conducted solely among the like-minded, safe from the challenges of other theoretical or contextual perspectives and disconnected from the realities of health care. We must ask: *For whom* is Catholic bioethics done? To whom—or rather, *with whom*—does it speak? Interlocutors matter. It is not simply that Catholic bioethics needs to be translated into or (to use the word often disparaged among academics) *applied* to the clinical or institutional setting where health care happens. Rather, it needs to engage patients and practitioners—in the United States and globally—as counterparts in the praxis of Catholic bioethics.

## *A Starting Point*

We agree with the liberationists that a necessary starting point for a Catholic social bioethics is—preferentially—the faces and lives of those marginalized, both in the United States and globally.[63] Catholic health care strives to make a preferential option for the poor and marginalized; Catholic bioethics must necessarily do the same. Such a shift is a matter not only of discipleship but also of epistemology. Such a locus supplies knowledge and resources that are crucial for an authentic Catholic bioethics but are inaccessible to those of us protected by privilege and power. From such a locus, for example, we would come to see not only that adult African Americans generally eschew advanced directives—the "problem" that needs to be solved, from the perspective of traditional bioethics. We would learn legitimate social, cultural, historical, and practical reasons for such resistance; would begin to understand the ways in which Catholic health care participates in intersectional structures of oppression; and would gain resources for reshaping bioethics and health care. Race, however, is but one epistemological lens; starting from the margins, Catholic bioethics will gain insight regarding gender, environmental degradation, and economic practices that enmesh both our culture and Catholic health care.

## *Sources*

No longer is it sufficient to simply draw on neo-Thomist principles or even a slightly more informed Thomism read through twentieth-century continental philosophy. As a Catholic scholarly discipline, Catholic bioethics must—at a minimum—integrate more intentionally the resources of the Catholic moral tradition, Catholic social tradition, systematic theology, liturgical practice, and the witness of those working in the relevant apostolates of the Church. As bioethics, it must also draw on the voices and experiences of those patients and practitioners who negotiate the daily realities of health care delivery. Additional engagement with secular resources—such as the UNESCO declaration, the Nuffield Report highlighting the importance of solidarity, the latest guidelines from the Council for International Organizations of Medical Sciences, and political philosophies—can potentially enhance the practice of Catholic bioethics itself. Each of these resources is necessary; none is sufficient. Yet critical questions remain about which resources are privileged in our methodology, and why.

### Norms

The trajectory of the method emerging from this analysis locates the path forward between the epistemological and structural questions of liberation theology and Cahill's participatory bioethics. Within such a trajectory, a primary norm becomes the foundational idea of solidarity—or, perhaps more carefully stated, pragmatic or preferential solidarity. Such a norm incorporates deep commitments to the dignity of all human persons and a consistent ethic of solidarity, in Blase Cardinal Cupich's new phrasing, as well as an integral and participatory understanding of the common good. It also makes clear that medicine is an institution and thus is embedded in social structures and social determinants of health that are materially relevant to Catholic bioethics.

### Theoretical Assumptions and Interpretive Strategies

Explicit assumptions shape the foregoing—that Catholic bioethics must engage the resources of the Catholic tradition as a whole, the priority of praxis, and the shape of epistemology. Likewise, we approach these sources with a particular hermeneutic—a commitment to revisioning an alternative way for health care professionals and Catholic health care institutions to care for patients and advocate for structural changes that more authentically embodies the mission and praxis of Catholic health care.

For example, one interpretive strategy shaping this project is to draw on the insights of both Cahill's participatory methodology and liberation theology. Cahill begins with a traditional set of Catholic bioethics issues and, by viewing them through a lens of political theory and policy, expands our ability to consider their social consequences outside the clinical setting. Liberation theology, however, takes a different starting point, from the place and experience of injustice, and demonstrates how social structures necessarily permeate clinical realities. By beginning with social injustices that infuse the walls of health care institutions, liberation theology enables bioethics to identify a new set of critical issues—racism, gun violence, immigration, and gender—living problems that play out in the health care setting but do not have a foothold in Catholic bioethical discourse. Once these are demonstrated as clinical concerns, Cahill's methodology enables Catholic bioethics to move the analysis and response to these issues into public discourse and practice in important new ways. *Theological bioethics* creates the opportunity to reflect on bioethics as a social ethic, and liberation theology frees us to confront social injustices within health care systems.

## Conclusion

Pursuing the foregoing methodological insights will transform not only how scholars contribute to the field of Catholic bioethics but also how health care is delivered. It is a robust and long-term agenda; and in conclusion, we suggest four next steps for advancing the work of Catholic social bioethics.

First, this approach calls scholars to more consistently and thoroughly examine *traditional* issues in Catholic bioethics—the various subquestions at the end of life, beginning of life, genetics, conscience, research, and more—through a CST lens. The work of transforming theological thinking on mainline Catholic bioethics issues has begun; traditional issues now need more systematic analyses from this perspective.

Second, this approach calls for Catholic bioethics to *expand the range of questions* absent from traditional engagements. By drawing on CST, new issues are brought to the forefront and emphasize the unjust experiences of many within Catholic health care. Victims of human trafficking and gun violence enter our institutions every day, yet are we educating physicians, nurses, social workers, chaplains, and administrators about the realities of this patient population? Although victims of gun violence may present with more acute conditions, undocumented patients and gender-questioning patients may silently navigate their health care while providers remain unaware of the challenges many of these patients face. In addition to clinical concerns, a social bioethics brings into view questions regarding the responsibility of health care institutions in caring for the environment and offering opportunities for clinicians and patients to think through the environmental impact of their decisions.

Third, it *challenges the current boundaries* between clinical ethics, organizational ethics, and political advocacy. Racism, for example, is not only a social determinant of infant mortality external to our institutions; it also inflects clinical dynamics, silently shapes hospital staffing practices, and underlies organizational decisions. Looking out of the hospital doors, this lens challenges Catholic bioethics to address how our institutions participate in maintaining the status quo of racism, sexism, and economic inequities, and how their clinical and institutional decisions affect the health of the community and better enable members of the community to participate in shaping their health care options.

Fourth, it *outlines an array of critically important theoretical and theological work* that remains to be done that addresses the connections, tensions, and contradictions in the tradition. What are the connections between, for example, the various meanings of "the dignity of the human person" in traditional Catholic bioethics and CST? How are both traditional Catholic bioethics and CST shaped by natural law commitments? How can they be augmented by the virtue tradition or interface with liturgical practices? Where, systematically, has magisterial teaching on Catholic bioethics already begun to integrate CST? How should Catholic bioethics integrate secular resources? Alternatively, how might bioethics inform CST and the field of social ethics via the latter's reflection on the realities of health care?

Scholars have begun fleshing out answers to these questions within the field of moral theology broadly construed; more research is needed here within Catholic bioethics. We invite our colleagues in the academy, our health care institutions, and their communities to join us in this project.

## Notes

1. Kaiser Family Foundation, "Infant Mortality Rate (Deaths per 1,000 Live Births) by Race/Ethnicity," August 6, 2015.

2. Michael Rozier, SJ, "The Medical Missions DTR: It's Not You, It's Me," *Jesuit Post*, May 2015.

3. Per the ATLA Catholic Periodical and Literature Index, a search—on the parameters 1980–2017, for academic journals, books, and essays—provides these results: for bioethics and Catholic, 1,351; for medical ethics and Catholic, 744; and for health care ethics and Catholic, 25. Expanding the search to ATLA Religion would augment these figures; accounting for duplicate entries would trim it. Overall, the ATLA-CPLI search provides a reasonable estimate of the scope of publications.

4. Issues include killing, fetus as patient, conscience, abortion, medically assisted nutrition and hydration, eugenics, the human person, resources allocation, health care reform, maternal-fetal conflict, John Paul II, HIV/AIDS, and the elderly.

5. For the purposes of this literature review, this list was limited to English-language titles.

6. Additional occasional issues include: (1) the clinical encounter, Nicanor P. G. Austriaco, *Biomedicine and Beatitude: An Introduction to Catholic Bioethics* (Washington, DC: Catholic University of America, 2011); (2) conjoined twins and embryo adoption, Jason T. Eberl, *Contemporary Controversies in Catholic Bioethics* (Cham, Switzerland: Springer, 2017); (3) Catholic identity, Anthony Fisher, *Catholic Bioethics for a New Millennium* (New York: Cambridge University Press, 2011); (4) global bioethics, David F. Kelly, Gerard Magill, and Henk ten Have, *Contemporary Catholic Health Care Ethics* (Washington, DC: Georgetown University Press, 2004); and (5) homosexuality, D. Brian Scarnecchia, *Bioethics, Law, and Human Life Issues* (Lanham, MD: Scarecrow Press, 2010).

7. Benedict M. Ashley, Kevin David O'Rourke, and Jean deBlois, *Healthcare Ethics: A Catholic Theological Analysis*, 5th edition (Saint Louis: Catholic Health Association, 2006).

8. William E. May, *Catholic Bioethics and the Gift of Human Life* (Huntington, IN: Our Sunday Visitor, 2000 and 2013); Willem Jacobus Cardinal Eijk, Lambert Hendriks, J. A.

Raymakers, and John Fleming, eds., *Manual of Catholic Medical Ethics: Responsible Healthcare from a Catholic Perspective* (West End, Australia: Connor Court, 2014); Scarnecchia, *Bioethics, Law, and Human Life Issues*; Peter J. Cataldo and Albert S. Moraczewski, eds., *Catholic Health Care Ethics: A Manual for Ethics Committees* (Boston: National Catholic Bioethics Center, 2001).

9. Ashley, O'Rourke, and deBlois, *Healthcare Ethics*.

10. Austriaco, *Biomedicine*; Fisher, *Catholic Bioethics*.

11. Alfonso Gomez-Lobo and John Keown, *Bioethics and the Human Goods: An Introduction to Natural Law Bioethics* (Washington, DC: Georgetown University Press, 2015).

12. Jason T. Eberl, *Thomistic Principles and Bioethics* (New York: Routledge, 2006); Martin Rhonheimer, *Vital Conflicts in Medical Ethics: A Virtue Approach to Craniotomy and Tubal Pregnancies* (Washington, DC: Catholic University of America Press, 2009).

13. Rhonheimer, *Vital Conflicts*; Austriaco, *Biomedicine*; Pia Matthews, *John Paul II and the Apparently "Non-Acting" Person* (Leominster, MA: Gracewing, 2013).

14. Kelly, Magill, and ten Have, *Contemporary Catholic Health Care Ethics*; Aaron L. Mackler, *Introduction to Jewish and Catholic Bioethics: A Comparative Analysis* (Washington, DC: Georgetown University Press, 2003); James J. Walter and Thomas A. Shannon, *Contemporary Issues in Bioethics: A Catholic Perspective* (Lanham, MD: Rowman & Littlefield, 2005).

15. To locate scholarly works at the intersection of Catholic bioethics and Catholic social thought, we searched ATLA-Religion, ATLA-CPLI, Amazon, and Google for these terms: "Catholic bioethics and social justice"; "Catholic bioethics"; "Catholic health care ethics"; "theological bioethics"; "Catholic social bioethics"; and "Catholic bioethics and Catholic social teaching." To ensure that we were capturing representation from Europe and other non-US locations, we queried the Catholic Ethics in a World Church website (www.catholicethics.com/network) for members of the network that had listed "medical ethics" as a specialty. We then ran ATLA-Religion/CPLI searches on the 97 international scholars identified. Altogether, these searches generated a bibliography of approximately one hundred titles (books/articles/essays) in English, Spanish, or Portuguese that were then reviewed. A review culled the final list to about seventy-five titles. Notably, twenty of these items—or roughly one-quarter—appeared in the journal *Christian Bioethics*, which devoted two issues to this interface—vol. 6, no. 3 (2000) and vol. 7, no. 1 (2001).

16. David Denz, "Catholic Social Teaching and Healthcare: Some Reservations," *Christian Bioethics* 6, no. 3 (2000): 252.

17. Ibid.

18. II. Tristram Engelhardt, "Roman Catholic Social Teaching and Religious Hospital Identity in a Post-Christian Age," *Christian Bioethics* 6, no. 3 (2000): 295–300; H. Tristram Engelhardt, "The Dechristianization of Christian Health Care Institutions, or, How the Pursuit of Social Justice and Excellence Can Obscure the Pursuit of Holiness," *Christian Bioethics* 7, no. 1 (2001): 151–61; H. Tristram Engelhardt, "A New Theological Framework for Roman Catholic Bioethics: Pope Francis Makes a Significant Change in the Moral Framework for Bioethics," *Christian Bioethics* 21, no. 1 (2015): 130–34.

19. Engelhardt, "Dechristianization," 152.

20. Engelhardt, "New Theological Framework," 131.

21. Paul Schotsmans, "Christian Bioethics in Europe: In Defense against Reductionist Influences from the United States," *Christian Bioethics* 15, no. 1 (2009): 17–30; Martien A. M. Pijnenburg, Bert Gordijn, Frans J. H. Vosman, and Henk ten Have, "Catholic Healthcare Organizations and How They Can Contribute to Solidarity: A Social-Ethical Account of Catholic Identity," *Christian Bioethics* 16, no. 3 (2010): 314–33.

22. Brenda Margaret Appelby and Nuala P. Kenny, "Relational Personhood, Social Justice and the Common Good: Catholic Contributions toward a Public Health Ethics," *Christian Bioethics* 16, no. 3 (2010): 296–313; Daniel J. Daly, "Unreasonable Means: Proposing a New Category for Catholic End-of-Life Ethics," *Christian Bioethics* 19, no. 1 (2013): 40–59; Christian Spiess, "Recognition and Social Justice: A Roman Catholic View of Christian Bioethics of Long-Term Care and Community Service," *Christian Bioethics* 1, no. 3 (2007): 287–301.

23. Bishop James McHugh, "Building a Culture of Life: A Catholic Perspective," *Christian Bioethics* 7, no. 3 (2001): 441–52; Norbert Mette, "Love as Evidence for the Truth and the Humanity of Faith: A Roman Catholic Perspective on the Significance of 'Caritas' in the Life of the Church," *Christian Bioethics* 15, no. 2 (2009): 107–18; William Newton, "The Link between Life Issues and Social Justice: Insights into Pope Benedict XVI's Social Encyclical *Caritas in Veritate*," *National Catholic Bioethics Quarterly* 12, no. 3 (2012): 449–60; Antoine Suarez, "The Social Question Is Radically an Anthropological Question: The Perspective of *Caritas in Veritate*," *Journal of Markets & Morality* 16, no. 1 (2013): 85–99; John A. Gallagher, "Pope Francis' Potential Impact on American Bioethics," *Christian Bioethics* 21, no. 1 (2015): 11–34.

24. Schotsmans, "Christian Bioethics," 22.

25. Pijnenburg et al., "Catholic Healthcare Organizations," 314.

26. Daly, "Unreasonable Means," 42.

27. Ibid., 46.

28. On *Deus Caritas Est*, see Mette, "Love as Evidence." On *Caritas in Veritate*, see Newton, "Link between Life Issues and Social Justice."

29. Gallagher, "Pope Francis' Potential Impact," 11.

30. James F. Keenan, Jon D. Fuller, Lisa Sowle Cahill, and Kevin T. Kelly, *Catholic Ethicists on HIV/AIDS Prevention* (New York: Continuum, 2000); Agbonkhianmeghe Orobator, *From Crisis to Kairos: The Mission of the Church in the Time of HIV/AIDS, Refugees, and Poverty* (Nairobi: Pauline Publications Africa, 2005); Agbonkhianmeghe Orobator, "Ethics of HIV/AIDS Prevention: Paradigms of a New Discourse from an African Perspective," in *Applied Ethics in a World Church: The Padua Conference*, ed. Linda Hogan (Maryknoll, NY: Orbis Books, 2008), 147–54; Agbonkhianmeghe Orobator, ed., *AIDS 30 Years Down the Line: Faith-Based Reflections about the Epidemic in Africa* (Nairobi: Pauline Publications Africa, 2012); Jacquineau Azetsop, ed., *HIV & AIDS in Africa: Christian Reflection, Public Health, Social Transformation* (Maryknoll, NY: Orbis Books, 2016).

31. Mary Jo Iozzio, Elsie M. Miranda, and Mary M. Doyle Roche, eds., *Calling for Justice throughout the World: Catholic Women Theologians on the HIV/AIDS* (New York: Continuum, 2009); Linda Hogan, ed., *Applied Ethics in a World Church: The Padua Conference* (Maryknoll, NY: Orbis Books, 2008).

32. José Roque Junges, "The Contribution of Theology to Bioethical Discussion," in *Applied Ethics in a World Church: The Padua Conference*, ed. Linda Hogan (Maryknoll, NY: Orbis Books, 2008), 183.

33. Darlene Forzard Weaver, "Embryo Adoption: Expanding the Terms of the Debate," in *Applied Ethics in a World Church: The Padua Conference*, ed. Linda Hogan (Maryknoll, NY: Orbis Books, 2008), 199.

34. Jorge José Ferrer, "Multinational Biomedical Research in Impoverished Communities: Toward a Theory of Global Justice," in *Applied Ethics in a World Church: The Padua Conference*, ed. Linda Hogan (Maryknoll, NY: Orbis Books, 2008), 189.

35. See, e.g., Hille Haker, "AIDS: An Ethical Analysis," in *Calling for Justice throughout the World: Catholic Women Theologians on the HIV/AIDS*, ed. Mary Jo Iozzio, Elsie M. Miranda,

and Mary M. Doyle Roche (New York: Continuum, 2009), 105–12; B. Andrew Lustig, "Reform and Rationing: Reflections on Health Care in Light of Catholic Social Teaching," in *Secular Bioethics in Theological Perspective. Theology and Medicine*, vol. 8, ed. Earl E. Shelp (Dordrecht: Springer, 1996).

36. Maura Anne Ryan, "Health and Human Rights," *Theological Studies* 69, no. 1 (2008): 144–63.

37. Paul Farmer, *Pathologies of Power: Health, Human Rights, and the New War on the Poor* (Berkeley: University of California Press, 2003), 239–42.

38. Ryan, "Health and Human Rights," 151–58.

39. Paul Farmer and Nicole Gastineau Campos, "Rethinking Medical Ethics: A View from Below," *Developing World Bioethics* 4, no. 1 (2004): 17; Ryan, "Health and Human Rights," 158.

40. Javier de la Torre Diaz and María Massé García del Carmen, "Bioética y derechos humanos," *Revista Pistis & Praxis* 6, no. 3 (2014): 845–67.

41. Ibid., 856.

42. Farmer and Campos, "Rethinking Medical Ethics," 17.

43. Lisa Sowle Cahill, *Theological Bioethics: Participation Justice Change* (Washington, DC: Georgetown University Press, 2005).

44. Ibid., 2.

45. Ibid., 60–61.

46. Ibid., 120–21.

47. Marcio Fabri dos Anjos, "Bioethics in a Liberationist Key," in *A Matter of Principles? Ferment in Bioethics*, ed. Edwin R. DuBose, Ronald P. Hamel, and Laurence J. O'Connell (Valley Forge, PA: Trinity Press International, 1994), 136.

48. Alexandre A. Martins, "Healthy Justice: A Liberation Approach to Justice in Health Care," *Health Care Ethics USA*, Summer 2014.

49. Marie J. Giblin, "The Prophetic Role of Feminist Bioethics," *Horizons* 24, no. 1 (1997): 37–39.

50. Shawnee Daniels-Sykes, "Code Black: A Black Catholic Liberation Bioethics," *Journal of the Black Catholic Theological Symposium* 3 (2009): 29–61.

51. Dos Anjos, "Bioethics," 131.

52. Farmer, *Pathologies of Power*, 175.

53. Dos Anjos, "Bioethics," 139.

54. Ibid., 136.

55. Ibid., 139; see also Giblin, "Prophetic Role," 45–46.

56. Giblin, "Prophetic Role," 41.

57. Ibid., 41–42.

58. Martins, "Healthy Justice," 2.

59. Ibid., 1.

60. Ibid.

61. Dos Anjos, "Bioethics," 136.

62. Anne Carr, "The New Vision of Feminist Theology—Method," in *Freeing Theology: The Essentials of Theology in Feminist Perspective*, ed. Catherine Mowry Lacugna (San Francisco: HarperOne, 1993), 5–30.

63. One recurring question is how this project differs from, builds on, and develops the groundwork laid by Cahill's *Theological Bioethics*. For us, Cahill's participatory methodology opens the door for theologians to demonstrate the social dynamic within the traditional issues addressed by Catholic bioethics. Theological bioethics can be enhanced by demonstrating the social issues and injustices that permeate the walls of health care institutions. Thus, when reflecting on the patients cared for in these facilities, the realities of racism, gun violence, immigration, and gender are living problems that the social tradition comments on, it takes us beyond the traditional scope of issues addressed by Cahill. Moreover, these social injustices correlate to bioethical concerns related to maternal-fetal outcomes, violence and public health, migrant access to health care, and limited service providers for gender-questioning patients. Although *theological bioethics* creates the opportunity to reflect on bioethics as social ethics, social injustices that confront health care systems come into better focus only when an alternative starting point is taken. We detail what Catholic bioethics looks like from this alternative starting point in our recent book, *Catholic Bioethics and Social Justice: The Praxis of US Health Care in a Globalized World* (Collegeville, MN: Liturgical Press, 2018).

# Aesthetics and Ethics: Women Religious as Aesthetic and Moral Educators

*Susan A. Ross*

This essay examines the particular contributions of three communities of women religious for the ways in which they incorporated concerns for the moral formation of their students together with a focus on beauty. These communities not only provided a basic "Catholic moral education" but also aimed to develop persons who saw their responsibility as building a better world that was not only good but also beautiful. Given recent attention to the relationship between ethics and aesthetics, this essay shows how the work of women religious makes a significant contribution to this field.

IN THE SPRING OF 1991, MUNDELEIN COLLEGE, THE LAST Catholic women's college in Illinois, closed, becoming a part of its next-door neighbor, Loyola University Chicago. When I joined the Loyola faculty in 1985, there was an eight-foot-high chain-link fence separating the two campuses; the fence was removed when the campuses merged. The following fall, the faculty of Loyola's Women's Studies Program welcomed the Mundelein College faculty who were engaged in feminist scholarship. As usual, we met in a conference room in a ten-story building that could best be described as utilitarian, with its concrete block structure, windows that did not open, and a single elevator.

As the Mundelein faculty introduced themselves, one of them was near tears as she talked about the stark contrast between the "gracious spaces" of Mundelein and those of Loyola. I remember feeling an immediate sense of recognition, because I had attended an all-girls' Catholic high school and an all-women's Catholic college, and I wondered whether I had lost my sense of the importance of beautiful spaces.

In this essay, I attempt to bring together several issues in aesthetics and ethics to use them as a lens for interpreting the educational work of Roman Catholic women religious, particularly in the years preceding Vatican II. I have

Susan A. Ross is professor of theology in the Department of Theology, Loyola University Chicago, 1032 West Sheridan Road, Chicago, IL 60660; sross@luc.edu.

*Journal of the Society of Christian Ethics*, 38, 2 (2018): 131–148

a couple of purposes in mind. One is to take a closer look at the work of a group that is often marginalized both historically and ethically. Women religious have been instrumental in Catholic education in the United States for at least two hundred years; their contributions have recently been the subject of much research, but little attention has been given to their work as playing a role in moral education, apart from the caricatures that can readily be found in popular culture.

Second, I offer a thick(er) description of the much-discussed and -contested relationship between aesthetics and ethics, incorporating embodiment, politics, feminism, and education. How does the educational work of women religious offer a way of giving these ideas practical traction while, in the process, showing how marginalized women's experiences can help to illustrate the larger discussion of aesthetics and ethics? My starting point is that ethics involves a stance oriented toward action in the world and that the stance and action always involve the corporeal, in the broadest sense, including the felt response to this stance and action. Aldo Leopold, quoted in Diane Yeager's very helpful article on ecology and ethics, puts it this way: "We can be ethical only in relation to something we can feel, understand, love, or otherwise have faith in."[1] Further, the kinds of artifacts, events, or activities usually classified as "aesthetic" are, in this essay, broadened to encompass not just "works of art" but also, in line with recent works on aesthetic theory, embodiment and the senses.[2] How human beings are educated to embody these stances and actions is my central consideration.

The relationship between aesthetics and ethics is a complicated one, and much ink has been spilled on its many permutations. From Hans Urs von Balthasar's focus on the scandalous splendor of the divine and our receptive openness to this revelation to philosophical reflections on how our bodies are mediators of meaning and value, there is something important about how it is that human beings are moved to become better persons, to make the world a better place, that is tied to the affective, the sensory, and the beautiful, as well as the ugly. This is not to say that ethics by definition is always *primarily* engaged with the aesthetic. Clearly, the need for obediential, virtue, or deontological approaches cannot be ignored. Given the recalcitrance of human nature—its tendency to be lazy, to avoid the hard choices, to simply not do anything in the face of a call for action—it is impossible to say that the motivation for doing what ought to be done is always and primarily tied to the aesthetic. Indeed, sometimes we need to ignore our feelings or our aesthetic response to a situation in order to undertake some kind of moral action. But it is important to note that the aesthetic, in the broadest sense, is never entirely absent.

Nevertheless, I want to argue here that we should pay more attention to the role of the aesthetic in moral formation. I am certainly not alone in making this statement.[3] How it is that human beings are encouraged and educated to the good needs to be attentive to the place of the aesthetic, the bodily, and the senses. I want to draw out some implications for the ways in which such an approach to moral formation might contribute to ongoing conversations about contemporary ethical issues.

Why explore women's religious communities? Although one recent survey noted that "the involvement of Catholic sisters in education has received scanty attention so far" and that "the literature on the contribution of women religious to education is only a fraction of the literature that exists on lay women teachers," scholarship on nuns' involvement in education has begun to grow, especially in recent years.[4] It has been commonplace in popular culture to caricature the involvement of women religious in education as threatening wielders of rulers on disobedient children's bodies;[5] but their contributions are in fact substantial—they matched and often exceeded the quality of public education.[6] My goal here is not so much to present a history—although their history does play a significant role—but rather to take some examples of their aesthetic and educational work as contributing to the developing discussion of ethics and aesthetics.

## Women's Religious Communities, Education, and Aesthetics

In turning to women religious ("nuns") as a "case study" for the relationship between aesthetics and ethics, I was initially inspired by my own experiences of Catholic girls' and women's education in the years before, during, and immediately after Vatican II.[7] As a student of the sacraments and the liturgy, I have often reflected on the surroundings, rituals, and practices that were central to my own education. Although many of these practices have long since been discontinued, especially since Vatican II, they nevertheless represented an approach to education that recognized the importance of the arts, embodiment, ritual, and space. My thesis is that these practices reflect an ethical concern that the aesthetic was essential for moral formation.

My research has drawn on the archives of the Sisters of Charity of the Blessed Virgin Mary (BVM Sisters) at Mundelein College, the Sinsinawa Dominican sisters at Dominican University (formerly Rosary College), historical records of women's religious communities including the Religious of the Sacred Heart and the Sisters of the Holy Child and their theories of education, and recent scholarship on women's religious communities and their practices. What these materials reveal are a number of commonalities across these communities in their attitudes toward the education of girls and women, particularly regarding the significance of the arts in their curricula but also with what I call here "embodied practices." The appropriateness of aesthetic education for girls and women is mentioned frequently, along with a concern that female education also include the traditional liberal arts and sciences. Gendered ideas of what was appropriate for women's education were not at all uncommon, often reflecting the idea that women were more suited to aesthetics than men. In addition, the importance of aesthetic education across classes and races was a frequent topic, especially as these communities considered their mission and whom they were educating.

In what follows, I discuss three themes. The first theme is the emphasis on the significance of the arts as particularly important for girls' and women's education but also as representing a distinctly "Catholic" approach to the arts. Although I have not researched the role of the arts in secular women's education as thoroughly, my guess is that there are similar emphases on the importance of the arts for girls and women in those contexts. What distinguishes this point for Catholic girls' education is its sacramental character and how it communicates deeply theological ideas about how divine beauty is revealed in music, literature, and art, as well as the moral significance of beauty. The approach of nuns in understanding beauty in the arts and in nature is not only aesthetic education but also education in virtue.

The second theme is the importance placed on what I call the "embodied context" of education. This includes both the physical surroundings of women's educational institutions as a means of "elevating" the students and attention to the "whole person" as affected by the arts and nature. The communities who built schools and colleges planned their institutions very deliberately in terms of architectural styles and physical surroundings. The assumption was that in order to learn well, one needed to be, as much as possible, surrounded by beauty.

The third theme has to do with agency—both of the women religious and their students. The worlds that these women inhabited were often set apart from secular society, especially in the nineteenth and the early part of the twentieth centuries. In addition, some of the religious orders were semicloistered, limiting their contact with the outside world.[8] But the space that students and their teachers inhabited gave them a significant measure of independence, albeit a circumscribed one. Their practices and traditions were how they defined their place in and contributions to the world. Despite their marginalization, these nuns and their students saw themselves as full contributors to church and society.

On the basis of these themes, I argue that the role played by the arts and an aesthetic focus in the broadest sense in women's religious communities and institutions was a means of developing their students not just in beautiful things or the ability to appreciate art but also in virtue and character. Ultimately, their work puts into practice the larger point that ethics needs to be attentive to the body: to feelings, affections, and desires as well as to the larger context in which they live and work. Later in this essay, I draw on recent work in philosophical aesthetics that stresses the role of beauty, embodiment, and the senses in ethics and that aligns with the ideas that were at work in these schools and colleges.

## Women's "Natural" Affinity for the Aesthetic

One of the main themes to emerge in my research is the "natural" connection of the arts with girls and women. The importance of the arts for female education was often mentioned as something particularly appropriate for girls and women. Teaching the arts in Catholic girls' schools is described by one historian as "central to the life of the school."[9] Statements like "all pupils were required to study art . . . as part of the daily schedule," were also common.[10] It was a given that any Catholic girls' school would strongly emphasize music, art, and literature. In her book *The Education of Catholic Girls*, Religious of the Sacred Heart educator Janet Erskine Stuart wrote:

> Rational principles of aesthetics belong very intimately to the life of women. Their ideas of beauty, their taste in art, influence very powerfully their own lives and those of others, and may transfigure many things which are otherwise liable to fall into the commonplace and vulgar. . . . The importance of all these in their effect on the happiness and goodness of a whole people is a plea for not leaving out the principles of aesthetics, as well as the practice of some form of art from the education of girls.[11]

Stuart's emphasis on "the happiness and goodness of a whole people" no doubt suggests that the education of girls would also eventually have a much larger effect on their families. But art was not simply instrumental; it was intrinsically significant. In addition, the idea of art as having the capacity to "transfigure" the commonplace is a frequent theme. And though one cannot deny what to our ears may in places sound elitist or classist, especially when referring to "vulgar" ideas, the point is that education in the arts allows the person to see the revelatory potential in what would otherwise be unremarkable. This is a training in vision, along the lines of what Iris Murdoch and Elaine Scarry have written regarding the effects of encountering a work of art.[12]

The educational work of Cornelia Connelly, the founder of the Sisters of the Holy Child Jesus, similarly emphasized that education in the arts was not to be seen simply as assisting young women in the "matrimonial stakes" or as "ephemeral or marginal" but rather as substantial.[13] This education was closely related to the religious dimension of their education. One scholar notes of Connelly's approach to the arts: "The fine arts, central to her philosophy of education, were the means by which she, as a Christian educator, sought 'to make visible the invisible' things of God. For Cornelia, art was 'a universal language.'"[14] For both Stuart and Connelly, there was an emphasis on what would be called today a "sacramental vision" that trained their students to see the transcendent in the ordinary. But the significance of the arts was to offfer not only a different way of seeing but also a different way of experiencing and learning about the world. Stuart writes about the lessons in discipline that the study of the arts can teach young girls:

> We have to brace our children's wills to face restraint, to know that they cannot cast themselves at random and adrift in the pursuit of art, that their ideals must be more severe than those of others, and that they have less excuse than others if they allow these ideals to be debased. They ought to learn to be proud of this restraint, not to believe themselves thwarted or feel themselves galled by it, but to understand that it stands for a higher freedom by the side of which ease and unrestraint are more like servitude than liberty; it stands for the power to refuse the evil and choose the good; it stands for intellectual and moral freedom of choice, holding in check the impulse and inclination that are prompted from within and invited from without to escape from control.[15]

Stuart is arguing that in the disciplined training in the arts, students learn self-control but also how they are to live. This was communicated by their teachers, who needed to be able to communicate "a whole-hearted love for real truth and beauty."[16] Both Stuart and Connelly saw training in the arts as training in life and in virtue.

Stuart also had a deep love of nature, which she expressed in poetry and letters. Her biographer writes, "When asked once about a programme of life, she answered, 'You are all God's property, and your life must be one wild bird song of praise, one wildflower's face looking up to [God]. Do not try to be a garden flower. I think He likes the wildflowers best, and I know that I do!'" And in a comment that summarizes her understanding of beauty: "We love beauty of scenery, of form, of art, of gifts of mind and talent, . . . because God is there. We love Earth because it is a parable to show forth Heaven, but we do not hold to the parable when we can have the truth unveiled."[17]

This emphasis on the importance of the arts, especially for women, was also found in higher education. In the United States, an astounding 190 two- and four-year Catholic colleges for women were established between 1919 and 1968.[18] Though many of them have closed, and most of the remaining institutions have become coeducational and/or secular, during this period they played a very important role for women's religious communities as well as for the young Catholic women they educated. Many of them were founded precisely because of fears of what "secular" education would do to Catholic women. As one scholar notes, "Americans were deeply ambivalent concerning the role of women in society, and the women's college was a social institution tailored to that ambivalence."[19] Catholic women's colleges, it was thought, would help to preserve the values of the church and protect women from the dangers of an increasingly secular American society.

These women's colleges sought to give women a first-class education while neither neglecting the arts nor violating their religious community's commitment to poverty. Countering ideas that educating women would ultimately be harmful, women's colleges included the arts and sciences, philosophy and theology, and the arts. Monika Hellwig observed, in relation to women's colleges, that "the religious practice of frugality does not exclude leisure or culture. It encourages the cultivation of appreciation, production, and enjoyment of the true, the good, and the beautiful. . . . God is to be found in the good, the true, and the beautiful."[20] These words echo the points that Stuart and Connelly made. This "natural affinity" between women and the arts was an expression of what was expected for women; yet it was also more than this. Education in the arts was also a means of training girls and women in virtue, in a sacramental vision of the world.

As I see it, the nuns' emphasis on the arts was a kind of strategic response to the double marginalization of women and the aesthetic in education—that is, the idea that women were best suited to the (fine and delicate) arts rather than the more difficult and "intellectual" fields of philosophy or the hard sciences that were more appropriate in men's education. In other words, both women and art were considered to be marginal. On one hand, the arts were emphasized because there was a "natural affinity" for them on the part of women. This was not challenged by women religious. The arts dealt with feeling, with delicacy, with beauty—all things that were seen as outside the male purview; indeed, the very idea that women possessed this delicacy helped to construct masculinity.[21] But on the other hand, the inclusion of the arts as they were understood by women religious was not to make women more marriageable but rather to educate them in truth, goodness, and beauty as virtues.

Women religious were also marginalized in society and the church. So the marginalization of art in education as well as the marginalization of women, including women religious, was taken for granted—yet at the same time was turned around for a higher purpose. There was an acceptance of this marginalization; yet it was seized on as a way of developing women's moral qualities. This "double marginalization" involves the surface assumption that women's education is nearly always inferior to men's and that the deliberate inclusion of the arts in women's education is meant to give women something "appropriate" to do. But this is not how the arts were understood by women religious or their students. They had a much more serious purpose but without disturbing the gender-based ideology that kept the arts in a feminine sphere.

## Beauty in Context

The women religious who built these colleges were very attentive to the aesthetics of their campuses and buildings. The three Catholic women's colleges in Philadelphia—Immaculata, Rosemont, and Chestnut Hill—all sought to be "a place apart" from the society outside their doors.[22] The location and architecture of the University of San Diego by the Religious of the Sacred Heart was a central concern, as was the establishment of the College of Saint Catherine in Saint Paul. Colleen Carpenter has written about the conflict between the founder of the college, a woman religious, and her argument with the local bishop on the placement and the architectural style of the college's chapel.[23] Rather than following the bishop's desire for a small, unobtrusive chapel, Mother Antonia McHugh built a large chapel, modeled on one in France, on the highest point of the campus, and also one of the highest points of the city. In her study of religious orders and the colleges they founded, Mary J. Oates notes that "whenever possible, [the sisters] instructed architects to incorporate female elements in the design of school buildings."[24] At Rosemont College, stained glass windows deliberately portrayed women saints, and the iconography of the Saint Catherine chapel was similarly dominated by female figures.[25]

One of the most revealing examples of this concern for the aesthetics of the college was demonstrated by the attention that BVM Sister Justitia Coffey paid to the construction of the "Skyscraper," the all-in-one building that served as the home of Mundelein College in Chicago. Mundelein College was established in 1929 at the behest of George Cardinal Mundelein, and it was intended to be a place where working-class Catholic women could receive a first-class college education. It was readily accessible by public transportation, and for the first decade or so, all the students commuted from their homes in the city.

Mundelein College was something of an exception to the tendency of a number of these colleges for women to be attractive, particularly to wealthier Catholics; this was certainly true of the institutions founded by the Religious of the Sacred Heart and the Visitation sisters. There were already two other Catholic women's colleges in Illinois—Rosary College, run by the Sinsinawa Dominican Sisters; and Barat College, run by the Religious of the Sacred Heart—but they were both located in wealthy suburbs and had both residential and commuter students. Mundelein, however, was an all-commuter school for the first decade of its existence, although it should be noted that Rosary, like Mundelein, educated many women who were the first in their immigrant families to go to college. The education offered by Mundelein and Rosary was intended to offer opportunities to the daughters of immigrants to become teachers or workers in other occupations.[26]

Construction on the Skyscraper began three days after the October 1929 stock market crash, but Sister Coffey was more concerned about her college than the stock market. A number of reports credit her with maintaining continuous employment (sometimes for twenty-four hours a day) for the men who worked on the building's construction during the early period of the Depression. The building—a fourteen-story, all-inclusive building, with classrooms, laboratories, gymnasium, swimming pool, art studios, music practice rooms, reception rooms, cafeteria, a chapel, and living quarters for the nuns—was completed just short of a year later, in September 1930.

Despite Cardinal Mundelein's plan for the building to be in a French Provincial style, Sister Coffey instead chose Art Deco, which she thought better reflected the times, and made sure that the building itself was designed and built with only the finest materials: "The main halls of the college were lined with imported Botticino marble, the bathroom areas with marble from Missouri. The wainscoting in the formal reception rooms was inlaid with ebony. The Art Deco elevator doors had etched metal inserts. The swimming pool, itself a luxury, had marble shower rooms."[27]

Such luxurious materials might suggest a lack of concern for the proper use of material reality and a violation of the spirit of poverty espoused by religious orders. But what is more significant for my purposes here was Sister Coffey's goal for her students. As one chronicler of her work put it, "The intent was to boost students' self-esteem; . . . to her, the beauty of the building was an educational opportunity and every element meant to elevate."[28] In other words, the students who attended Mundelein were for the most part not raised with such luxury; Coffey's intent was to ensure that her students were as worthy of such beauty as anyone and that they would be inspired by this beauty. She arranged for students to attend performances of the opera, ballet, and symphony, and brought in experts to lecture the students ahead of time. Regular on-campus music performances were scheduled, art exhibitions were hung, and alongside the focus on a well-rounded education, including the sciences, the arts were always in the forefront.[29]

In addition to making sure that students were exposed to the arts in their education and that their environments were intended to be beautiful and "elevating," women religious also included many traditions and ceremonies that involved music, dance, and drama. Again, this was not uncommon in women's schools and colleges in the United States, but the traditions in the Catholic schools always had a religious connection. In elementary and secondary girls' schools, there were required uniforms, which were in part intended to erase visible economic distinctions among the students.

There are many more examples of the focus on the incorporation of the arts, their surroundings, and embodied practices; but these suffice for the present as examples of ways in which women religious paid specific attention to the aesthetic and embodied dimensions of education. On the surface, these practices may seem unremarkable, but I want to argue that there is more here than meets the eye. The larger contexts of society and the Catholic Church essentially marginalized women and were also often suspicious of efforts to educate women. But the smaller arenas in which women religious exercised autonomy provided a context within which they could influence their students, take their bodies and their responses to the arts seriously, and understand that their development as mature Catholic women was not only in ideas, important as they were, but also in their lived corporeal contexts. These would ultimately affect the families from which their students came and the ones they would eventually form.

## Women's Aesthetic Agency

In the world of Catholic girls' and women's education, particularly in the years before Vatican II, women were the authorities. Women's schools and colleges—and also Catholic hospitals run by women's religious congregations, but that is another story—were, for the most part, established by women and staffed by women. In these institutions, students experienced their women teachers as the authorities in their fields and also as models of women's leadership. The kind of aesthetic agency that I want to highlight briefly here had to do with what later feminist theologians would call "ritual" agency.[30] I describe it here in the somewhat broader language of aesthetic agency because it is difficult to separate the aesthetics from the rituals.

Students in both the schools and colleges participated in a number of aesthetic/ritual practices that included processions, personal altars, rituals involving the Virgin Mary, and other ceremonies that marked important academic achievements and saints' feasts. These practices were related to but still distinct from the formal sacraments. In some cases, these ceremonies involved choosing a student to represent the student body or to portray a saint, or even the Virgin Mary, in a dramatic presentation. Feast days honoring Mary and the other saints and holy women, often the religious order's foundress, were celebrated, often with pageants. As I have already noted, today, most of these practices have largely disappeared from schools, and especially colleges; my point is to note that these were practices developed, planned, and executed by the students and their teachers. This ritual/aesthetic agency is worth noting; before explicitly feminist ritual practices that countered androcentric liturgy came into being in the 1970s and beyond, girls and women were already doing feminist liturgy, although it was not named as such. The kinds of practices that later feminist ritual theorists would write about—involving the circle, honoring the ordinary, women's crafts, community, and memory—were all part of the aesthetic and ritual practices of the girls' and women's schools and colleges, guided by women religious.[31] As Don Saliers notes in a classic essay on liturgy and ethics, "Beliefs about God and world and self which characterize a religious life are dramatized and appropriated in the mode of the affections and dispositions focused in liturgical occasions."[32]

The incorporation of the arts into educational curricula, the aesthetic dimensions of educational and social practices, and the ability to take on leadership roles in these activities were not primarily intended to make women "more refined" but rather sensitive and thoughtful moral agents. I think it is fair to say that most of those involved in serious efforts at women's education in non-Catholic contexts would have agreed on this point. All serious educators of girls and women were determined that their students receive first-class educations. But the aesthetic dimension of education held a special place in Catholic girls' and women's education as a way of seeing the divine in the earthly, as developing a distinctly Catholic sacramental vision and agency for a world in which women were largely excluded from power. The arts were both significant in and of themselves but also as lenses for understanding the world.

## Aesthetics and Ethics

I now turn to recent literature on aesthetic theory, which I argue helps both to underscore and to make sense of these practices as having not just historical or aesthetic but also ethical significance. In a book that has been influential on my own thinking, *The Meaning of the Body: Aesthetics of Human Understanding*, the philosopher Mark Johnson makes the case that all human knowing and valuing is rooted in the body. Drawing on a wide array of scholarship, including psychology and neuroscience as well as philosophy and aesthetics, Johnson makes a strong case that the very structures of human knowledge cannot be adequately understood apart from their rootedness in the complexity of physiological functions. Johnson challenges the idea that human beings and animals experience meaning in completely different ways, with animals learning through the body and humans as learning through the mind. He points out that the human sociocultural environment is on a continuum with other species, although language marks a crucial difference.[33] For human beings, language allows the representation of reality in conceptual terms, but his more significant point is that these same conceptual terms are based not purely "in the mind" but rather are rooted fully in embodied experience. The "classical representation" of the mind/body split is a false one because our brains are inextricably entwined with our bodies.[34] To underscore his point, Johnson develops a number of schemas (container, source-path-goal, etc.) that illustrate how ideas that we assume are "mental" are in fact fully grounded in embodied experience. To use his words, "According to this view [that is, the view that Johnson is espousing] we do not have two kinds of logic, one for spatial-bodily concepts and a wholly different one for abstract concepts. There is no disembodied logic at all. Instead, we recruit body-based, image-schematic logic to perform abstract reasoning."[35] Within the human sociocultural environment, the capacity to develop language and abstract reason develops, but it is never separate from the body.

Johnson develops this idea to make the point that it is not just that human intellectual concepts are rooted in the body. It is, even more, that these concepts are by their very nature metaphorical, that they operate on a fundamentally aesthetic level. Thus, Johnson writes, "Aesthetics must become the basis of any profound understanding of meaning and thought. Aesthetics is properly an investigation of everything that goes into human meaning-making, and its traditional focus on the arts stems primarily from the fact that arts are exemplary causes of consummated meaning."[36]

Johnson's point is that aesthetics is not a sphere ancillary to human thinking; rather, it is the very foundation of human thinking, acting, and meaning. Contrary to what he refers to as the "pervasive cultural misunderstanding of, and consequent prejudice against, aesthetics . . . as a minor, nonpractical, wholly subjective dimension of human life," he argues that any form of human meaning-making must take seriously the embodied, and therefore aesthetic, dimensions of human existence.[37] His is thus a fundamentally epistemological argument; but it also has profound ethical implications. That is to say, how we know and what we value are rooted in our bodily experiences and responses to the material realities we encounter. In his earlier book *Moral Imagination*, Johnson emphasizes the importance of developing a moral capacity that is able to imaginatively inhabit other people's experiences.[38]

In a similar way, the political theorist Jane Bennett argues for "an aesthetic disposition" rooted in embodiment for ethics. In her book *The Enchantment of Modern Life: Attachments, Crossings, and Ethics*, she writes that "ethics requires both a moral code (which condenses moral ideals and metaphysical assumptions into principles and rules) and an embodied sensibility (which organizes affects into a style and generates the impetus to enact the code)."[39]

Her point, similar to Johnson's, is that without engaging bodily affect, ethics remains a set of rules without an impetus to act. Without the body, ethics is only a disembodied idea. She argues for cultivating a sense of *enchantment*, both as a counter to the idea that the contemporary world is utterly disenchanted and as a necessary factor in developing ethical ways of living. Enchantment, Bennett argues, "can aid in the project of cultivating a sense of presumptive generosity . . . of rendering oneself more open to the surprise of other selves and bodies."[40] Bennett's attention to enchantment has a number of similarities to a Catholic sacramental sense, although she does not develop them. I just note that it is interesting how theological ideas of the aesthetic are largely absent from philosophical discussions of ethics and aesthetics. My point is not to hijack Bennett's use of enchantment as a sacramental theology in disguise but rather to indicate how startlingly similar her ideas are to the educational practices of women religious.[41]

As I have tried to show thus far in this essay, the importance of bodily and aesthetic engagement was central to the educational work of women religious. It is interesting to note how Janet Stuart connected the embodied spirituality of Catholic education for children, especially children of the "lower classes," with the concreteness of Catholic sacramentality and piety. She mentions the "friendly protection" of Mary, the angels, and saints, all mediated through iconography, in contrast to Protestant piety, which, she argued, "broke up . . . ceremonial observance in which [these relationships] found expression."[42] She also notes how the Church's rituals allow an outward expression of inward faith in a chapter on "manners," which, though sometimes sounding more than a bit dated, nevertheless shows how the outward sign of the inward is essential to moral action. "Manners," for these women, were not so much affectations of the wealthy as they were "a school . . . in which we may learn how human intercourse, may be carried on with the most perfect external expressiveness."[43]

A second related point to the work of women religious is the marginalization of the aesthetic and of the feminine. Philosophers of aesthetics and ethics have long noted the marginalization of the aesthetic. Hans Urs von Balthasar, the theologian who has been credited with the contemporary revival of theological aesthetics, argued that rationalist categories had so colonized theology that the aesthetic had been relegated to the inessential and trivial; his life's work was to restore the centrality of the aesthetic to the theological, to argue that the human relationship to the divine was not fundamentally a rational one but one based in feeling.[44] Although I find many problems with Balthasar's theology, not least with his gendered ideology, the point that he makes about the aesthetic is nevertheless significant. For Balthasar, the Enlightenment and modern rationality were responsible for the relegation of truth to the merely factual, the good to duty, and beauty to the ornamental.

Along the same lines, Johnson argues that Kant's conception of the aesthetic has played a negative role in marginalizing it in both conceptual meaning and in ethics. He charges that Kant relied on "Enlightenment faculty psychology, where feeling is contrasted with thought,"[45] ultimately resulting in the idea that "nothing connected with the aesthetic can have any role in meanings, conceptualization, and reasoning."[46] Bennett, however, while acknowledging Kant's efforts to exclude feeling or any kind of somatic experience in moral sentiments, nevertheless sees in Kant a kind of "dark acknowledgment" of the "affective dimension of ethics," because one's imagination is inevitably involved when considering the good.[47]

Women religious, as I noted above, saw the arts as central to their educational work and as a means of developing virtue and character, despite their own marginalization in church and society and the marginalization of the arts to female education. The potential of the arts and of embodied practices rooted in a sense of their significance for human development were taken very seriously.

A third point to note very briefly in philosophical discussions of aesthetics and ethics is that of the embodied agent. Here, Johnson's emphasis on the embodied dimension of human meaning-making underscores the work done by women religious and their recognition of the role of embodiment, and the sensible and perceptible context in which education took place.

The material that I have presented so far provides a new way of thinking about the relationship between art and moral formation in pre–Vatican II women's religious communities: how education in the arts developed the whole person, how women's marginalized role in society and the similarly marginalized place of art nevertheless worked to empower women religious and their students, and how context was significant and helped shape the person. These more recent treatments of aesthetics and ethics find resonance in the work of women religious.

## Conclusion

After Vatican II, women's religious communities experienced drastic declines in their numbers. Education for the daughters of the middle and upper classes no longer seemed relevant when the needs in poor communities were much more pressing. Single-sex education came to be seen as limiting girls and women from having greater opportunities offered by men's or coeducational institutions. Women joined the workforce and pursued new career options in ways never envisioned by the founders of these communities. The traditions and practices of girls' and women's education were discarded as the Catholic Church and women embraced the twentieth century. So the question remains whether their aesthetic and moral educational work has any lasting significance.

In this last section, I draw very briefly and suggestively on some of the ideas of the French thinker Jacques Rancière, who explicitly connects politics and aesthetics, to argue that there is lasting significance. Rancière argues that politics and, I would add, ethics, is not just a question of its content and ideas but of *how* it is presented—that is, the form that politics and political organizations take. If the aesthetic is understood as the sensible and perceptible, not only specifically "works of art" but also the ways in which ideas are presented, then the aesthetic *is* a mode of presentation. The philosopher Robin James, in an article on Rancière, asserts that in his thinking "the aesthetic is the *primary* medium in which privilege and oppression are maintained."[48] Rancière argues that it is not simply the *content* of what is said in social and political contexts that is important; it is *how* what is said that matters.[49] And it is also through the aesthetic that privilege and oppression are countered. James points out that "reorganizing events, though rare, can take place primarily through the aesthetic, so if we want to change society, if we want a more just society, we have to use and engage the aesthetic."[50]

From this perspective, one could say that women religious both represented the maintenance of privilege, particularly in their role as educators of women through the arts, yet also resisted the oppression of women. They did this by both cooperating with an aesthetic/political system that marginalized and idealized women while also using this system as a way to further their educational goals within it. This system was also one that privileged whiteness and wealth, whether implicitly or explicitly. As James observes, "Rancière's point is that advantage and disadvantage are distributed primarily via the sensible/aesthetic."[51] There is no question that Catholic women's educational institutions were places of white privilege.

However, I suggest that the very aesthetic practices that women religious and their students were engaged in during the pre–Vatican II years worked to empower many of them to take on new roles in a post–Vatican II world. Their understanding of the aesthetic was broadened in an awareness of its social context and power. The same attention to embodiment, context, and agency was now marshaled to support education and social justice in new ways. Women religious looked for new opportunities to educate children, particularly those in marginalized areas.[52] Many of them came to understand their own privileged context critically and engaged in acts of ritual and moral agency in public ways.

This is not to say that racism and white privilege were not issues for women religious. The fact of black women's exclusion from religious orders is a deep wound on the history of religious communities in the United States.[53] The story of Sister Thea Bowman, whose own work for justice drew heavily on music, is a powerful example of the link between aesthetics and ethics in the struggle for racial justice.[54] Although I have just begun to explore this literature, my sense is that such a focus on the aesthetic would be as much emphasized if not more so, given the triple marginalization of African American women religious.

Although women religious are no longer occupying the enclosed spaces of the pre–Vatican II Church, they did not, for the most part, abandon their commitment to the sensible and aesthetic. I suggest that there is a "counter-aesthetic," in the broader sense of this term used by Rancière, that progressive women religious have developed and maintained as their ethos. The marginalized spaces that women have always occupied continue to be the places where service of and to the body are lived out, not only in education but also in ecclesial ministries and in social justice work. At the same time, they are actively resisting the aesthetic of power and privilege that has characterized the all-male hierarchy.

The women religious and the girls and women they educated have taken on multiple leadership roles in the post–Vatican II Church, much to the dismay of many conservatives. Women dominate ministries to the body (education especially of children, nursing, service to the poor, refugees) and, although marginalized officially, nevertheless use this "weaker" position to live out their moral commitments. Not unlike their place in the pre–Vatican II Church, women today take on what is seen as lesser: ministry to the sick, to the marginalized.

In interpreting the educational work of women religious as both aesthetic and ethical, I have tried to show that attention to the arts, to context, and to agency all played a role in moral education. Although much of the educational work of women religious has changed greatly over the last fifty years, this commitment to embodiment, context, and agency has remained. Rather than dismissing their earlier work as a sad and limited example of women's oppression, it is possible to see them as making a significant contribution to an embodied and aesthetic ethics. Moreover, their contributions raise larger questions about the relationship between aesthetics and ethics. The work of women religious shows how attention to the whole person—intellect, emotions, and bodily sensations—needs to be at the center of ethics. Too often, the theological anthropology that undergirds ethics fails to account for the multidimensionality of people, whose social, historical, and familial contexts have powerful influences on responses to issues that require a moral response. Although an aesthetic approach is not a sufficient element of moral education, it is nevertheless a necessary part of this process.

## Notes

1. D. M. Yeager, "'Suspended in Wonderment': Beauty, Religious Affections, and Ecological Ethics," *Journal of the Society of Christian Ethics* 35, no. 1 (2015): 122. The literature in theological aesthetics is too vast to enumerate here. Some helpful resources that relate aesthetics to ethics would include Alexander Garcia-Rivera, *The Community of the Beautiful: A Theological Aesthetics* (Collegeville, MN: Michael Glazier, 1999); Maureen O'Connell, *If These Walls Could Talk: Community Muralism and the Beauty of Justice* (Collegeville, MN: Liturgical Press, 2012); Laurie Cassidy and Maureen O'Connell, eds., *She Who Imagines: Feminist Theological Aesthetics* (Collegeville, MN: Michael Glazier, 2012); and Roberto Goizueta, *Christ Our Companion: Toward a Theological Aesthetics of Liberation* (Maryknoll, NY: Orbis Books, 2009).

2. Here, I draw on the French philosopher Jacques Rancière's understanding of the aesthetic as involving the senses and perception. See Jacques Rancière, *The Politics of Aesthetics*, ed. and trans. Gabriel Rockhill (London: Bloomsbury, 2004).

3. See, e.g., Martha Nussbaum, *Upheavals of Thought: The Intelligence of Emotions* (Cambridge: Cambridge University Press, 2001); Jane Bennett, *The Enchantment of Modern Life: Attachments, Crossings, and Ethics* (Princeton, NJ: Princeton University Press, 2001); and Mark Johnson, *The Meaning of the Body: Aesthetics of Human Understanding* (Chicago: University of Chicago Press, 2007).

4. Bart Hellingkx, Marc Depaepe, and Frank Simon, "The Educational Work of Catholic Women Religious in the 19th and 20th Centuries: A Historiographical Survey," *Revue d'histoire ecclésiastique* 104, no. 2 (2009): 529–48, at 531–32.

5. See, e.g., the documentary *A Question of Habit*, www.youtube.com/watch?v=atOD8S-rcLA.

6. See Hellingkx, Depaepe, and Simon, "Educational Work," esp. 538ff.

7. I use the terms "nuns," "women religious," and "sisters" more or less interchangeably, although there are technically canonical differences in these names.

8. Unlike "cloistered" nuns, who for the most part do not leave their communities, "semi-cloistered" women religious are able to leave their convents for education, medical needs, etc., but their primary apostolic work is within their community. This is distinct from "active-contemplative" women's communities, whose work is outside the convent.

9. Lorna Bowman, "Women's Religious Education," *Religious Education* 1, no. 93 (1993): 36.

10. Ibid.

11. Janet Stuart, RSCJ, *The Education of Catholic Girls* (London: Longmans, Green, 1922), 71–72.

12. See, e.g., Iris Murdoch, *The Sovereignty of Good* (London: Routledge, 1970); and Elaine Scarry, *On Beauty and Being Just* (Princeton, NJ: Princeton University Press, 1999).

13. Bowman, "Women's Religious Education," 36.

14. Ibid.

15. Stuart, *Education*, 194.

16. Ibid., 195.

17. Maud Monahan, *Life and Letters of Janet Erskine Stuart, Superior General of the Society of the Sacred Heart, 1857–1914* (London: Longmans, Green, 1922), 206.

18. *Catholic Women's Colleges in America*, ed. Tracy Schier and Cynthia Russett (Baltimore: Johns Hopkins University Press, 2002), 65. Half of all colleges for women in the United States were founded by women's religious congregations.

19. Ibid., 63.

20. Ibid., 19.

21. See Robin James, "Oppression, Privilege, & Aesthetics: The Use of the Aesthetic in Theories of Race, Gender, and Sexuality and the Role of Race, Gender, and Sexuality in Philosophical Aesthetics," *Philosophy Compass* 8, no. 2 (2013): 111, referencing Carolyn Korsmeyer, *Gender and Aesthetics: An Introduction* (New York: Routledge, 2004).

22. James, "Oppression," 126.

23. Colleen M. Carpenter, "Knowing the Ground beneath Our Feet: A Spirituality of Place-making," paper presented at Catholic Theological Society Annual Convention, San Diego, June 2014, 7–9. I am grateful to Professor Carpenter for sharing her paper with me.

24. Mary J. Oates, "Sisterhoods and Catholic Higher Education, 1890–1960," in Schier and Russett, *Catholic Women's Colleges*, 164.

25. Ibid.

26. For an account of Cardinal Mundelein's efforts to found a Catholic women's college, see Edward R. Kantowicz, *Corporation Sole: Cardinal Mundelein and Chicago Catholicism* (Notre Dame, IN: University of Notre Dame Press, 1983), 88–95.

27. Margery Frisbie, "Mundelein College," *New World*, October 14, 1994, 24.

28. Ibid. Frisbie recounts Coffey's insistence that the grand pianos for the Music Department (bought on credit and never fully paid for) be carried up seven flights of stairs by movers without their shoes on so the marble would not be scratched. Frisbie, *New World*, October 21, 1994, 44.

29. One of the first doctoral degrees in chemistry awarded to a woman was that of a BVM sister.

30. See, e.g., Lesley Northup, *Ritualizing Women: Patterns of Spirituality* (Cleveland: Pilgrim Press, 1997).

31. Ibid., chap. 2, "Emerging Patterns in Women's Ritualizing," 28–51.

32. Don Saliers, "Liturgy and Ethics: Some New Beginnings," *Journal of Religious Ethics* 7, no. 2 (Fall 1979): 173–89, at 175.

33. Johnson, *Meaning of the Body*, 147.

34. See especially the section "Embodied Concepts," 157–70, although the entire chapter ("The Brain's Role in Meaning") is pertinent.

35. Johnson, *Meaning of the Body*, 181.

36. Ibid., xi.

37. Ibid.

38. Mark Johnson, *Moral Imagination: Implications of Cognitive Science for Ethics* (Chicago: University of Chicago Press, 1993), 198–99.

39. Bennett, *Enchantment*, 131.

40. Ibid.

41. It is worth noting that Martha Nussbaum focuses on a "sense of wonder" in her *Upheavals of Thought*, esp. chap. 4, "Emotions and Infancy," 174–237.

42. Stuart, *Education*, 201.

43. Ibid., 213. For Stuart, "manners" were much more than knowing what fork to use or how to introduce oneself. She writes: "In any class of life, in school or home, wherever a child is growing up without control and 'handling,' without the discipline of religion and manners, without the yoke of obligations enforcing respect and consideration for others, there a *rough* is being brought up, not so loud-voiced or uncouth as the street rough, but as much out of tune with goodness and honour, with as little to hold by and appeal to, as troublesome and dangerous either at home or in society, as uncertain and unreliable in a party or a ministry, and in any association that makes demand upon self-control in the name of duty" (200).

44. See the first part of his trilogy: Hans Urs von Balthasar, *The Glory of the Lord I*, 7 vols., trans. Joseph Fessio and John Riches (San Francisco: Ignatius Press, 1983–91). See also Christopher Steck, *The Ethical Thought of Hans Urs von Balthasar* (New York: Crossroad, 2001).

45. Johnson, *Moral Imagination*, 217.

46. Ibid., 218. One might also note the critique of thinkers such as M. Shawn Copeland of the enduring role of the Enlightenment in racism; see M. Shawn Copeland, *Enfleshing Freedom: Body, Race, and Being* (Minneapolis: Fortress Press, 2009).

47. Bennett, *Enchantment*, 136. Bennett notes that "the kind of qualitative distinction Kant makes between ideas and feelings constrains him from pursuing the issue [of archetypes and their influence] further and pushes him to distinctions in kind when differences in degree would be more credible" (137).

48. James, "Oppression," 101–16.

49. Ibid., 105.

50. Ibid., 104.

51. Ibid.

52. See, e.g., Suellen Hoy, "No Color Line at Loretto Academy: Catholic Sisters and African Americans on Chicago's East Side," *Journal of Women's History* 14, no. 1 (Spring 2002): 8–33.

53. See Shannen Dee Williams, *Subversive Habits: Black Nuns and the Long Struggle to Desegregate Catholic America*, 2013, https://rucore.libraries.rutgers.edu/rutgers-lib/40733/.

54. Kim Harris, "Sister Thea Bowman: Liturgical Justice through Black Sacred Song," *US Catholic Historian* 35, no. 1 (Winter 2017): 99–124.

# Constructive Agents Under Duress: Alternatives to the Structural, Political, and Agential Inadequacies of Past Theologies of Nonviolent Peacebuilding Efforts

## *Janna L. Hunter-Bowman*

This essay explores the viability of theologies of nonviolent peacebuilding through reflection on constructive agents under duress. John Howard Yoder's messianic theology was once a default model of peacebuilding in Christian ethics, but he mixes eschatologies, with problematic results. This essay extends insights from participant observation in Colombia to suggest that if we relate distinct accounts of messianic and gradual eschatologies without mixing them, we articulate a relationship between church and state that is fruitful for theological peacebuilding. This relationship is best described as an interplay that allows for transformative displacement.

THIS ESSAY GROWS OUT OF MY FRUSTRATION AS A HUMAN rights and peacebuilding field worker in war-torn Colombia, South America: frustration that the rights-based frameworks of peacebuilding were unable to detect the transformative agency and generative activity of war victims on the ground there.[1] I argue that when the dominant option remains focused on the individual autonomy of the rights-constituted subject, we need another approach for thinking about the moral agency of peacebuilding amid constraints on autonomy. When persons enact change amid high levels of constraint, injustice, and direct violence endemic to situations of armed conflict, they participate in what might be called constructive agency under duress.

This agency under duress, which is crucial to peacebuilding that decenters state institutions and lifts up grassroots participation, has escaped the notice of those adhering to the dominant framework for evaluating armed conflict. So I turned to theology for alternative notions of power, authority, and agency that open new vistas for thinking about participation and change. I have found that messianic theology is the best theoretical framework we have for illuminating how beleaguered Colombian communities live in a world at war and

Janna L. Hunter-Bowman is assistant professor of Christian social ethics and peace studies at Anabaptist Mennonite Biblical Seminary, 3003 Benham Ave, Elkhart, IN 46517; jhunterbowman@ambs.edu.

*Journal of the Society of Christian Ethics*, 38, 2 (2018): 149–168

experience the Ultimate in ways that enable and mandate their agency under duress. The communities that interest me are marginalized and vulnerable as well as transformative and generative. Their embodied proclamation of God's action in history is simultaneously liturgical and political. Reflection on their witness has made it evident that a partnered gradual eschatology is also necessary to account for their engagement with state institutions and their cooperation with moral others that transforms unjust structures and reconstitutes public space.

Methodologically, the theological peacebuilding that interests me is partially embedded in and partially a reflection on Christian communities' action for social transformation, including the action of doing normative theory. I deploy theology in three ways: as social fact that shapes communities' actions, as normative theory for thinking about peacebuilding, and as academic reflection in need of critique from the standpoint of the agents under duress. To this last point, the featured nonviolent Christian communities that should vindicate the Mennonite theologian John Howard Yoder's peace theology not only help to point out the limitations of his theology but also gesture toward a more robust and practical framework of participatory theological peacebuilding.

This essay begins with vignettes from my sixteen years of engaged fieldwork that exhibit constructive agency under duress. I extend the insights of the Colombian case to suggest that the interplay of (1) a messianic apocalyptic ("now time") and a (2) gradual eschatology ("gradual time") constitutes a framework for nonviolent peacebuilding that centers such communities. The messianic moment, in which God proleptically comes to agents under duress, sends the witnesses toward a horizon constituted by the culmination of God's purposes, the experience of time I call a gradual eschatology. Also, in the context of a gradual eschatology, emergent sociohistorical processes are unpredictable; they do not follow the sequential steps of linear time. I go on to show that Yoder mixes the two, with problematic results. In the last section, I distinguish the two in a way that allows us to think about church and state as enabling transformative displacement that centers the agents under duress without delegitimizing institutional political systems. Transformative displacement is enactment of radical change in present experience that simultaneously opens possibilities for historical processes of social and political change.

## Vignettes of Colombian Communities: Manifestations of Messianic and Gradual Eschatologies

Four vignettes of Colombian communities manifest messianic and gradual eschatologies. These scenes are from different points in time.

## Scene 1, August 5, 2009: Northwest Colombia, in the Department of Córdoba

Dozens of unarmed women and men suddenly leave their fields, vegetable stands, and workshops to protect Isaac, a civilian wanted by the paramilitary armed group. The state army is within easy walking distance of the impending assassination but does not respond to the urgent calls for help. In contrast, church members quickly gather in supplication at the slat-walled church, where Isaac has sought refuge. Isaac is in their midst, held by the community that is interceding and, by their account, intervening with God on his behalf. They remain and protect him throughout the night, then smuggle him out in predawn shadows, out from under the watchful eye of the paramilitary.

Amid extreme political tensions in an embattled area abandoned by the state, the members of the community neutralized and counteracted violence through their corporate practice of theological agency. Through their participation, they transformed a space of terror that was enclosing the nearly dead in a firm grip into one of relative peace. Why did they risk their lives for Isaac in this way? "We had nowhere and no one else to turn to but God," the pastor responded to my question. "We participate with the Spirit," other participants chimed in. Such partnering with ultimate power allows them some sense of being able to protect and extend their life. It gives them a sense of agency in a situation of terror and chaos.

Providing protection is an exercise of constructive agency under duress: The communities redressed an instance of injustice in a situation of exigency, meeting the goal of rights even though rights were not in place. The liberal peace assumes that human rights are necessary to save life and limb, yet the communities' constructive interventions realize the goal when rights regimes are unsuccessful. Rights regimes fail to understand crucial engagement by agents under duress, because they assume that the goal of rights can only be reached if a minimum threshold of autonomy is met.[2] Moreover, because those enmeshed in situations of injustice do not enjoy conditions necessary for free agency, rights frameworks seem to assume that they are not agents at all. Because agency under duress is outside the scope of rights-based evaluation, which is shaped by negative prohibitions that protect the conditions of free agency, rights-based theories neither pretend nor aspire to capture them. Nevertheless, failure to attend to these forms of agency forfeits opportunities for transformative peacebuilding, so we need to find other ways of attending to constructive agents under duress and theorizing about them.

My notion of "constructive" agency is linked to how I understand the term "duress" and its place in Catholic moral theology, where it refers to constraints on autonomy that might lead someone to cooperate with evil acts from which he or she would have extricated himself or herself if it were not for forced choices.[3] It is an analogical extension, however, in that I am not talking about how people have been forced into entanglements with evil but rather about what people have been able to accomplish under duress. Amid conflict and adversity, communities operating independently of institutional political systems redressed instances of injustice by relying on divine action. This kind of agency is a manifestation of the messianic. Generally speaking, the apocalyptic or messianic are types of eschatologies in which the Ultimate—as telos—is understood to have interruptive qualities. Messianic eschatologies thematize unpredictable disruptions that disconnect the present from the threatening past and disclose the hopeful horizon of expectation as future. The apostle Paul characteristically uses the expression *ho nun Kairos*, "now time." In Giorgio Agamben's translation of 2 Corinthians 6.2, "Behold, now is the time to gather, behold the day of salvation." In now time, communities under duress enact conditions of peace, as the absence of direct violence. Such disruptive experiences of the Ultimate not only effect change in immediate reality; the communities also share Gustavo Gutiérrez's insistence that there is much to come *in* messianic breaks.[4] The next three scenes illustrate how these breaks spur *relational shifts* in the community, uncover the *malleability of oppressive structures*, and produce a particular *political body* that contributes to plural processes and spaces.

## Scene 2, 2004–5

Now practiced in crisis intervention, small groups interceding on behalf of hostages break the brittle air between themselves and heavily armed paramilitary soldiers by making small talk. One twenty-something-year-old soldier says he is tired of war. Another shows a worn photograph of his daughter. The civilians learn about fragments of the stories and complex lives of these feared men and women. "Sometimes we touch humanity," one woman remarked. Sometimes the soldiers touch their humanity. Almost imperceptibly, relationships shift. In a few cases, soldiers abandoned the paramilitary ranks and sought relationship with the communities. In these experiences, perception shifts and identities flex—if only slightly.

## Scene 3, 2007

As we rattle along in his pickup truck, past expansive paramilitary-protected cattle ranches on our way to a resettlement community for internally displaced persons, the community leader Pedro Acosta comments, "We're now asking why [mass internal displacement] continues to happen. Why do the rivers still run red?" Terror aims for a hallucinogenic effect, the anthropologist Michael Taussig observes, one that turns persons in on themselves and into increasingly small identity groups. Yet by turning together toward others in need, the community members countered the tendency to withdraw and expanded the scope of their questions and their engagement. In spite of threats and reprisals, they helped found the interinstitutional, pluralistic Working Group for the Defense of Land and Territory in Córdoba.[5] By cooperating with other groups with converging goals, they acquired new ways of thinking about problems and new tools for redressing them. Reflecting on collaborative efforts with government entities, the community leader Juana Ruiz commented, "We listen carefully in meetings and then discuss among ourselves. These are lessons in navigating the world of the state and institutions."

Such scenarios suggest that redressing those structural issues that produce and sustain direct violence—and that cause suffering and death, even when a shot is not fired—requires engaging moral others. Forming coalitions with other violence-affected groups and concerned counterparts in order to address structural problems is an exercise in agency under duress in which proximity to an ongoing crisis provides valuable knowledge of the problem, which in turn shapes strategies.

### Scene 4, 2016

Pictures of the Colombian president posing with religious leaders from around the country—including from Córdoba—flit across my computer screen.[6] A moment later, his social media feed highlights a community that actualizes the kind of change he is searching for on a national level. Representatives of the state drew on the moral power and authority of the communities' achievements to leverage support in the international community for a peace process with the Revolutionary Armed Forces of Colombia (Fuerzas Armadas Revolucionarias de Colombia), the oldest guerrilla group in Latin America. Colombia will be "reborn" from "the ground up" by "building on what is already built," the administration promised.[7] To paraphrase: If these remote communities in subaltern spaces can enact transitions from violence to peace amid war, then surely we can do so on a national level. But these communities did not just serve the process; this recognition and acknowledgment—enabled by messianic eschatology—nurtured the social processes and dignity of these heretofore multiply-excluded persons.

The latter three scenes are distinct from the first one in what they reveal about eschatology: Messianic interventions enable shifts in relationships and generate processes in gradual eschatological time. The emphasis on redressing a crisis here and now, in messianic time, shifts to the unacceptable relationships and circumstances that produce a crisis in the delay of the Ultimate culmination of God's purposes. The telos now creates a distant vanishing point, a horizon of purpose that guides the pilgrims on a long journey. To engage systems and structures in need of change, the newly constituted extrajudicial political body intersects with other moral communities in civil society and institutional political systems (scenes 3 and 4). In messianic time, proximate communities accomplish what the state cannot; in gradual time, the state can do what churches cannot do.

Taken together, the eschatological point of all four of these scenes is that the communities did not live indefinitely in staccato messianic moments peppering history; these groups are not self-sufficient bodies standing against all others, participating exclusively in implosions of (negative) peace amid monolithic systems that overwhelm history. The messianic-cum-experiential élan is such that groups derive their identities and transformative processes with reference to it. Messianic interventions may generate something novel and transformative for the communities themselves, their neighbors, and the nation. Agents born against hegemonic power structures may discover that threatening systems and structures are malleable; they may not only find common cause with moral others and the state but also directly benefit from coalition formation and a more responsive state. Such shifts make it necessary to pair messianic time with a gradual eschatology, the time afforded by messianic breaks with linear progression and stage-dependent ways of thinking, that extends to the Parousia. Gradual time intersects with linear time through its institutions and programs, but it must not be mistaken for what it confronts and transforms. Gradual eschatology is the context for engaging structures as systems to transform; it is a time when the possibilities of the newly formed community are oriented by a vision of a shared future.

## The Blending of Messianic Eschatology and Gradual Eschatology in the Work of John Howard Yoder

John Howard Yoder's messianic theology, once a default model of nonviolent peacebuilding in Christian ethics, does not properly distinguish between these two eschatologies, nor does it provide a fine-grained account of a gradual eschatology. As a result, Yoder did not articulate how the two relate within his theological framework. Rather, under the heading of a messianic political ethic, he mixed the two eschatologies in ways that enabled some forms of violence while obscuring others.

To identify the conceptually confusing mixing more precisely, I sketch a form of messianic eschatology and a form of gradual eschatology found in Yoder's work: Eschatology 1, a two-aeon (messianic) eschatology, and Eschatology 2, an eschatology of social processes (gradual eschatology).

In Yoder's messianic vision, taken from Pauline sources, God is sovereign and Jesus Christ is God's divine representative, who became the Messiah by challenging the hegemony of the "Powers" (plural)—the political, religious, and intellectual structures of human life.[8] In Yoder's work, what the Lordship of Christ means for history shifts, with the result that the two eschatologies emerge.[9]

## Eschatology 1

In texts including *The Politics of Jesus*, "Peace without Eschatology," and *The Christian Witness to the State*, Yoder describes Christ's relation to the Powers as creating communities of renewed living ("the church") that, in their diametric "otherness," provide countercultural witness to peace, over and against "the rebellious world."[10] This church/world distinction manifests an eschatology of two eons: "These aeons are not distinct periods of time, for they exist simultaneously. They differ in nature or in direction; one points backward to human history outside of (before) Christ; the other points forward to the fullness of the kingdom of God, of which it is a foretaste. Each aeon has a social manifestation: the former is the 'world,' the latter is the church or the body of Christ."[11] In the two eons, "a split in the cosmos" creates collective identities and oppositional relationships,[12] which are manifest in "two social systems"—"the old order" and "the order to come";[13] "the former is the world and the latter is the church."[14] The messianic relationship between penultimate and final things is on display. In this context, the state—"the fundamental phenomenon that society is organized by the appeal to force as ultimate authority"—is the functional equivalent of the world.[15] The choice for humans is between "responsibility" as "nationalism and pragmatism," on one hand, and "obedience" to Jesus as "cross and resurrection," on the other hand.[16] At the point of emphasis, it becomes a decision: Do we choose the politics of the state as channeled evil or the politics of Jesus as "suffering love?"[17]

For the Colombian communities, this framework is of limited usefulness because they do not live in the staccato of the messianic. For example, collective identities are at odds with flexible identities (scene 2), and juxtaposing the politics of the church and the politics of the state renders the experience of the state building up the church as logically incoherent, in the context of ad hoc collaboration (scene 4). As adduced above, Yoder posits dualisms in the two-aeon eschatology.[18] I presuppose what feminist insight makes clear: Dualisms thinly mask asymmetries of power and subtle forms of violence that may coexist with an absence of war or direct ("bloody") violence.[19] Furthermore, the messianic option ultimately "does not promise to 'work,'" in the sense of transforming history or systems,[20] but rather *"accepts the structures"* of society on the assumption that "they are about to crumble away" anyhow.[21] This assertion is problematic, given what God subsequently enabled and required of the communities (scenes 3 and 4). In this framework, the penultimate (state) cannot impinge on ultimate reality (the church), which accepts oppressive structures.

## Eschatology 2

The meaning that Christ's relation to the Powers has for politics and history in Yoder's later work better illuminates the experience of the communities that interest me. It is solidified in *For the Nations*, in which Yoder teaches that Jesus Christ's action upends the Powers of domination and makes marginal communities that "performatively proclaim" Ultimate (ontic) power-in-vulnerability to be a conduit of generative political energy in history.[22] In this context, "What Jesus came to do was light a fire on earth, to initiate an authentically historical process of reconciliation and community formation."[23] In place of an emphasis on Christian ethics for Christians,[24] here he stresses that "God's purposes are for the whole world, that they are knowable, [and] that they are surely about to be fulfilled."[25] The practices of the church represent an invitation because the distinctive patterns offer a way for those outside the church to understand their lives and social processes.[26] In this context, what makes the Christian community distinct is not its "otherness" but its knowledge of humankind's common destiny.[27] Yoder emphasizes that "Christ's final victory" is not yet,[28] and "the world to come is the real world. The question becomes how we get from here to there."[29] The church becomes "the new world on its way," and so signals that history is heading in a particular direction.[30] In place of churches against the world or against the "enemy nation," churches are rather in civil society "for the nations," sometimes cooperating with existing institutions,[31] always as "pulpit and paradigm."[32] Now there is a reason for our obedience:[33] Social science verifies that churches' alternative patterns of behavior are matters of historical causation."[34] In this context, what God makes possible is more clearly about transformation catalyzed by "underdogs" alongside other moral communities with whom they find common cause.[35]

Yoder's eschatology of social processes better illuminates the experience of the Colombian communities by providing a language to talk about agents under duress who enable changed patterns of relationship—at various levels—and contribute to government-oriented change processes and the nation without being consumed by them. For example, it illuminates communities' cooperation with the state to prepare the fractured region for peace-deal implementation (scene 4). But it confusingly mixes a messianic eschatology—in which churches could not expect the state to play a positive role and which operates within oppressive structures—with a gradual eschatology, which entails engaging structures of oppression. In the latter, oppressive structures are, Yoder (quoting Paulo Freire) asserts, "limiting systems [victimized communities] can transform."[36] The experience of the Colombian communities signals three areas of problematic ambiguity that result.

### *Three Areas of Ambiguity*

First, Yoder's account is ambiguous with regard to the possibility of transforming structures. The coexistence of transformative social processes and constructive use of the concept of "revolutionary subordination" in *For the Nations* is an example of this ambiguity.[37] Throughout his extensive corpus, Yoder makes "revolutionary subordination" the internal order of the messianic community and a precondition for enacting an alternative to the order of domination.[38] In this political system, "a subordinate person becomes a free ethical agent in the act of voluntarily acceding to subordination in the power of Christ" and accordingly maximizes freedom available *within the limits*.[39] This is a just and precise description of the conditions under which agents under duress emerge (scene 1). Yet their witness lends support to feminist and womanist theologians who draw attention to various problems with the concept, including the way a call to accept the power structure "as it exists" sits in tension with Yoder's emphasis on egalitarian dialogical discernment and contradicts his later "rejection of God language that supports power gradients instead of undoing them as the gospel."[40] Agents under duress (scenes 1 and 3) provide evidence for the need to distinguish what Yoder mixes in his evocation of revolutionary subordination in *For the Nations*: It is possible to affirm that there is no foreclosure of power, such that one can be addressed as a moral agent in a situation of subordination, and one can—at the same time—*reject* oppressive structures with the hope of transforming them. The verbs "accept," "challenge," and "transform"—used to discuss revolutionary subordination in relation to structures—have different meanings, so what precisely Yoder affirms in this normative delineation is ambiguous. Yoder is mixing eschatologies, which are his social theories, and therefore is bequeathing us conceptually sloppy categories for thinking about agency and structural change.

A second limitation of Yoder's work arises with the relationship between messianic time and institutional political systems. As illustrated in the opening scene, where the army betrays and the community saves, the messianic eschatology is manifest in disconnection from the institutions on which people enmeshed in a desperate historical situation would otherwise rely for protection. Yoder calls this a new pattern of relationship.[41] For Yoder, the idea of seeking safety from the state or state intervention in the messianic regime is (theo)logically incoherent, so recourse to the state is not a viable option for members of the messianic community. In Eschatology 2, Yoder helpfully distinguishes between "state" and "nation," but he makes the crucial distinction in the service of articulating the unidirectional movement of the church's contributions to the world.[42] From the communities' standpoint, it becomes difficult to even talk about the more responsive state's positive contributions to church members (scene 4).

Yoder's inattention to psychological and relational dynamics experienced by the individual unit is the third and final point. Yoder makes "transformation of enmity to neighborliness" a messianic movement,[43] but the collective identities that pit "us" against "them" are inadequate to describe the psychological dynamics and nearly imperceptible relational shifts that occurred in the encounters between individual civilian community members and paramilitary soldiers (scene 2). As Alex Sider observes, Yoder acknowledges but does not study in detail the personal and interpersonal dimensions of the social practices that he emphasizes and, furthermore, "evacuate[s] of psychological content."[44]

The way moral power proceeds in history, in Eschatology 1, is of a piece with these problems. Yoder emphasizes "servanthood *in place* of domination" (emphasis added)[45] as an "*alternative* to how kings of the earth rule" (emphasis added),[46] and the church's order of service as a replacement for the order of domination.[47] The two-aeon messianic theology is structured by cross–crown relationships: The power of the cross, not the crown, determines the meaning of history.[48] The relation between ultimate power and penultimate realities is structured by the Pauline *katargein*, meaning "to render inoperative."[49] In Yoder's interpretation, Christ's rule cannot mean to "destroy" the Powers (the penultimate) but rather proceeds to confront, overturn, "dispossess," and thus *replace* forms of repressive power with alternative power.[50] This logic pinpoints how Christ's relation to the Powers exists as a social and political possibility in Yoder's messianic regime: as replacement and dispossession. According to this dualistic logic, Yoder posits the move from enmity to neighborliness as mechanistic: The external structures that generate the threat remain intact, and the church replaces the state.

In sum, Yoder provides a way to talk about how communities under duress can be addressed as moral agents and contribute to state processes, but he fails to provide a fine-grained account of structural change, church–state relations in different temporal contexts, or interpersonal relationships. The lack of clarity stems from Yoder's mixing of the structure of the messianic—in which the Ultimate cannot be impinged on by the penultimate—with a gradual eschatology. A gradual eschatology recognizes moral and epistemic communities in civil society, and it recognizes the state as, in principle, able to live into its creative, God-given purpose for general welfare. Thus, gradual time logically ought to allow for what Yoder's account obscures: the state as an actor from which the church could receive and that could intervene in the church. Moreover, in messianic time, persons operate with moral freedom within oppressive structures. In gradual time, persons apprehend oppressive structures as systems to change, which entails engaging state systems as other than evil.

The existence of constructive agents under duress signals problems with Yoder's eschatologies that his predatory behavior seems to confirm. I am referring to Yoder's sexual predation and abuse of power.[51] Yoder's mixing of eschatologies functionally protected him in his abuse of women by providing an eschatological language for talking about how the church could exist in society and contribute to the nations without being accountable to an external authority (because, in messianic time, the Ultimate cannot be impinged on by the penultimate).

Consider Yoder's ambiguity about the possibility of transforming limiting systems. His long pattern of abusing others relied on women, colleagues, and church members accepting patterned asymmetries of power in the church and seminary. This structural issue is especially troubling when we recall the logical impossibility for Yoder of state intervention in the messianic body politic. Remember the structure of the political regime in which this ambiguity about structural change is enmeshed: Yoder claimed to operate in the register of the messianic throughout his career. We have said that the messianic is manifest in disconnection from the institutions that people in a desperate historical situation could otherwise rely on for protection. Institutional political systems claiming to offer salvation are revealed as ideological. Inadequate resources to account for the personal, interpersonal, and psychological dimensions further compound the problems. If Yoder's resources are inadequate to address the *external* relational dynamics (scene 2), the lack is accentuated *within* the community. The practices Yoder "evacuate[s] of psychological content" are consistent with what Sider calls "the alienating structures of Yoder's thought,"[52] such that the person who experiences the direct violence Yoder emphasizes and finds inevitable may find himself or herself psychologically alienated from those with whom his or her life is deeply intertwined.[53] If the alienated person accepts the structures as they exist and is unable to seek recourse from the state, to whom shall he or she turn? These are categories of fit—not entailment—with Yoder's behavior. The issue is one of correlation—not causation—that creates space for violence.

The crux of the problem is that Yoder describes a kind of gradual eschatology in his later work, but he does not name or fully develop it, and he does not adequately distinguish it from the messianic politics he had made normative for Christians. More clarity on the relationship between these two modes of eschatology and politics is imperative for Christian peacebuilding.

## The Distinct Yet Intimately Related Messianic and Gradual Eschatologies

A more robust account of structural change and increasingly flexible church–state and interpersonal relationships have places in an eschatological framework of nonviolent peacebuilding that parses what Yoder blends. I hold out the possibility of distinction amid inseparability. Perhaps it is useful to think about the relationship thus: The presence of the Messiah sends the pilgrim on the road.[54] Key for theological peacebuilding is this simultaneity of two times—the messianic "now" and the gradual—in relation to each other, the shift in perception that comes with delineating the doubleness of times, the multiple forms of participation and politics that the distinction draws, and the different contributions toward a just peace that they enable.[55] Both eschatologies are necessary in order to think about how witnessing to God's interruptive action in history allows for agency and how witnessing to the delay of the end entails engaging structures that are in need of change. The two eschatologies are manifest in different kinds of relationships with institutions of political systems, different epistemologies, distinct social-political-psychological dimensions, different kinds of activities and practices, and different achievements. For communities in the midst of open conflict, responses to episodes of direct violence require different forms of knowledge, different capacities, and different relationships than redressing the deep-seated destructive patterns on structural levels. For politically, socially, culturally, geographically, and economically excluded communities, knowledge of God's in-breaking presence is integral to tactical participation and key to messianic time. In contrast, Ruiz's reflection on newly acquired forms of knowledge and strategies (scene 3) indicates the multiple forms of knowledge that mark gradual time, the context in which agents under duress engage forms of structural violence as systems to transform. The ability to participate independently of dominant systems that threaten survival is key in messianic time; so too the ability to intersect with the state and foster strategic alliances, coalitions, and networks is key to transform social, political, and economic systems in gradual time. All are necessary, often simultaneously, for reducing violence and pursuing a just peace.[56] Thinking eschatologically, we might say that "now peace" of now time ought not be reduced to, but minimally entails, the absence of direct violence, what Galtung called a negative peace. The "gradual peace" of gradual time is the slow, arduous work of deep relational, institutional, and systemic transformation. The peace that we seek and pursue entails both.

We need to consider the interplay of messianic and gradual eschatologies—the ability to move back and forth between messianic tactical politics and the gradual strategic politics of engagement. The eschatological perspective provides theoretical clarity about differentiated relationships between moral communities while also underscoring different modes of pragmatic action for faithful communities. It is always both/and.

## A Distinction and a Method for Thinking about the State

How communities negotiate with the state in different contexts illustrates a distinction that can be drawn from the two eschatologies: It is possible to distinguish between (1) accepting the ideology, assumptions, and epistemology of the state and (2) accepting the state's claim to power. It is possible to reject the ideology, assumptions, and epistemology of the state while accepting the state's claim to power, but on terms different from those that the state articulates.

The eschatological distinction and the temporal interplay make sense of the need for distance when the communities experience state violence, weakness, and failure as threats to survival—physically or in terms of identity. The interplay can also comprehend the contributions of a more responsive state, including the dignifying value of acknowledgment and multidirectional learnings enfolded in ad hoc collaboration. It helps us think with particular communities negotiating both the state's pull to sameness and the forces making for difference, when political systems are apparently engaged constructively, as is the case with a multilevel peace process.[57]

The notion of the Powers described by the systematic theologian Hendrik Berkhof provides a framework in which we can move from replacement of the state to a flexible account of the state and transformative displacement, which are consistent with the distinction. The communities are not theoreticians, and thus do not articulate an account of the state, but they do model a stance toward the state: They engage independently of the state (they often "negotiate" with the state in its absence), but they do not consider themselves sufficient alternatives to the state, and they do receive from the state. A rereading of the Powers framework illuminates their stance toward the state. Like Berkhof and those he inspired, including Yoder and Walter Wink, I place the state under a Pauline rubric of "the Powers"—structures that were created good but are fallen (sinful) and nevertheless redeemable.[58] The state becomes a locus of sovereign power with a legitimate claim to power, meaning that the community reliant on ontic power sometimes works in spite of, sometimes against, and at other times in common cause with the state.

Wink makes a crucial point when he emphasizes that, in the rubric, the three natures coexist.[59] This quality means that we must speak of disparate realities that exist concurrently, and so conform to distinct church–state relationships at the same time, without losing theoretical coherence. The folly of any particular theory of the state is that it reifies one of the three eschatological realities of the state—created good, fallen ("violent"), and redeemable. Definitions of the state tend to locate church communities in relation to the state in ways that overdetermine what everyday interaction looks like. Such formulas for thinking about the state make it difficult to recognize that these realities are often present simultaneously. I incorporate the threefold reality of the state into the political eschatological peacebuilding framework in order to offer a dynamic, context-contingent method for thinking about the state that has the flexibility to account for the existence of different kinds of community–state relationships, even simultaneously. It helps us think about relationships (1) of collaboration, when the state is working to make incremental improvements (e.g., overcoming exclusion by incorporating different moral agents into a multilevel peacebuilding process—scene 4) and (2) of protest against its inadequacies, when it fails in its positive role in other ways (e.g., supporting agroindustry and mining, historically fomented by paramilitarism, that strips residents from the land—scene 3). Furthermore, the created nature of the state means it can contribute to the life of the church in gradual time, perhaps even reaching into the church community. State acknowledgment can contribute to a sense of dignity for Colombia's agents under duress, and the state can intervene in cases of sexual predation in the church. This is another way in which a fine-grained account of the two eschatologies is necessary for Christians and corrects Yoder.

As the Powers metaphor helps us to see, the institutions involved in a peace process are still less than they can be. All the same, this eschatological foundation for the state provides ground for the communities to stand on as they pursue less violent and more just conditions in national peace processes. It moves beyond the oppositional relationships of two-aeon messianic eschatology—and other frameworks that juxtapose church and state and therefore locate Christian communities in a fixed relationship with the state without resources to hope for or imagine something different. Locating the church and state in flexible relationship allows for changes in church–state relations as the context changes.[60]

The Powers metaphor also allows us to distinguish between the state and the nation. It accommodates the reconstitution of public space (e.g., "the nation") as distinguished from institutional political systems. Together, the interplay of times and the Powers metaphor allows us to theorize about a political body that emerges independent of state power but does not live indefinitely in the staccato moment of messianic "otherness." Rather, it engages without dominating or consuming others, as a minority that is not assimilated and dissolved. We can imagine how Christian communities once excluded many times over could participate in the profound pluralism that William Connolly espouses—as minorities amid other moral minorities in a world where "multiple ways of life" negotiate and cooperate.[61]

In this context, multiple epistemologies and moral communities contribute to the nation. We catch a glimpse in the land reform working group struggling to change the structures that threaten rural populations' survival (scene 3). Another glimpse is provided by the state's reliance on power produced outside the political system to leverage support for a historic peace process. The communities were precipitating and clamoring for such a peace deal for decades (scene 4). Because gradual time is not about harmony realized—only on the far end do we have hope that full communion will be achieved—moral minorities do engage in an agonistic struggle amid deep pluralism, in which democratic institutions are defended. These agents under duress help us recognize that theological peacebuilding can and must, at least, transform antagonism to agonism.[62] *How* remains a question.

## *Transformative Displacement*

To complement a nontriumphalist, context-sensitive account of the state, I offer the notion of transformative displacement—enactment of radical change in present experience that simultaneously opens possibilities for historical processes of social and political change—as a messianic-cum-eschatological discourse of transformation. Several Jewish-inflected parables of the Messiah suggest that to enact peace, it is not necessary to start the world over again, to destroy everything, or, as Yoder said, to replace one thing with another. The philosopher Giorgio Agamben reports what Ernst Bloch learned from Walter Benjamin: "It is sufficient to displace this cup or this bush or this stone just a little, and thus everything. But this small displacement is so difficult to achieve and its measure is so difficult to find that, with regard to the world, humans are incapable of it and it is necessary that the messiah come."[63]

In this formulation that I adopt, things are rendered different with the coming of the Messiah, even as some things of history remain. The label "displacement" acknowledges more readily than "replacement" that the systems in place (armies in a war and the systems that give rise to them) are—at present—not dismantled by the coming of the Messiah but are instead spatially dislodged. The experience of the penultimate is "transformed," but not yet transformed are the interlocking powers that are operative in that moment.[64] An end is accounted for, but only by implication. A change is enacted that introduces what is needed to pursue more expansive change. Transformative displacement accommodates discussion of asymmetries of power and types of violence in ways that Yoder's truncated definition of violence, defined as deadly violence, obscures.

The subtle shifts in perception, relationship, and identity that the community members and soldiers experienced through the communities' recurrent interventions—through participating in the advent of the Messiah again and again (scene 2)—illustrate the relational dynamics of transformative displacement. Here, I follow the New Testament scholar Brigitte Kahl, who maintains that messianic movement occurs when the "Other" is transformed into "Another."[65] Reimagining the *allelon* (which is usually translated as "one another") includes movement from "one-and-otherness" to "one anotherness."[66]

Where the dualism-inflected notion of replacement assumes oppositional collective identities, Kahl presupposes the malleability and elasticity of identities and relationships at various levels. That the *allelon* also seeks to ensure ongoing social movement and a dynamic flow of power within the community is an expression of this flexibility.[67] Therefore, the element that helps to illuminate the Colombian communities' experience with external structure also redresses a problem in Yoder's account of the internal structures of the community—what Sider calls the alienating structure of Yoder's thought. Furthermore, because we can distinguish between overcoming polarity and dissolving boundaries, dualisms become dualities relative to particular descriptive and normative distinctions.

The notion of transformative displacement helps us think about how triumphs in messianic time relate to confrontation with constraints in gradual time. Persons under duress extend the life of the almost-dead (scene 1), transformatively displacing inert victims with witnesses to the possibility of change amid what seemed like hegemonic powers that overwhelmed history—constructive agency under duress. The idea of transformative displacement helps us think about how transitions occur in a world of thick relationships, long memories, and entrenched structures in a way that does not involve starting over, destruction, or counterdualisms.

## Conclusions

I have argued that messianic and gradual eschatologies—now time and gradual time—are necessary to illuminate peacebuilding in the neglected context of agency in duress. Yoder mixed these two eschatologies, with problematic results. But if we offer distinct, fine-grained accounts of each eschatology without mixing them, we articulate a relationship of church and state that is fruitful for peacebuilding. This relationship is best described as an interplay that allows for transformative displacement.

The crucial importance of the interplay of messianic and gradual eschatologies and political regimes was on display in the first year of a post–peace accord Colombia (2016–17). Colombia's historically innovative and unprecedented comprehensive peace agreement officially ended more than fifty years of war.[68] But "the end" is not a promise that governments can keep. Months into a post-accord (not postconflict) Colombia, the communities that interest me again relied primarily on knowledge of God in history and each other to confront new dynamics of direct violence in a local relapse of state abandonment while simultaneously strengthening democratic institutions that could make specific peace accord commitments a lived reality. They are still agents under duress. Their existence points out the inadequacies of the agential, structural, and political inadequacies of past theologies of nonviolent peacebuilding and gesture toward new ways of understanding theological peacebuilding.

## Notes

I thank Jerry McKenny for the teaching and mentoring that shaped this essay. My thanks also to the anonymous reviewers of the *Journal of the Society of Christian Ethics* whose insightful comments helped sharpen it. All mistakes are my own.

1. I worked in Colombia with Justapaz, an institution of the Colombian Mennonite Church, through the Mennonite Central Committee from 2001 to 2004 and from 2006 to 2010.

2. For a justification of rights suggesting highly constrained possibilities or inability to engage if rights are not respected, see Michael Ignatieff, *Human Rights as Politics and Idolatry*

(Princeton, NJ: Princeton University Press, 2001), 55, 75–83. For the philosophical underpinnings, see Isaiah Berlin, *Two Concepts of Liberty: An Inaugural Lecture Delivered before the University of Oxford on 31 October 1958* (Oxford: Clarendon Press, 1958), 52–54. Atalia Omer, who directed me to the above sources, further observes that such limitations for conflict transformation do not diminish rights usefulness for other diagnostic, comparative, and legal purposes. See Atalia Omer, *When Peace Is Not Enough: How the Israeli Peace Camp Thinks about Religion, Nationalism, and Justice* (Chicago: University of Chicago Press, 2013), 89.

3. Thomas Kopfensteiner, "The Meaning and Role of Duress in the Cooperation in Wrongdoing," *Linacre Quarterly* 70, no. 2 (2003): 153; Lisa Sowle Cahill, *Theological Bioethics: Participation, Justice, Change* (Washington, DC: Georgetown University Press, 2005), 8, 78, 103, 117–20, 146, 172.

4. Gustavo Gutiérrez, *A Theology of Liberation: History, Politics, and Salvation*, trans. Caridad Inda and John Eagleson, rev. edition (Maryknoll, NY: Orbis Books, 1988), 94.

5. In Spanish, Grupo por la Defensa de la Tierra y el Territorio en Córdoba.

6. Colombia, Office of the President, "Más de 100 líderes religiosos de todo el país le dicen sí a la paz," July 4, 2016, http://es.presidencia.gov.co/noticia/160704-Mas-de-100-lideres-religiosos-de-todo-el-pais-le-dicen-si-a-la-paz.

7. Colombia, Office of the High Commissioner of Peace, "Learn about the Peace Process in Colombia," June 6, 2014, www.altocomisionadoparalapaz.gov.co/procesos-y-conversaciones/proceso-de-paz-con-las-farc-ep/Documents/Learn_about_the_peace_procces_in_Colombia_22_sept_VF.pdf.

8. John Howard Yoder, *The Politics of Jesus: Vicit Agnus Noster*, 2nd edition (Grand Rapids: Eerdmans, 1994), 138, 145.

9. For an analysis of Yoder's thought that supports the distinctions drawn here, see Paul Martens, *The Heterodox Yoder* (Eugene, OR: Cascade Books, 2012); and Paul Martens, "Universal History and a Not-Particularly Christian Particularity: Jeremiah and John Howard Yoder's Social Gospel," in *Power and Practices: Engaging the Work of John Howard Yoder*, ed. Jeremy M. Bergen and Anthony G. Siegrist (Scottdale, PA: Herald Press, 2009), 131–46.

10. Yoder, *Politics of Jesus*, 161.

11. John Howard Yoder, "Peace without Eschatology," in *The Royal Priesthood: Essays Eschatological and Ecumenical*, ed. Michael G. Cartwright (Grand Rapids: Eerdmans, 1994), 146.

12. Yoder, *Politics of Jesus*, 161.

13. Ibid., 96.

14. Yoder, "Peace without Eschatology," 146.

15. John Howard Yoder, *The Christian Witness to the State*, 2nd edition (Scottdale, PA: Herald Press, 2002), 12.

16. Yoder, "Peace without Eschatology," 149.

17. Yoder, *Christian Witness to the State*, 12–13, 18; John Howard Yoder, *Discipleship as Political Responsibility* (Scottdale, PA: Herald Press, 2003), 18, 45.

18. On this point, I depart from Gerald Schlabach, "The Christian Witness in the Earthly City," in *A Mind Patient and Untamed: Assessing John Howard Yoder's Contributions to Theology, Ethics, and Peacemaking*, ed. Ben C. Ollenburger and Gaule Gerber Koontz (Telford, PA: Cascadia, 2004), 232; and I agree with Martens, *Heterodox Yoder*, 124–25.

19. For a discussion of the limitations of apocalyptic eschatology in feminist perspective, see Catherine Keller, *Apocalypse Now and Then: A Feminist Guide to the End of the World* (Boston: Beacon Press, 1996).

20. Yoder, *Royal Priesthood*, 151; Yoder, *Christian Witness to the State*, 7.

21. Yoder, *Politics of Jesus*, 187; cf. Yoder, *Royal Priesthood*, 151.

22. John Howard Yoder, "Armaments and Eschatology," *Studies in Christian Ethics* 1, no. 1 (1998): 53.

23. John Howard Yoder, *The War of the Lamb: The Ethics of Nonviolence and Peacemaking*, ed. Glen Stassen, Mark Thiessen Nation, and Matt Hamsher (Grand Rapids: Brazos Press, 2009), 82.

24. Yoder, *Christian Witness to the State*, 28.

25. John Howard Yoder, *For the Nations: Essays Evangelical and Public* (Grand Rapids: Eerdmans, 1997), 218.

26. See John Howard Yoder, "Firstfruits: The Paradigmatic Role of God's People," in *For the Nations*, by Yoder, 29; and John Howard Yoder, "Sacrament as Social Process: Christ the Transformer of Culture," *Theology Today* 48, no. 1 (1991), 36–37.

27. E.g., contrast Yoder, *For the Nations*, 24, with Yoder, *Christian Witness to the State*, 17, 42, 72–73.

28. John Howard Yoder, "To Serve Our God and to Rule the World," in *Royal Priesthood*, by Yoder, 136.

29. Yoder, *For the Nations*, 134.

30. In contrast, the church and world move in opposite directions in Yoder, *Christian Witness to the State*, 9.

31. Yoder, *For the Nations*, 84.

32. Ibid., 37–50.

33. Yoder, *Royal Priesthood*, 203.

34. Yoder, *For the Nations*, 135, 131.

35. Yoder, *War of the Lamb*, 178.

36. Yoder, "Armaments and Eschatology," 53.

37. Yoder, *For the Nations*, 89n20, 116.

38. Yoder introduces "revolutionary subordination" in *Politics of Jesus*, 172–74, and affirms the concept throughout his career; see Yoder, *For the Nations*, 89, 166.

39. Yoder, *Politics of Jesus*, 186–87.

40. Nekeisha Alexis-Baker, "Freedom of the Cross: John Howard Yoder and Womanist Theologies in Conversation," in *Power and Practices: Engaging the Work of John Howard Yoder*, ed. Jeremy M. Bergen and Anthony G. Siegrist (Scottdale, PA: Herald Press, 2009). Yoder indicates that he agrees with the feminist perspective of Elisabeth Schüssler Fiorenza; yet *if* things "as they are" actually can be altered, *how* they could be altered is a matter that remains unreconciled with the eschatological context in which the concept is developed. See Elisabeth Schüssler Fiorenza, *Bread Not Stone: The Challenge of Feminist Biblical Interpretation* (Boston: Beacon Press, 1984), 83; Yoder, *Politics of Jesus*, 192. Contra the earlier feminist Yoder interpreters, Karen Guth understands revolutionary subordination to be about appropriate methods for challenging structures in need of change. I find her argument unpersuasive because she reads revolutionary subordination out of context (Eschatology 1) and through the lens of a second, distinct political regime (Eschatology 2). Karen Guth, *Christian Ethics at the Boundaries* (Minneapolis: Fortress Press, 2015), 125.

41. John Howard Yoder, "Thinking Theologically from a Free-Church Perspective," in *Doing Theology in Today's World*, ed. John D. Woodbridge and Thomas Edward McComiskey (Grand Rapids: Zondervan, 1991), 259.

42. John Howard Yoder, *The Original Revolution: Essays on Christian Pacifism* (Scottdale, PA: Herald Press, 1972), 29–30.

43. Yoder, *For the Nations*, 234.

44. J. Alexander Sider, "Friendship, Alienation, Love: Stanley Hauerwas and John Howard Yoder," *Mennonite Quarterly Review* 84, no. 3 (2010).

45. Yoder, *Politics of Jesus*, 123.

46. Ibid., 39.

47. John Howard Yoder, *Preface to Theology: Christology and Theological Method* (Grand Rapids: Brazos Press, 2002), 126.

48. John Howard Yoder, *Karl Barth and the Problem of War, and Other Essays on Barth* (Eugene, OR: Wipf & Stock, 2003), 158–67.

49. Giorgio Agamben, *The Time That Remains: A Commentary on the Letter to the Romans* (Stanford, CA: Stanford University Press, 2005), 121.

50. Yoder, *Politics of Jesus*, 144; See also Hendrik Berkhof, *Christ and the Powers* (Scottdale, PA: Herald Press, 1977), 40, 42.

51. See Rachel Waltner Goossen, "'Defanging the Beast': Mennonite Responses to John Howard Yoder's Sexual Abuse," *Mennonite Quarterly Review* 89 (January 2015): 7–80.

52. Sider, "Friendship, Alienation, Love," 423.

53. Ibid., 417.

54. I am following Giorgio Agamben, *The Church and the Kingdom*, trans. Leland de la Durantaye (London: Seagull Books, 2012), 1–40; and Gutiérrez, *Theology of Liberation*, 93–94.

55. Eleanor Kaufman, "The Saturday of Messianic Time (Agamben and Badiou on the Apostle Paul)," *South Atlantic Quarterly* 107, no. 1 (Winter 2008): 38.

56. For my account of the relationship between Anabaptist peace theology and conflict transformation articulated by John Paul Lederach—including a discussion of terms addressed in this essay, e.g., justpeace—see Heather DuBois and Janna Hunter-Bowman, "The Intersection of Christian Theology and Peacebuilding," in *The Oxford Handbook on Religion, Conflict, and Peacebuilding*, ed. R. Scott Appleby, Atalia Omer, and David Little (New York: Oxford University Press, 2015), 569–96.

57. Charles Taylor, "Modernity and Difference," in *Without Guarantees: In Honour of Stuart Hall*, ed. Paul Gilroy, Lawrence Grossberg, and Angela McRobbie (London: Verso, 2000), 366–67.

58. Walter Wink, *Engaging the Powers: Discernment and Resistance in a World of Domination* (Minneapolis: Fortress Press, 1992), 67.

59. See Berkhof, *Christ and the Powers*, 22–41. Yoder follows Berkhof in *Politics of Jesus*, 138–43.

60. For a discussion of notions of the state that position religious agents, see Slavica Jakelic, "Secular-Religious Encounters as Peacebuilding," in *The Oxford Handbook of Religion, Conflict, and Peacebuilding*, ed. Atalia Omer, R. Scott Appleby, and David Little (Oxford: Oxford University Press, 2015), 124–45.

61. William Connolly, "Europe: A Minor Tradition," in *Powers of the Secular Modern: Talal Asad and His Interlocutors*, ed. Charles Hirschkind and David Scott (Stanford, CA: Stanford University Press, 2006), 80.

62. Chantal Mouffe writes that, in an agonistic struggle, "the others are not seen as enemies to be destroyed, but as adversaries whose ideas might be fought . . . but whose right to defend those ideas is not to be questioned." Chantal Mouffe, *Agonistics: Thinking the World Politically* (London: Verso Books, 2013), 7. Also see Chantal Mouffe, "Religion, Liberal

Democracy, and Citizenship," in *Political Theologies: Public Religions in a Post-Secular World*, ed. Hent de Vries and Lawrence E. Sullivan (New York: Fordham University Press, 2006), 318–26.

63. Giorgio Agamben, *The Coming Community*, trans. Michael Hardt (Minneapolis: University of Minnesota Press, 1993), 53.

64. Agamben, *Church and the Kingdom*, 19.

65. Brigitte Kahl, *Galatians Re-Imagined: Reading with the Eyes of the Vanquished*, reprint edition (Minneapolis: Fortress Press, 2014), 269.

66. Ibid., 24–25.

67. Ibid., 17.

68. John Paul Lederach, "Colombia's Peace Agreement," *New York Times*, November 25, 2016.

# Liberal Domination, Individual Rights, and the Theological Option for the Poor in History

*David M. Lantigua*

The theory and practice of liberalism has historically justified the dispossession of non-European peoples through the ideological deployment of individual rights—private property being the most prominent. Rather than discarding rights language altogether owing to its colonialist background, the theological option for the poor in the postconciliar Church of Latin America establishes a criterion of authenticity that contributes to its prophetic renewal. The methodological turn toward the poor evident in the liberation theology of Ignacio Ellacuría can wrest rights from its crippling association with political, economic, and cultural forms of liberal domination as seen in the Americas. Latin American theologians provide historical and constructive resources for demythologizing the sacred right to private property in liberalism's neo-colonial present and historical past, as typified by John Locke. Specifically, the theme of *integral liberation* outlines the material, social, and transcendent dimensions of justice for the dispossessed as an ecclesial alternative to liberal individualism.

> The church does not receive its prophetic inspiration from adherence
> to a liberal program, but from its roots in a world of poverty.
> —Gustavo Gutiérrez, *The Power of the Poor in History*

WESTERN LIBERALISM IS IN CRISIS. PUBLIC INTELLECTUALS are signaling the retreat of this dominant political and economic ideology that victoriously outlived its twentieth-century competitors of fascism and communism in the West. North Atlantic societies felt the brunt of the economic recession in the previous decade, whereas China and India experienced tremendous economic growth. Americans, in particular, are increasingly aware of a shrinking middle class. Authoritarian regimes are on the rise as democracies wane. Populism and nativism appear to be taking a stronger moral hold over the pluralism that previously defined liberal societies, especially those marked by

David M. Lantigua, PhD, is assistant professor of moral theology / Christian ethics at the University of Notre Dame, 130 Malloy Hall, Notre Dame, IN 46556; lantigua.1@nd.edu.

*Journal of the Society of Christian Ethics*, 38, 2 (2018): 169–186

immigration from the Global South and a demographic implosion self-induced by reproductive technology.

Even if we are on the cusp of a postliberal era in the West, that is no reason for elation in the field of moral theology and Christian ethics. We may well see a loss of a liberal faith in fundamental human rights, so that to future generations it might look like one more utopia in the Western political dreamscape. Surely, some antiliberal Christian ethicists would gladly welcome this demise. Yet I would strongly caution against such blanket dismissals of human rights. As important as critics of liberal conceptions of justice have been in the field of Christian ethics, my argument shares Nicholas Wolterstorff's view that inherent rights provide an indispensable language for naming and recognizing wrongs committed against individuals and peoples. The issue of rights remains an essential component of modern Christian moral vocabulary, though its ongoing importance demands a recalibrated meaning corrective of the ideology of liberal individualism.

This essay looks to an unlikely source for vindicating fundamental rights—theologians from Latin America who have been among the most forceful critics of Western liberalism during the past half century. The theological insights of the postconciliar Church in Latin America provide critical and prophetic resources for wresting rights from liberalism's colonial past and its neocolonial present. The option for the poor has both *historical value* in the task of demythologizing the sacred individual right to private property and *constructive value* for promoting the integral liberation of dispossessed peoples. The historical turn to the poor and oppressed in Latin American theology reconstitutes the authentic subject and agent of human rights according to the preferential option.

## Theology, Poverty, and Human Rights in Latin America

Since its emergence in the 1960s, liberation theology, and Latin American theology more broadly, have been critical of the Western idea of individual human rights. Gustavo Gutiérrez's foundational *Teología de la liberación* makes little mention of rights, but that does not imply Latin American theologians initially avoided the idea, as some have contended.[1] Much like the papacy's turn to human dignity and the rights of the person to combat political totalitarianism after World War I, Church leaders in Latin America opposed the human rights abuses of emerging national security states that began with Brazil's military coup in 1964. By the 1970s, arbitrary imprisonments, disappearances, and death squads characterized Latin American dictatorships and thus elevated the necessary role of human rights in the Church's historical struggle for justice.[2]

Nevertheless, the Latin American theological perspective on justice avoided naïveté because it immediately recognized the ambiguity, and even deceptiveness, of human rights language.[3] In large part, this insight stemmed directly from a pastoral decision at the Second Vatican Council to align the institutional Church with poor, mostly indigenous, populations. A month before the council's meeting, Pope John XXIII delivered a radio address summoning the Church in the third world to present "itself as it is, and how it wants to be, as the church for everyone . . . as the church of the poor."[4] Pope John's summons was a catalyst for a group of cardinals, bishops, and theologians known as the "Church of the poor" at Vatican II. Just days before the closing of the council in December 1965, the bishops in the "Church of the poor" group made a "Pact of the Catacombs." These forty bishops gathered in the ancient catacombs of Domitilla outside Rome, agreeing that after the council they would return to their respective flocks and live in a manner that reflected the simplicity, service, and voluntary poverty characteristic of the apostles.[5] They also dedicated themselves to promoting the cause of justice, especially for the world's population living in substandard conditions. More than half the bishops who signed the pact were from Latin America (twenty-two), and they went on to organize and inspire the teachings of Medellín.

The significance of the Latin American bishops' meeting at Medellín in 1968 is well known. Church leaders who gathered in Colombia were keen on the human rights language of the Second Vatican Council but decisively focused on "*los derechos de los pobres y oprimidos*" (the rights of the poor and oppressed) as the Church's evangelical line of pastoral praxis.[6] In the spirit of the Catacombs Pact, they formally positioned the institutional Church within the ambit of el Pueblo de Dios (the People of God), signaling a momentous ecclesial turn toward the poor. The lived faith of the poor provided a new theological locus, or a source of theological reflection alongside scripture and tradition, for the universal Church. The meeting of bishops at Puebla in 1979 would explicitly designate this shift as the "preferential option for the poor."

The challenge of the poor became the prominent Church–world theme of Latin American liberation theology, thereby distinguishing it from North Atlantic progressive theology's focus on the question of unbelief.[7] More than the *nonbeliever*, the *nonperson* disturbed the conscience of these Latin American theologians. But who were the poor? Theologians and bishops taking stock of Medellín critically reflected on the material degradation in their midst—or the evil of "real poverty."[8] The episcopal choice at Medellín to defend "the rights of the poor and oppressed" demonstrated that the response to abject poverty did not strictly belong to the Church's ministry of charity but rather to its mission of pursuing justice in the world.

In scripture, the narrative arc of salvation makes it abundantly clear that God's revelation has unfolded in the history of the oppressed and their liberation from the powerful worldly domination of Pharaoh, Caesar, and, ultimately, death. Scripture concretizes the poor and oppressed at the hands of those who conquer, enslave, injure, and maim the innocent and powerless. Oppression is the chief cause of poverty in the biblical narrative. Its principal motive comes from "the eagerness to pile up wealth," which takes the form of an idolatrous attachment.[9] The Puebla meeting would identify those concrete poor in Latin America who are lacking both life's necessities and a dignified existence, in contrast to a minority that accumulates vast wealth to the detriment of indigenous peoples, rural farmworkers, laborers, and the marginalized—especially women, who are doubly oppressed.[10] These vulnerable groups—*los rostros reales*, or "real faces" of the suffering Christ—were very often the target of extrajudicial killings, kidnappings, and the torture campaigns of national security states.

The attention to socioeconomic oppression that informs a dialectical analysis of poverty in the Latin American theological context shows a Marxian influence. However, the hermeneutic frame of theology within a biblical worldview accounts for the injustice of poverty as the deprivation and dispossession "of the requirements of human dignity, from the fruits of labor, and from the original common destination of the earth's goods."[11] Faith informs this socioeconomic analysis with its Christological view of the poor, who serve as the definitive witnesses at the eschatological judgment of God's reign.[12] The socioeconomic dimension—although not exhaustive of other forms of oppressive poverty linked to racism, sexism, ageism, ableism, and religious persecution—remains foundational for understanding the concrete material situation of the poor. It provides, in the words of Ignacio Ellacuría, the "analogical starting-point" (*analogatum princeps*) for analyzing all other forms of poverty.[13]

The conflictual nature of poverty in a sinful world means that human rights represent a concrete historical struggle against oppression in order to safeguard the material necessities of life due to the most vulnerable. As early as 1969, the liberation theologian Ellacuría analyzed fundamental rights in terms of a struggle between rights that favor the self-interest of the dominant versus rights put into service by those dominated. Only an objective baseline in concrete reality (*la realidad*) and the necessities of human life can guarantee an ascertainment of truth about rights. This baseline establishes a certain hierarchical ordering of rights (*jerarquización*), beginning with the fundamental right to life (*el derecho a la vida*) and its negation in death.[14] The hierarchical ordering of rights is a key step toward surmounting superfluities and resisting liberal capitalism's inescapable scenario, as noted by Marx, whereby "force decides" the conflict "between equal rights."[15]

It is particularly important that the *negative* phase of the dialectical struggle—the violation of a human being denied what he or she needs to live—provides the primary datum for claiming human rights. Ellacuría's point here bears striking resemblance to Nicholas Wolterstorff's argument that *wronging*, or the failure to render certain life goods to someone, is the source of rights.[16] Ellacuría further explains: "The concrete reality of injustice as it has happened and is shown historically offers a stronger first principle than a presumed human nature from which there derives a basic collection of 'human' rights. Structural injustice in its diversely manifested forms is a fact prior to 'rights.' Rights are formulated because there is an injustice and this injustice is recognized before the expression of any specific right."[17]

From the perspective of the dialectical struggle for liberation in history, the truth about rights must flow from the first truth about injustices committed.[18] The prioritization of injustice to right does not undermine the intellectually important task of associating rights with human nature, basic needs, human dignity, and the common good. Rather, it keeps rights authentically linked to overcoming real injustices instead of being held captive by the interests of the powerful and elite.

Approaching human rights in view of a concrete historical struggle enables us to analyze it first from the negative dialectic of dispossessed peoples.[19] Ellacuría uses the term "historization," a neologistic translation of *historización*, to denote the method of treating human concepts as always already embedded in history and situated within specific political contexts shaped by the human struggle for existence and survival. Ellacuría gave substantial attention to the concepts of human rights and private property, both of which have a particularly important colonial background in the Americas. These concepts have undergone "ideologization" (*ideologización*), or mythologizing, which attributes a fixed universal status to something abstract and independent of its political deployment in history.[20] For Ellacuría, ideologized concepts like rights and property are touted as noble and just "without adequately accounting for the actual historical situations to which they are being applied and, what is worse, without attending to the scandalous fact that they can be employed to bring about circumstances that utterly contradict the truths they proclaim."[21] They can give sanction to the status quo by distorting reality and masking injustice. "Historization" therefore is the method appropriate for the de-ideologization (*desideologización*) of these kinds of sacralized concepts.

The bishops at Puebla in 1979, working out of the Catholic social tradition and the liberationist current, identified liberal capitalism as one of the most pressing ideologies within Latin America next to Marxist collectivism and national security.[22] Following the collapse of communism worldwide and right-wing national security states in Latin America, liberal capitalism has remained the most relevant ideological force in the West during the last three decades. Liberal ideology adheres to an individualist anthropology that subsumes labor under capital and social duty under economic gain.[23] Its "illegitimate privileges derived from an absolute right to property," write the bishops, "lead to scandalous contrasts and a situation of dependency and oppression on the national and international levels."[24] The philosophy of "getting to the top" (*arribismo*) corrupts the value of social duties among the youth, only exacerbating the gap between rich and poor for future generations.[25]

Liberalism as an ideological commitment characteristically abhors poverty, attributing its existence not to oppression but to backwardness and nonindustriousness, and something overcome by development and economic dependency.[26] Its compatibility with democratic societies and its global economic promise of raising the standard of living in underdeveloped countries have made it a neocolonial international force. For the remainder of this essay, I rely on the methodological option for the poor and dispossessed to start "historizing" a key ideological dimension of the individual right to private property in the Americas before briefly outlining a constructive theology of integral liberation as an ecclesial alternative to liberal individualism.

## De-Ideologizing the Individual Right to Property in the Americas

> The indigenous reality offers a unique perspective for reconstructing a new world and *inventing a new historical method of human rights.* That is because the condition of the oppressed majority adds the particularity of a tradition that can cast doubt on rights accepted ideologically as *natural* and *universal* human rights.[27] (emphasis added)

From its inception, the practice of liberalism has been wedded to colonial and imperial expansion outside Europe, all under the banner of the individual right to private property and civilizational progress. The colonial ideology of liberalism has a deeply entrenched social-political and legal history in the Americas, extending across both continents and garnering support from US presidents. Theodore Roosevelt's *The Winning of the West* (1889–96), a multivolume work launching his presidential bid that celebrates the right of Manifest Destiny among white English-speaking settlers on the frontier delivers a poignant illustration. It opens with an encomium to European colonialism: "During the past three centuries the spread of the English-speaking people over the world's waste spaces has been not only the most striking feature in the world's history, but also the event of all others most far-reaching in its effects and importance."[28]

According to Roosevelt, there was no injustice perpetrated against Native Americans by white settlers, who simply "moved into an uninhabited waste." Without a proper understanding of private property to claim the vast uncultivated lands as theirs in the first place, the natives "never had any title to the soil." Besides, if settlers and pioneers had not chopped down trees, erected buildings, cleared the ground for tillage, and put up fences, America would have been "nothing but a game preserve for squalid savages."[29] Roosevelt's unabashed brand of Manifest Destiny drew the stark conclusion that "the man who puts the soil to use must of right dispossess the man who does not, or the world will come to a standstill."³⁰

Roosevelt recognized the long-standing rationale for the English settlement of land in North America that gained ideological prominence in nineteenth-century white European readings of the past: the improvement of wasted space through the cultivation of soil. This agricultural argument posited an individual's claim to possess uncultivated land in vacant or wasted spaces by *occupying* it; that is, making proper use of it without need of another's consent. The activities of "enclosing" and "improving" the land through labor—physically represented by fencing off an area and planting the ground—were the chief markers for demonstrating individual ownership.³¹

The agricultural argument had strong ideological support from John Locke and the Puritans who first arrived in Plymouth, Massachusetts. Settlers often remarked about the sharp contrast they observed between the land's natural wealth and the poverty of the natives, who appeared to them like English beggars.³² The Puritan deacon Robert Cushman, for example, offered a popular crude description of the native way of life to advance the colonialist rationale. "Their land is spacious and void," he wrote. "They are not industrious, neither have art, science, skill, or faculty to use either the land or the commodities of it, but all spoils, rots, and is marred for want of manuring, gathering, ordering, etc."³³ This image of the nonindustrious and impoverished native strengthened the moral force of the argument in the Americas.

The most notable of the early Puritan defenders of colonization was the lawyer and first governor of the Massachusetts Bay Colony, John Winthrop, who constructed an influential legal interpretation of the agricultural argument for his "city on a hill."³⁴ Winthrop distinguished between two kinds of property rights given by God to conveniently label the division between Europeans and Native Americans: a natural right and a civil right. A *natural right* to property pertained to people holding things in common, who used only what they needed at their disposal for survival. In contrast, a *civil right* to property belonged to advanced agricultural societies, whereby individual men "appropriated certain parcels of ground by enclosing and peculiar manurance [cultivation of land]." Winthrop then relegated the Indians to an inferior status, saying, "they enclose no land neither have any settled habitation nor tame any cattle to improve the land by, and so have no other but a natural right to those countries."³⁵

The communal right of a village to use the land for various ecological purposes—as practiced by native tribes of the Northeast, for example—was an insufficient basis for claiming what the English settlers were after in the New World: private land ownership. Winthrop's juxtaposing a natural right of *using* common property to a civil right of *owning* private property was a rhetorically effective distinction denying indigenous political agency and civilization. It was this categorization of natural right (or common right) and civil right (or individual right) that made John Locke's labor theory of property so compatible with English colonial settlement in North America.

In chapter 5 of the *Second Treatise of Government*, Locke advanced a proto-liberal agricultural argument for property reliant on the twofold distinction outlined by Winthrop.[36] For Locke, the state of nature was not merely an a priori universal concept for his political theory. It was, instead, empirically demonstrable and geopolitically useful because "in the beginning all the world was America."[37] Locke's colonial interests in North America were significant, and they undoubtedly shaped his theoretical commitments. As an administrator of the Carolinas who was personally involved in revising its constitutions of 1682, he was also among those persons apportioned land by its proprietors, receiving some 75 square miles in the Carolina colony.[38] Contemporaneously, in Locke's England, the enclosure of the commons by individual proprietors claiming exclusive right to land was well under way. This "revolution of the rich against the poor" deprived the latter of traditional access to and a customary share of common lands.[39]

Because of Locke's important influence on the colonial American liberal tradition, he gives a particularly strong example of the ideologization of private property.[40] According to his conception of private property, "the wild Indian, who knows no enclosure," may have a right to his hunted game and gathered fruits, but it was only a common right of using the divinely bestowed goods of the Earth for natural sustenance.[41] America, however, was in large part "wild woods" and an "uncultivated waste."[42] Labor, expressed through tilling and planting the soil, was the agricultural indicator distinguishing a European civilized right from an Indian natural right focused on hunting and gathering. Like Winthrop, Locke attributed a common natural right of using unclaimed lands to Indians who still belong to that unpredictable and savage state of nature.

Though "God gave the world to men in common," for Locke, this did not mean that "it should always remain common and uncultivated."[43] By means of labor, Europeans have used their reason and industriousness to lay claim of God's gift of creation and turn it into something far more beneficial to people than the nonindustrious Indians could ever do. Locke (and many other European colonists) considered the American Indians as a people "rich in land, and poor in all the comforts of life."[44] In Locke's estimation, European settlers in North America fulfilled the divine mandate of Genesis 1:28 to make the Earth more fruitful by tilling the soil and improving it for everyone, thus embodying the biblical idea of dominion in a colonial mode.

The absence of private land ownership among the Indians implied not only their poverty but also their lack of legitimate political authority. After all, one of the chief purposes of political authority in European social contract theory was the regulation and protection of individual private property, as Locke frequently noted. Without a recognizable native political order premised on a quasi-liberal conception of private property, Locke could fundamentally skirt the requirement of respecting their consent.[45] It deserves mentioning that land purchases and treaties between the English and native peoples historically did occur as a seemingly more just alternative. But at least two conditions attenuated native consent in practice: First, the English exerted pressure on natives with threats and denied any native right of refusal; second, Native Americans most likely did not conceive of the title to land in European terms.[46] When native chiefs (sachems) conceded a right of using the land to Europeans, they likely did so without relinquishing their own jurisdiction over it. They would not have transferred an exclusive right of possession to land as some kind of tradable commodity, for the notion was utterly foreign to them.[47]

The vanishing space of native consent in Locke's political theory occurs in his discussion of money—the engine of industry in frontier colonial worlds. Inconsumable commodities like gold and silver become most useful through the "tacit and voluntary consent of men."[48] Money is what measures the value of industriousness beyond the perishable and necessary, and does so independently of the state's jurisdiction. Money represented more than a medium of exchange by offering the means "to store the *value* created by labor without letting it decay and return to the waste of the common."[49] Whereas the fruit of labor for hunters and gatherers was subject to the condition of spoilage, the monetary wealth derived from laboring the land in agricultural societies satisfied the nonspoilage condition. Settler families who enclosed and cultivated great tracts of land in North America were morally obligated and economically inclined to join the world of agricultural commerce; otherwise, their land remained wasteful because of excessive production of unused goods.[50]

Money was a form of capital permanently storing the surplus value from land improvement through labor. Locke therefore believed the enlargement and accumulation of one's possessions by hoarding up silver and gold was no injustice to anyone, because money did not rot.[51] Yet this did not necessarily translate into an aggressively violent and crude form of possessive individualism.[52] The ideological basis of Locke's protoliberalism was far more subtle and humane from the colonialist standpoint, similar to John Stuart Mill's liberal imperial defense of civilizing the backward peoples of India out of paternal benevolence. In Lockean terms, dispossessed natives were served better by an unequal possession of the Earth because the cultivation of land by industrious individuals would increase "the common stock of mankind."[53] Moreover, the dispossessed, who have tacitly consented to a monetized economy, have only been deprived of the common right to unowned lands.

In a commercial society where ingenuity creates new industry and money generates new wealth, the dispossessed are still individual masters of themselves. They have self-ownership and the ability to sell their labor on the market and receive its rewards.[54] Locke ultimately compares European and Amerindian societies to drive home his colonial argument that an English day laborer is better off than a native chief in America.[55] Escaping the state of nature through a superior civilized society that protects private ownership is *freedom from poverty* for everyone. The kernel of liberalism's appealing ideology is on full display here: The privatization of property benefits common human welfare.

## Neocolonialism and the Integral Liberation of Dispossessed Peoples

As Ignacio Ellacuría explains, "The powerful nations of today tell us they come to the Third World to make us 'rich' and to make us 'democratic.' But these 'generous propositions' contain a distinctive political and economic project. To discover and unmask the truth of such a project, one should not look *within the borders* of dominant nations in the West, but instead look precisely *beyond their borders.* There the ultimate effects of the Western project—its chief representative and carrier being the US—become manifest, showing what it really is and what it pretends to be" (emphasis added).[56]

John Locke's colonial agricultural argument on behalf of the individual appropriation of wasted spaces and uncultivated lands became the de facto norm in revolutionary America and the westward expansion of manifest destiny. It captivated presidents from Thomas Jefferson to Theodore Roosevelt and beyond. Jefferson appropriated Locke's concept of the state of nature by identifying the American Indians as peoples without government and law concerning private property.[57] Jefferson's policy was not the eradication of Native American persons as such but one of civilizing and assimilating them into the way of settler agricultural life through technological improvement of the land.[58] Refusal to do so was met with a persistent policy of further displacement into hunting lands beyond the American frontier until no more unappropriated land remained. Of course, the American frontier and its liberal justification for land improvement through privatization and wealth accumulation by dispossession did not end at the Pacific Ocean. In a prominent way for the United States, it went south.

The spread of neocolonial liberalism in the twentieth century at the hands of the United States took formal political shape by exposing the economic veins of Latin America. The unilateralist interventionism of the United States in Latin America developed, tellingly, during President Roosevelt's administration (1901–9), also termed "the imperial presidency."[59] His corollary to the Monroe Doctrine sought to push European nations out of the Western Hemisphere by bringing all territories of the Americas under the protection or possession of the new "international police power," the United States.[60] Roosevelt's corollary also required other American nations to strictly abide by the "primary laws of civilized society," or risk inviting US intervention through war. Shortly after Roosevelt and World War I, President Woodrow Wilson's version of liberal internationalism would advance the universal cause of civilized society by making democracy the principle of stability for a new world order.

US efforts to stabilize Latin America for purposes of national security under subsequent Cold War–era presidents bore out Wilson's legacy of liberal internationalism in a contradictory manner. Beginning in the 1960s and strengthening during the 1970s and 1980s, US political ideology strengthened the cause of military coups and dictatorships across Latin America in common resistance to the international communist threat against democracy.[61] The national security system emerging out of postwar United States established a federal model of control and secret service through its National Security Council and the Central Intelligence Agency. With clandestine US operations and arms supply across Latin American nations during the Cold War, the national security state was, according to the liberation theologian José Comblin, America's "farthest-reaching export."[62]

The moral and economic dimensions of US foreign interests coalesced under presidents Jimmy Carter and Ronald Reagan (1977–89), signaling an era of neoliberalism that culminated in the "Washington Consensus" of the 1990s. Trade liberalization, greater privatization of once public assets, commodification of nature and the commons, and deregulation of the financial sector have been key policies of liberalism's economic globalization directly affecting Latin America. Concurrent with this economic policy initiative was the moral rhetoric of human rights and democracy so characteristic of Carter and Reagan on behalf of the free world. Carter's inaugural address proclaimed an "absolute" commitment to individual human rights at home and abroad. Latin American theologians did not see the concurrent rise of neoliberalism and international human rights as mere coincidence but as part of a common ideological rubric of Western neocolonialism.[63]

An important nexus for this connection was the Trilateral Commission, which was first organized in the 1970s by Chase Bank executive David Rockefeller. The commission, which is still in existence, brought together the United States, Western Europe, and Japan under an international vision of cooperation and development responsive to the socioeconomic polarity between North and South, or rich and poor nations, rather than the Cold War ideological divide. Underdeveloped nations subject to military regimes had become an obstacle to the global free market, hindered in their ability to provide raw materials and to consume manufactured goods.[64] Revealingly, the Trilateral Commission's moral doctrine was none other than human rights, the "soul" of Carter's foreign policy. Carter, selected to the commission when he was governor of Georgia, appointed one of the commission's founding members as his national security adviser.

Jimmy Carter's inaugural address and Amnesty International's receipt of the Nobel Peace Prize in 1977 both signified a "breakthrough" year for individual human rights on the world political stage.[65] The Latin American Church's option for the poor and the liberationist critique of individualism enabled theologians to dissect and scrutinize the liberal breakthrough of international human rights espoused by governments and organizations from the North, especially the United States. Theologians immediately grasped the ideological significance of liberalism's catchwords of human rights and democratic freedom, progress, and development. But this did not mean that human rights were unsalvageable, as we have seen. The Brazilian theologian Hugo Assmann, like Ellacuría, recognized the important point of contrast between liberal human rights and the third world alternative discourse (*discurso alternativa*) of rights. He remarked that one of the most difficult points for progressivists to accept from Latin America was "the necessity of subordinating certain (derivative) rights to others more fundamental" like the right to life.[66]

Latin American theology has proposed integral liberation as an alternative to liberal individualism's sacred expression of rights in terms of propertied possessions of the neoliberal economic or social progressivist variety. The preferential option for oppressed communities marked by real poverty and injustice allows for a "historization" of human rights that can prophetically reach toward their authentic universality by exposing the ambiguity of rights asserted in the abstract.[67] Ellacuría's principle of de-ideologizing concepts brings into sharper relief the ethical difference between integral liberation and liberal individualism on the matter of justice. The historization of private property begins from a fundamental recognition that the common right of everyone to partake of the Earth's goods takes precedence over private ownership, whose existence "is justified only when it is the best possible way to make the goods of the Earth fulfill their primary purpose and to achieve solidarity among human beings."[68] Concerning common goods, Ellacuría echoes a long-standing Christian tradition that the Earth's bounty found in the sea, air, mountains and forests, and rivers and lakes, and its natural resources for production, use, and enjoyment, do not need privatization for experiencing shared life together.[69]

Private property is a reasonable concession to humanity's flawed but thoroughly social nature. From this anthropological truth, modern Catholic social teaching has consistently asserted the prior principle of the universal destination of goods for delimiting private property. Similarly, the scholastic theological tradition identified the common right of using the Earth's goods with natural law (*ius naturale*) and associated private property with the law of nations (*ius gentium*), thus accentuating the primacy of natural law to the law of nations.[70] These were not abstract ideas in the Christian West, but concretely realized and stratified in the distinctively chosen lifestyles of the poor religious and the propertied laity. Representative liberal political thinkers would abandon this metaphysical order for an empirically driven or formally asserted individualist anthropology that offered normative justification to leave behind the savage state of nature and its common right forever once the more civilized individual right to private property emerged.

Christian social doctrine overlaps remarkably with indigenous conceptions of ownership, where the ongoing struggle of the poor and oppressed over natural resources against foreign extractivism has continued in Latin America and the Global South. The ethical confluence of Christian and Andean theologies of creation on the issue of common goods, for example, helped inspire social, constitutional, and even international reform after the "Water War" of Bolivia in 2000.[71] At the behest of the World Bank, Bolivia's government enacted a neoliberal policy permitting a multinational company's privatization and allocation of water in the capital city of Cochabamba, which prompted public protest for substantial price hikes. Soon thereafter, owing to mobilized resistance efforts, the multinational organization withdrew its control of water. The Church expressed its solidarity with the indigenous community and the city's poor in a 2003 pastoral letter by the Bolivian bishops titled *Water, Fountain of Life and Gift for All*. The document's social vision referred to water as "a good destined for all," and its access a fundamental human right necessary for life, health, and the realization of all other rights.[72] Water's true sacred value resists commodification and therefore entails responsibility on the part of all citizens to contribute proportionately toward its clean and public access under the protection of the state rather than foreign businesses. In 2009, the new Bolivian government proclaimed that access to water is a human right against any future privatization. The following year, Bolivia went on to sponsor a similar resolution at the United Nations.

The primacy of the right to water in this brief example—consonant with the fundamental right to life—illustrates the theme of integral liberation in the Latin American theological approach to human rights. On this score, the Puebla meeting has been a crucial theological source for promoting integral liberation across three dimensions of human life: the material (relationship with the world), the social (relationships with others), and the transcendent (relationship with God).[73] These three dimensions are inseparable with respect to the effects of sin and the pursuit of justice for the dispossessed. Integral liberation outlines primary rights that correspond to each dimension of human life yet mutually implicate one another in a holistic nexus of relations.

The fundamental right to life, whether recognized through the injustice of denying public water access or denying a fair wage to laborers, requires a people's right of self-determination and a people's right to organize at the social level. Latin American theology's continued emphasis on the poor as agents of their own historical struggle for liberation and justice is an abiding feature in the effort to convert oppressors and prompt social and political transformation.[74]

The right of historically dispossessed people to decide for themselves or participate collectively on matters pertaining to their social welfare, shared land usage, access to resources, and cultural integrity is the last remaining vestige of self-determination in a supposedly decolonized world of sovereign nation-states.

The practice of land grabbing in Latin America, Asia, and Africa by agribusiness multinationals and foreign nations seeking to acquire arable space because of a rising commodities market and food shortages looms large as a neocolonial frontier. Western support for these large-scale land acquisitions rehearse the familiar liberal argument of making good and effective use of underutilized land or wasted space. They also promise to be good for the global market economy by feeding the world's poor. Nevertheless, global land grabs in regions historically beset by European colonialism often directly conflict with and displace the subsistence agriculture of rural farmers and indigenous communities currently occupying and using the land, forcing them to migrate elsewhere or sell their labor on the cheap.[75]

The postconciliar Church has served a crucial mediating role in conflicts involving indigenous communities and governments in Latin America.[76] Ecclesial public witness in the struggle for the rights of dispossessed peoples is possible only because of the Church's transcendent mission to carry on the liberating work of Jesus Christ in a world marred by personal, social, and structural sin. The chief right for securing the integral liberation of peoples at the basic material and social dimensions is the *freedom to proclaim the truth* about the reign of God's justice and mercy in the face of evil and injustice. Undoubtedly, the exercise of this God-given right has brought violent conflict and even death for those courageous enough to pursue it. Bishops of accompaniment, from Saint Óscar Romero to Bishop Samuel Ruiz García in Highland Chiapas, and numerous others in Bolivia and throughout Latin America, in the spirit of the Pact of the Catacombs, provide rich and challenging examples of solidarity with the poor and dispossessed. To the end, Ellacuría believed the university was the necessary place where the search for the truth about injustices using extensive social-scientific analysis could occur.[77] His assassination at the Central American University in San Salvador proved how right he was.

The rhetoric of human rights may have staying power for the time being, even as nativism, populism, and the international importance of China grow. But if global human rights remain locked in a neoliberal frame, with its overwhelming emphasis on the individual's civil and political rights stemming from private property, we should expect its pitiable collapse before larger, more powerful, and concentrated forms of collective self-interest. Regardless of modest achievements in assisting the poor, the liberal project cannot accomplish what it never set out to do. Its economic proponents can and often do acknowledge a minimum floor of well-being and the raising of living standards, but they will stop short of questioning, much less limiting, the height of wealth's ceiling.[78] As long as this ceiling continues to rival the Tower of Babel, *the gap between rich and poor* will violently expand, thereby undermining liberal ideals of equality on which its notion of justice abstractly rests. Inspired by the theological option for the poor, Christians must continue to call this injustice greed, or idolatry, which is the root of all sin and is a supreme obstacle to authentic freedom. Only then will the discourse on human rights move beyond the ambiguity and deception that have marked its deployment in a neoliberal global context.

## Notes

1. See Mark Engler, "Toward the 'Rights of the Poor': Human Rights in Liberation Theology," *Journal of Religious Ethics* 28, no. 3 (Fall 2000): 339–65; Ethna Regan, *Theology and the Boundary Discourse of Human Rights* (Washington, DC: Georgetown University Press, 2010), chap. 4.

2. José Comblin, *The Church and the National Security State* (Maryknoll, NY: Orbis Books, 1979), 104–5.

3. Consider the perspective from 1966 of Brazilian archbishop Dom Hélder Câmara, an early liberationist critic of national security and developmentalism who was among the bishops of the poor at Vatican II: "Absurd privileges are upheld in the name of the principle of property. The dignity of the human person is invoked as if the dignity of the workers were nonexistent." See Dom Hélder Câmara, *Essential Writings*, selected with an introduction by Francis McDonagh (Maryknoll, NY: Orbis Books, 2009), 77.

4. Pope John XXIII, Radio Address, September 11, 1962: "Para los países subdesarrollados la Iglesia se presenta como es y como quiere ser, como Iglesia de todos, en particular como la Iglesia de los pobres."

5. Maria Clara Bingemer, *Latin American Theology: Roots and Branches* (Maryknoll, NY: Orbis Books, 2016), 49–54.

6. Medellín (1968), "Document on Peace," in *Las cinco conferencias generales del episcopado Latinoamericano* (Bogotá: CELAM, 2014), no. 22.

7. Gustavo Gutiérrez, *The Power of the Poor in History* (Portland, OR: Wipf & Stock, 2004), 92.

8. Gustavo Gutiérrez, "Option for the Poor," in *Mysterium Liberationis: Fundamental Concepts of Liberation Theology*, ed. Ignacio Ellacuría and Jon Sobrino (Maryknoll, NY: Orbis Books, 1993), 235–50.

9. Elsa Tamez, *Bible of the Oppressed*, trans. Matthew O'Connell (Maryknoll, NY: Orbis Books, 1982), 3.

10. Puebla (1979), in *Las cinco conferencias generales*, §§31–39, 1135n326.

11. Ignacio Ellacuría, "Pobres," in *Escritos teológicos* II (San Salvador: UCA Editores, 2000), 174–75.

12. Ibid., 182–83, citing Mt 25:31–36.

13. Ibid., 174.

14. Ignacio Ellacuría, "Historización de los derechos humanos en los países subdesarrollados y oprimidos," in *La lucha por la Justicia: Selección de textos de Ignacio Ellacuría (1969–1989)*, ed. Juan Antonio Senent (Madrid: Universidad de Deusto, 2012), 299–301.

184 · Liberal Domination, Individual Rights, and the Theological Option

15. Karl Marx, *Capital*, in *The Marx-Engels Reader*, 2nd edition, ed. Robert Tucker (New York: W. W. Norton, 1978), 364. For Marx, this represented the class conflict between the rights of the owners of capital and the rights of workers.

16. Nicholas Wolterstorff, *Justice: Rights and Wrongs* (Princeton, NJ: Princeton University Press, 2008), 293.

17. Ellacuría, "Respuesta a CETRAL," in *Lucha*, 295: "La realidad concreta de la injusticia tal como se ha dado y se da históricamente es un principio de arranque más firme que una presunta naturaleza humana de la que se desprenderían originariamente un conjunto de derechos 'humanos.' La injusticia estructural con sus diversas formas de manifestarse es un dato anterior a los 'derechos.' Se formulan derechos porque hay injusticia y esta injusticia es reconocible anteriormente a la formulación de cualquier derecho."

18. Ibid., 296: "El hecho primario de la injusticia clama por su superación y regula todo otro tipo de derechos."

19. Gutiérrez, *Power of the Poor*, 20–21.

20. Ellacuría, "Ideología e inteligencia," in *Lucha*, 124.

21. Kevin Burke, SJ, *The Ground beneath the Cross: The Theology of Ignacio Ellacuría* (Washington, DC: Georgetown University Press, 2000), 124.

22. For a discussion of each of these ideologies within the Puebla document and Catholic social teaching more broadly, see Ricardo Antoncich, *Christians in the Face of Injustice: A Latin American Reading of Catholic Social Teaching*, trans. Matthew O'Connell (Maryknoll, NY: Orbis Books, 1987), chap. 10.

23. Puebla (1979), §47.

24. Ibid., §542.

25. Ibid., §95.

26. Clodovis Boff, "Epistemology and Method of the Theology of Liberation," in *Mysterium Liberationis*, 75–76.

27. Ellacuría, "Respuesta a CETRAL," in *Lucha*, 296: "La realidad indígena ofrece una perspectiva peculiar para la reconstrucción de un mundo nuevo y para la invención de un nuevo sistema histórico de derechos, porque a su condición de mayorías oprimidas añade la peculiaridad de una tradición que puede poner en tela de juicio derechos que ideologizadamente se aceptan como derechos humanos universales o naturales."

28. Theodore Roosevelt, *The Winning of the West*, vol. 1 (New York: G. P. Putnam's Sons, 1907–8), 1.

29. Ibid., 89–90.

30. Ibid., 92.

31. Patricia Seed, *American Pentimento: The Invention of Indians and the Pursuit of Riches* (Minneapolis: University of Minnesota Press, 2001), chaps. 1 and 2.

32. William Cronon, *Changes in the Land: Indians, Colonists, and the Ecology of New England* (New York: Hill & Wang, 2003), 33.

33. Robert Cushman, "Reasons and Considerations Touching on the Lawfulness of Removing out of England into the Parts of America (1622)," in *The Puritans in America: A Narrative Anthology*, ed. Andrew Delbanco and Alan Heimert (Cambridge, MA: Harvard University Press, 2009), 43–44.

34. Notably, Roger Williams was an important dissenting voice among the early Puritans, arguing in defense of native political sovereignty and right to land. See Jack L. Davis, "Roger Williams among the Narragansett Indians," *New England Quarterly* 43, no. 4 (December 1970): 593–604.

35. John Winthrop, "Reasons to Be Considered for . . . the Intended Plantation of New England (1629)," in Delbanco and Heimert, *Puritans in America*, 73.

36. I use the term "proto-liberal" to situate Locke's ideological commitments in his early modern context and to distinguish the economy as a predominantly commercial or mercantile system in contrast to the self-regulating market economy associated with liberal capitalism.

37. John Locke, *Second Treatise of Government*, ed. Ian Shapiro (New Haven, CT: Yale University Press, 2003), chap. 5, §49, p. 121.

38. See the important studies by Barbara Arneil, *John Locke and America: The Defense of English Colonialism* (New York: Cambridge University Press, 1996); James Tully, *An Approach to Political Philosophy: Locke in Contexts* (New York: Cambridge University Press, 1993), chap. 5; and David Armitage, *Foundations of Modern International Thought* (New York: Cambridge University Press, 2013), chaps. 5, 6, and 7.

39. Karl Polanyi, *The Great Transformation: The Political and Economic Origins of Our Time* (Boston: Beacon Press, 2001), 37.

40. Craig Yirush, *Settlers, Liberty, and Empire: The Roots of Early American Political Theory, 1675–1775* (New York: Cambridge University Press, 2011), chap. 4.

41. Locke, *Second Treatise*, chap. 5, §26, p. 111.

42. Ibid., §37, p. 116.

43. Ibid., §34, p. 114.

44. Ibid., §41, p. 117.

45. Tully, *Approach to Political Philosophy*, 139.

46. Seed, *American Pentimento*, 20–21.

47. Cronon, *Changes in the Land*, 67.

48. Locke, *Second Treatise*, chap. 5, §50, p. 121.

49. Onus Ulas Ince, "Enclosing in God's Name, Accumulating for Mankind: Money, Morality, and Accumulation in John Locke's Theory of Property," *Review of Politics* 73 (2011): 43.

50. Locke, *Second Treatise*, chap. 5, §48, p. 121.

51. Ibid., §50, p. 121.

52. Though an otherwise thought-provoking study, the critical essay by the liberationist thinker Franz Hinkelammert tends toward this extreme reading of Locke, thereby losing sight of liberalism's neocolonial appeal. Franz Hinkelammert, "The Case of John Locke: The Inversion of Human Rights in the Name of Bourgeois Property," in *Property for People, Not for Profit: Alternatives to the Global Tyranny of Capital* (New York: Zed Books, 2004), 43–76.

53. Locke, *Second Treatise*, chap. 5, §37, p. 116.

54. Michael P. Zuckert, *Natural Rights and the New Republicanism* (Princeton, NJ: Princeton University Press, 1994), 269–71.

55. Locke, *Second Treatise*, chap. 5, §41, p. 117–18.

56. Ignacio Ellacuría, "Quinto Centenario de América Latina, ¿descubrimiento o encubrimiento?," in *Lucha*, 348.

57. Arneil, *John Locke and America*, 189–90.

58. Maureen Konkle, "Indigenous Ownership and the Emergence of US Liberal Imperialism," *American Indian Quarterly* 32, no. 3 (Summer 2008): 303–5.

59. Brian Loveman, *No Higher Law: American Foreign Policy and the Western Hemisphere since 1776* (Chapel Hill: University of North Carolina Press, 2010), chaps. 6–7.

60. Theodore Roosevelt, "The Roosevelt Corollary to the Monroe Doctrine" (1904), in *Latin America and the United States: A Documentary History*, 2nd edition, ed. Robert Holden and Eric Zolov (New York: Oxford University Press, 2011), 97–98. The Monroe Doctrine (1823), ascribed to President James Monroe and to his secretary of state, John Quincy Adams, unilaterally defended the noncolonization of lands in the Americas against foreign European powers.

61. Loveman, *No Higher Law*, chap. 11.

62. Comblin, *Church and the National Security State*, 64.

63. Consider the two-volume work on Jimmy Carter's economic and political interests toward Latin America, whose contributors are mostly Latin American liberationists and social scientists: *Carter y la lógica del imperialismo*, 2 vols., ed. Hugo Assmann (San José: Editorial Universitaria Centroamericana, 1978).

64. Pablo Richard, *Death of Christendoms, Birth of the Church: Historical Analysis and Theological Interpretation of the Church in Latin America*, trans. Phillip Berryman (Maryknoll, NY: Orbis Books, 1987), 84–86.

65. Samuel Moyn, *The Last Utopia: Human Rights in History* (Cambridge, MA: Harvard University Press, 2010), 155.

66. Hugo Assmann, "El tercer mundo comienza a crear un lenguaje alternativa sobre los derechos humanos," in *Carter y la lógica del imperialismo*, 2:455.

67. Ignacio Ellacuría, "Historización de los derechos humanos desde los pueblos oprimidos y las mayorías populares," in *Lucha*, 373.

68. Ignacio Ellacuría, "The Historicization of the Concept of Property," in *Towards a Society That Serves Its People: The Intellectual Contributions of El Salvador's Martyred Jesuits*, ed. John Hassett and Hugh Lacey (Washington, DC: Georgetown University Press, 1991), 132.

69. Ignacio Ellacuría, "Utopia and Prophecy in Latin America," in Hassett and Lacey, *Towards a Society*, 76.

70. Ignacio Ellacuría, "Historicization of the Concept of Property," in Hassett and Lacey, *Towards a Society*, 129–31.

71. Terrence McGoldrick, "The Religious Case for Water as a Human Right from the Andes," *International Journal of Design and Nature and Ecodynamics* 12, no. 4 (2017): 470–81.

72. Conferencia Episcopal Boliviana, *Agua Fuente de la vida y don para todos* (2003), §16.

73. Gutiérrez, *Power of the Poor*, 144–48.

74. Enrique Dussel, *History and the Theology of Liberation*, trans. John Drury (Maryknoll, NY: Orbis Books, 1976), 145–46.

75. Derek Hall, *Land* (Malden, MA: Polity Press, 2013), 95–102.

76. Alison Brysk, *From Tribal Village to Global Village: Indian Rights and International Relations in Latin America* (Stanford, CA: Stanford University Press, 2000), chap. 5.

77. Ignacio Ellacuría, "The University, Human Rights, and the Poor Majority," in Hassett and Lacey, *Towards a Society*, 211.

78. Cf. Samuel Moyn, "A Powerless Companion: Human Rights in the Age of Neoliberalism," *Law and Contemporary Problems* 77, no. 4 (2014): 149.

# Book Reviews

# Tolerance Among the Virtues

John R. Bowlin

PRINCETON, NJ: PRINCETON UNIVERSITY PRESS, 2016. 280 PP. $39.50

John Bowlin has produced a comprehensive and fine-grained analysis of, and argument for, the virtue of tolerance in contemporary Western democratic societies. His account relies heavily on Thomas Aquinas, yet he believes that the case for tolerance should have force beyond Christian communities because liberal democracies are necessarily concerned about maintaining just relationships among people with different understandings of the good. This is a precise and thorough treatment of an important quality in these contentious times.

Bowlin argues, first, that criticisms of tolerance often arise from mistaking the virtue for one of its semblances, typically a sort of truculent self-restraint. In response, drawing on Aquinas and Wittgenstein, he makes an extended case for true tolerance as part of the virtue of justice. Tolerance is necessary to any human life ("natural" in Aquinas' terms) because of the social nature of humanity and the inevitable rise of interpersonal or intergroup differences. The virtue consists of "patient endurance of objectionable difference" for the sake of peaceful society and shared autonomy (130). Peaceful society and autonomy are goods shared in common by members of a democratic society, and so all are owed tolerance in respect of that membership. Obviously, not all differences should be tolerated. Tolerance as a virtue includes the ability to distinguish between what is truly objectionable and what is not, along with between what is objectionable and what is unendurable. The accuracy of these distinctions, of course, depends on circumstances and context.

When Bowlin returns to the issue of opposition to tolerance (chap. 5), he points out that disputes about tolerance are actually often about a particular community's lists of what is tolerable and what is not. Tolerance, therefore, is not a possession of either the political right or left, for any human group develops and exercises tolerance for some of the inevitable differences among its members. Rather, the right and the left cling to different lists of what is properly tolerated. This section of the book seems particularly helpful, as it provides an instructive perspective on differences that often seem unfathomable.

Finally, Bowlin discusses the relationship between "(1) tolerance annexed to justice and acquired by natural means; (2) forbearance as a perfection of friendship's love; and (3) a forbearance that, by Christian confession, comes by grace, expresses God's love, and participates in God's life" (207). Drawing on Paul here, Bowlin asserts that though natural tolerance has limits, gracious forbearance—grounded in love—does not. Even if sinners must be restrained by just coercion, they must at the same time be patiently endured while their forbearing community hopes for their transformation through grace.

Bowlin has written a strong argument for tolerance as an important virtue. The latter chapters are broadly accessible, whereas the earlier sections require at least some familiarity with Thomistic assumptions and methods. This is an excellent contribution to virtue ethics, political theology, and scholarship on pluralism and democracy.

Laura Yordy
Bridgewater College

REVIEW OF
## Global Justice, Christology and Christian Ethics
Lisa Sowle Cahill

NEW YORK: CAMBRIDGE UNIVERSITY PRESS, 2013. 328 PP. £62.00 / £20.99

Given this book's title and its cover photo of Catholic Relief Services workers in Kenya, I was expecting an examination of global issues with case studies. But chapter titles such as "Creation and Evil," "Kingdom of God," "Christ," "Spirit," and "Cross" tipped me off that my original expectations were incorrect.

Perhaps this is Cahill's summa, an attempt to bring together current understandings of major themes in Christian systematic theology and to show how those are tied to Christian ethics. As the series editor, Robin Gill, notes, as opposed to specific moral issues, Cahill's "aim now is to supply a sustained theological basis for global justice" (xi). Cahill herself explains that she hopes "to give biblical and theological reasons for Christian commitment to justice, to show why just action is necessarily a criterion of authentic Christian theology, and to give grounds for Christian hope that change in violent structures is really possible" (1). This is a bold attempt that I feel works on some levels. Cahill draws from key historical and current theologians, including feminist thinkers and marginalized groups.

As an ethicist, much of this was a fascinating read in current systematic theology, while some seemed like an overview. I found the chapter on creation and evil somewhat of a plodding summary, yet the chapters on the Kingdom of God, Christ, and the Cross are interesting reads on current discussions in Christology. I would recommend this book for academics and graduate students. Selected sections might work well for undergrads. Sections such as "Historical Research on Jesus" could be great current summaries for undergraduates.

The chapter on the Spirit was interesting but problematic because Cahill's overall approach could err too strongly on the presence of the Spirit primarily in the church itself rather than the world. The chapter on the Cross illustrates interesting historical and current discussion on the necessity of Jesus' death. At this point (246), I feel we primarily have a summary of Christian systematic theology. She acknowledges this as well: "The chapters thus far have been primarily biblical and theological in orientation, but ethical ideals and standards have played a key part in readings of scripture, doctrines, and theologies" (247).

Then the book seems to abruptly shift to traditional ethics. With the chapter title of "Nature," I was expecting an examination of environmental ethics but instead got a helpful read on the natural law and virtue ethics approach of Thomas Aquinas. This chapter includes examples of "War as a Test Case" and "Ecology." The final chapter, "Hope," speaks of the need for hope in working toward just and peaceful societies. It includes the longest and only real case study in the book, describing how "Liberian peace activist Leymah Gbowee won the Nobel Prize for spearheading a grassroots women's movement against the civil war" there (295). This is a fascinating account of women using their power and perseverance to overcome an unjust regime, noting that "women had become the 'toy of war'" (298). Finally, observing that "peacebuilding practices reflect the vision of Christian politics that has shaped the previous chapters of this project" (302), she offers seven key points that tie previous chapter topics to current Christian ethics. It seems like an abrupt ending, finishing on point seven and not offering an overall reflection on the book itself.

Given this structure, I wish that it had been written as a text for undergrads because the systematic topics covered, and their tie to and conclusion on Christian ethics, would be a nice format for an introductory course. But Cahill's work has always been current, progressive, and concerned with global ethics and the common good. This book is no different, and it is a welcome part of the New Studies in Christian Ethics series.

Keith Soko
Saint Ambrose University

**REVIEW OF**

*Liberating Sexuality: Justice Between the Sheets*

Miguel A. De La Torre

SAINT LOUIS: CHALICE PRESS, 2016. 232 PP. $27.99

What lies at the heart of Miguel De La Torre's provocative and refreshing collection of essays *Liberating Sexuality* is his lifelong commitment to a justice-based society. He is deeply concerned with "how oppressive social structures, rooted in a two-thousand-year-old misunderstanding of Christian sexuality, prevent us from a more just social order" (vii).

De La Torre rigorously engages with the biblical literature and considers it a vital ground for ethical reflection. He first returns to Genesis and successfully argues that "God blesses sex and declares it good" (4). He closely examines the story of the first man and woman and proposes the concept of "cleave to" in Genesis 2:24–25 as the guiding definition for a healthy marriage in our modern society. By revisiting and creatively retelling the stories of women in the Bible—Lot's wife, Sarah, Dinah, Rebekah, and Tamar—he restores the humanity and dignity of women and calls for our responsibility to dismantle the patriarchal structures that foster sexual abuse. He also provides alternative interpretations of the troubling biblical texts for LGBTQ communities to consider. After thoroughly surveying the biblical justification of patriarchy and the subjugation of women in the Hebrew Bible, he proposes that "the entire Bible should be read through the lens of the Gospel message, specifically passages like John 10:10" (13). Though a creative attempt to liberate the sacred text from oppression, this approach requires caution, as there may be possible anti-Semitic ramifications for reading the Hebrew Bible through a New Testament lens.

One of the major contributions of De La Torre to the field of sexual ethics is the proposal of "orthoeros" through a liberative method that seriously considers liberation theology and goes beyond the inadequate approaches of both conservatives' sexual legalism and liberals' permissiveness toward sexual ethics. "Orthoeros" promotes a "familial relationship based on mutual giving and vulnerability" (21) and is made up of five biblically based principles: safe, consensual, faithful, mutually pleasing, and intimate.

As an ethicist who is invested in the public discourse, De La Torre actively and boldly engages with issues of various sexual practices. He critiques *Fifty Shades of Grey* and envisions an ethical, Christian-based sadomasochism by employing "orthoeros" principles. He also examines the historical reasons against masturbation and argues for its constructive role in the sexuality of Christians.

Deeply disturbed by the prevailing injustice that corrupts our society, De La Torre focuses much of the volume on exposing the sources and the detrimental effects of sexism, heterosexism, and racism. He reveals misogynist legislation by mapping out the "war on women," specifically the issues of equal pay, rape, reproduction rights, and global sexism. He reflects on his own "sin of heterosexuality" of being a macho man, conquering, and celebrating *cojones*. He also examines the Euro-American history of owning black bodies and critiques the stereotyping of Latino bodies in Hollywood.

Another major contribution of De La Torre is the indecent approach to justice-based praxis—an ethics *para joder*—that "screws" with the prevailing power structures by utilizing a nonviolent survival strategy based on love, designed to liberate the abused and the abusers from the death-dealing social structure.

*Liberating Sexuality*, situated at the intersection between Christian ethics, biblical hermeneutics, and cultural studies, is a successful interdisciplinary endeavor. The essays gathered here remain highly engaged with the public reality and should benefit both general readers and scholars. Furthermore, this volume provides much-needed guidance on how a sexual ethics should be implemented and is, hence, a vital resource for those engaged in the practices of ministry.

Simeiqi He
Drew University

■

REVIEW OF
*Christian Martyrdom and Political Violence:*
*A Comparative Theology with Judaism and Islam*
Rubén Rosario Rodríguez
CAMBRIDGE: CAMBRIDGE UNIVERSITY PRESS, 2017. 318 PP. £74.99

Responding to the conflation of martyrdom and political violence in the public imagination in the post-9/11 global context, Rosario makes a constructive liberationist argument for a nonviolent theology of martyrdom emerging from Christianity, Judaism, and Islam. He surveys depictions of political violence in these scriptural traditions, arguing that martyrdom—properly understood—is fundamentally political but nonviolent in character. This comparative angle allows him to address the histories of violence of each tradition alongside their liberative possibilities. Although Rosario's project has a strong comparative theological dimension, he emphasizes that the work is grounded in Christian theology. He integrates several distinctive theological methods—systematics, scripture, history, and ethics—toward making a constructive argument about martyrdom that grapples with its complex and multifaceted manifestation in Christian thought and practice. He uses a Christian liberationist lens to bring the contributions of each of these conversations to bear on his argument.

After defining sacred scripture in Christianity, Judaism, and Islam and examining the role of political violence therein, the first chapter offers comparative exegesis of the book of the prophet Jonah in these traditions as the basis for a liberative reading of scripture that emphasizes nonviolence and interreligious encounter. Chapter 2 engages early Christian martyr narratives to explore how early Christians employed them in resistance against inhospitable social conditions. In the third chapter, Rosario argues for the nonviolent character of martyrdom in these scriptural traditions, critiquing ideologies and practices within each tradition that manipulate martyrdom for political gain (Islamic terrorist violence, Israeli nationalism, Christian Zionism, and the so-called just war against terror). Chapter 4 interprets the martyrdom of Óscar Romero, arguing that nonviolent witness is the most faithful witness to scripture. The final chapter argues for a full and embodied view of Christ's life as a necessary context for understanding his death. Rosario contends that a holistic Christological view is essential for appreciating the nonviolent character of authentic Christian martyrdom.

This text illustrates a dynamic approach to Christian ethics that uses the broad range of the theological and scriptural resources available in the field. At times, this ambitious approach can obscure the text's most significant arguments. This multifaceted work demands slow and careful reading by even the most experienced ethicist, making it difficult to assign the text in its entirety to groups that might otherwise benefit from engaging its arguments (undergraduate students, church groups, and grassroots community organizations). But there are rich rewards for patient attention to Rosario's methodologically intricate argument. For scholars of Christian ethics, he demonstrates that liberation theology is an essential literature for Christian ethics in the twenty-first century with almost unprecedented persuasion. With derision for "contextual theology," many Christian ethicists continue to doubt liberation theology's capacity to speak to our most urgent global problems. Rosario's work ought to disabuse the field of this shallow dismissal, demonstrating liberation theology's enormous potential to grapple with the problem of political violence across religious traditions. Conversely, scholars of liberation theology should receive Rosario's work as a challenge to explore the constructive possibilities for creative engagement with problems beyond local contexts and sources of the liberationist canon toward cultivating scholarship that is of even greater interest and relevance to the broader academy and public life.

Nichole M. Flores
University of Virginia

REVIEW OF

## *The Altars Where We Worship: The Religious Significance of Popular Culture*
Juan M. Floyd-Thomas, Stacey M. Floyd-Thomas, and Mark G. Toulouse
LOUISVILLE: WESTMINSTER JOHN KNOX PRESS, 2016. 250 PP. $25.00

*The Altars Where We Worship: The Religious Significance of Popular Culture* is notable for interested readers of religion and contemporary popular culture. The authors expand scholarly understandings of religion and the sacred, but more important, the spaces where they appear in society by providing analysis of the religious nature of six aspects of American culture. These "meaning-making" aspects of popular culture function as "altars of worship." They are the body and sex, big business, entertainment, politics, sports, and science and technology. How religious devotion and worship are manifest in everyday life of Americans is fully examined. This book offers an alternative entry to classical secularization debates that have garnered the attention of religious scholars across fields of study. Resisting polarized battle lines in which secularization debates have positioned the death of religion on one hand, and its resilience in industrialized societies on the other hand, this book considers the idiosyncratic nature of secularization by foregrounding historical, national, and local differences that exist in various contexts.

The authors argue that "religion *is* important to Americans. But the religion we practice is often *not* the religion we confess" (1, emphasis in the original). According to them, Americans basically believe in a serviceable, friendly "God" who meets their every desire and need. In contemporary American culture, the objects that are deemed to fulfill Americans' desires and passions become their God(s) and thus their religion(s). They support their argument by citing studies by the Pew Research Center on "America's Changing Religious Landscape" and "'Nones' on the Rise," which indicate a decrease in religious affiliation among adults and a notable tension between Americans' professed religious beliefs and their actual religious practices. Given these trends, they contend that Americans discover and produce religious meaning in places outside traditional or conventional sacred spaces. Consequently, they confess, Americans have "laid our fair share, if not our all" (186) on the six altars of American popular culture. Thus, though studies indicate a trending decline in traditional religious affiliations, for the authors, this does not "sound the death knell of religion" (185). Religion, they insist, exists in different shapes and practices.

In *The Religious Experience of Mankind* (1969), the religious historian Ninian Smart offers a seven-dimensional scheme for the interpretation of religion: doctrinal, mythological, ethical, ritual, experiential, institutional, and material. This scheme is adopted in the book as a framing device for interpreting the religious nature of popular culture. The sevenfold scheme is paralleled in each of the six chapters dedicated to a particular altar. Making their case, the authors draw on and weave thinkers from across disciplines and over time as critical interlocutors—from Friedrich Nietzsche, Rudolf Otto, Paul Tillich, and Robert Bella to Cornel West, Audre Lord, and bell hooks, among many others—in examining the religious significance of popular culture.

Although a truly engaging and provocative book, *The Altars Where We Worship* is not without challenges. Some readers may find certain categories of analysis underdeveloped. For example, what makes big business or politics sites of popular culture? This line of inquiry may raise questions for readers about what constitutes popular culture in general. Such challenges, however, do not detract from the overall accomplishments and contributions this book offers the study of religion in the United States.

Michael R. Fisher Jr.
Vanderbilt University

REVIEW OF

## Christian Ethics at the Boundary: Feminism and Theologies of Public Life

Karen V. Guth

MINNEAPOLIS: FORTRESS PRESS, 2015. 231 PP. $39.00

In her promising first book, Karen Guth does "ethics at the boundary," reading the central figures of Martin Luther King Jr., John Howard Yoder, and Reinhold Niebuhr with an uncommon generosity that allows for synthesis and opens up new potential for collective action. She challenges the Christian realists, witness theologians, and liberationists in contemporary Christian ethics to see overlap in their theologies, hear the questions that others bring to their work, and join together in bringing theology to the public square.

This moment in politics and political theology seems to call for the kind of argument that Guth wants to make. Polarization in the academy mirrors that of the church and society, and potential for moving beyond it seems more elusive than ever.

The key contribution of the book is shedding light on what is often overlooked in three key figures who continue to influence Christian ethics. At the "boundaries" or edges of their work, Guth retrieves Niebuhr's attention to ecclesiology as an essential part of his realist ethic; Yoder's willingness to learn from liberalism and translate theology for a diverse audience; and King's liberation theology of the streets, which enacted transcendence of the witness/realist divide.

Equally significant is attention to overlooked feminist themes in all three thinkers. Guth argues that Yoder has the most developed feminist theology (especially evident in unpublished memos, 138–40), whereas King and Niebuhr, though often rightly criticized by feminist thinkers, have in their writings and sermons significant overlap with central feminist themes. By reading King and Niebuhr alongside feminist thinkers, we can begin to see King's "'feminist' and 'womanist' politics of love," which inspires a view of "churches as potential sites of divine creation" (183), and Niebuhr's call for the church to "confess its complicity with the world" for its failures, which coheres with feminist insistence that the church must "confess its complicity in women's oppression" (111). In retrieving feminist themes, Guth offers a corrective to political theology's frequent lack of attention to sexism.

Guth is careful to note that, in their personal lives, all three theologians failed to live up to their professed concern for gender justice. Despite this qualification, it is particularly difficult to read of Yoder's professed feminism in light of the overwhelming allegations of sexual abuse against him by over one hundred women. His perverse theological justification of the abuse and the ongoing tension among Christian ethicists about how to respond compound the problem. In 2017, SCE members held a prayer service to honor the testimony of Yoder's victims and to address the SCE's complicity in the harm done by him. Guth's response is that it is now even more important to correct misperceptions and uphold feminist themes in Yoder's work. However, it seems all but impossible to redeem his thought in this area. Yoder justified his abuse by melding together themes from scripture and liberalism. In light of what we know now, his justification of "revolutionary subordination" (even in the 1994 version of *Politics of Jesus*) is even more troubling. In these times, silence about Yoder may be the more appropriate way to honor his victims.

Still, Guth's emphasis on intellectual charity, her articulation of the desire for beloved community as essential to the ethicist's task, and her willingness to risk standing at the boundary in order to illuminate the common concerns of those who see themselves as opponents are great gifts to Christian ethics. By complicating the reader's location of Yoder, Niebhur, and King, Guth makes a strong case that ethicists can form a better "community of argument" (190). In a course on social ethics, or in public or political theology, reading Guth would provide a way for students to synthesize the contributions of key thinkers, grapple with both personal and theoretical limitations, and think creatively about how to do their work with generosity and humility.

Julie Hanlon Rubio
Saint Louis University

REVIEW OF
## *God's Command*
John Hare
OXFORD: OXFORD UNIVERSITY PRESS, 2015. 368 PP. $110.00

Divine command theory has received a significant amount of high-powered philosophical attention in recent years, notably in works by C. Stephen Evans, Robert Adams, and Philip Quinn. John Hare's book *God's Command* joins this discussion and advances it by attending not only to the Christian tradition but also to Judaism and Islam, and by engaging with evolutionary psychology. Central to Hare's account of divine command theory is the claim that human nature is a "mixture," characterized by the dual affections for advantage and for justice. Against theories that assume a single-source account of motivation (e.g., eudaimonism), Hare contends that human beings experience the pull of competing motivations, toward morality and self-interest. Any adequate moral theory will account for both motivations and indicate how they can be reconciled. Hare contends that his version of divine command theory is up to this task.

It is on this point that Hare most clearly adheres to his claim at the beginning and the end of *God's Command* that the book "defends the thesis that what makes something morally obligatory is that God commands it, and what makes something morally wrong is that God commands us not to do it" (1). Elsewhere in the book, this kind of philosophical defense recedes. After an initial chapter describing divine command theory in general, and two chapters on eudaimonism and naturalistic deductivism, Hare provides three chapters illustrating how divine command theory is worked out by representative thinkers in the traditions of Christianity, Islam, and Judaism, followed by a chapter on how divine command theory can accommodate the findings of evolutionary psychology. The book ends with a summary, showing how the various pieces of the book, which at times read like a series of independent essays, constitute a single picture. In these latter chapters, Hare seems to leave behind the philosophical defense of divine command theory, turning instead toward a discussion of what kind of divine command theory theists should adopt, given their predetermined commitment to theism and divine command theory in general.

In one sense, this shift can be understood in terms of audience. Initially, Hare addresses anyone interested in ethics. By the second half of the book, Hare has shifted to convincing theistic ethicists that the best way to hold together their various commitments is to adopt a divine command theory, as opposed to other options such as Eudaimonism. This shift arises as an attempt to fend off a potential criticism of divine command theory—the possibility that people will do terrible things in the name of God's command. Hare suggests that Kant provides one solution to this problem, which is that if we *think* God is commanding us to do something that is at odds with practical reason, we ought to doubt that God is *really* commanding us to do this thing. Hare is sympathetic to Kant here, but he also seems to think that Kant's solution would undermine his own project, insofar as it makes God's command appear superfluous. Hare's alternative approach involves acknowledging that religious traditions possess safeguards to protect against the possibility that appeal to a divine command is used to justify horrendous evils. For Hare, the Abrahamic traditions provide historical evidence that the benefits of divine command ethics can be enjoyed without accepting the apparently bad aspects.

Hare himself notes that there is a kind of circularity here. He has made the point as a kind of hypothetical: If you already believe in God as the divine commander, and adhere to one of the Abrahamic traditions, you will possess resources to overcome this problem. As he admits at the end of chapter 5, he has not addressed the question of why someone who does not already believe in God as the source of morality ought to begin to do so. Nevertheless, the question of whether thinkers within religious traditions have provided compelling answers to the epistemological problems at the center of divine command theory will be of interest to many, both inside and outside various religious traditions. By bringing a high level of philosophical rigor to the study of theological sources in Judaism, Christianity, and Islam, Hare has charted a course that others in the fields of religious ethics and moral philosophy would do well to follow.

Joshua T. Mauldin
Center of Theological Inquiry,
Princeton, New Jersey

**REVIEW OF**

## *The Wiley Blackwell Companion to Religion and Ecology*

Edited by John Hart

OXFORD: JOHN WILEY & SONS LTD, 2017. 560 PP. $195.00

If ecology is the study of "relationships in a place," as John Hart reminds readers in the preface of the *Wiley Blackwell Companion to Religion and Ecology*, it is fitting that this volume centers its thrust relationally (xxiv). Throughout its pages, a diverse community of authors explores the relationships among religious and spiritual traditions, human life, and care for the Earth. Defining religion as a language with which to grapple with meanings assigned to cultural values (xxi), this volume turns to the meanings that humans have historically placed on their relationship to the Earth within spiritual and religious frameworks. It further ponders how our religions and spiritual traditions reflect a relationship to the Earth that is conscious of the status of our planet's health today. Offering insights from Buddhism, Hinduism, Islam, Judaism, Eastern and Western Christianity, and indigenous perspectives, the authors reflect on new and old insights from within their tradition that speak to specific ecological issues. The volume is split into four parts, flowing thematically from conceptual and descriptive, to concrete visions for practical steps toward healing the Earth.

Part 1 describes the various ways religious and spiritual traditions enhance ecological consciousness. Seyyed Hossein Nasr shows how the Qur'an depicts the created order as a reflection of God's face, suggesting that we are literally defacing the face of God in our industrial recklessness. David Mevorach Seidenberg presents a Jewish eco-theology, which decenters the human as the pinnacle of creation. In part 2, the authors further draw out the socioecological implications of religious teachings. Melanie Harris argues that religious communities must open their eyes to the link between structural violence against black women to structural violence against the Earth. She maintains that this analysis is key to finding solutions for ecological reparations. When Harris argues that social justice is Earth justice, she is claiming that the dismantling of both white supremacy and colonial ecology go hand in hand.

Part 3, titled "Ecological Commitment," highlights the specific contexts in which the relationship between religion and ecology are embedded. Myrna Perez Sheldon and Naomi Oreskes trace the entanglement of evangelical identity with the politics of scientific doubt. In response, they suggest a new framework for evangelical participation in environmental restoration that moves beyond a political identity that is chained to right-wing doubt about climate change. In asking how "Korean Christianity can become more Nature-conscious, Nature-related, and Nature-integrated," Yong Bum Park points to Chondogyo, a Korean indigenous religion (333). This tradition is shown to take seriously the ecological crisis as a "crisis of consciousness and conduct," encouraging religious people to foster a socioecological vision of restoration (333).

Part 4, which provides examples of concrete visions and projects on the ground, ends with John Hart's reimagining of the Earth as a "common commons." The notion that the Earth is a sacred "common commons" of "interdependent, integral, evolving relational community" requires conversion in light of how religious people relate to the Earth today (437). According to this commons ethic, land should be "commonized and communalized" rather than rendered private property (476).

I highly recommend this volume for teaching undergraduate and graduate courses that are exploring the intersection of religion and ecology, especially courses focusing on religious ethics. Though the breadth of this work might strike the reader as boundless, herein lies its strength, especially for teachers of Christian ethics. This resource broadens the conversation recently highlighted by Pope Francis in *Laudato Si'* beyond the Christian perspective on ecology. The *Companion* models interreligious dialogue, opening to the diverse ways many different religious and spiritual traditions demand action for environmental restoration.

Dannis M. Matteson
Loyola University Chicago

■

REVIEW OF
# A Culture of Engagement: Law, Religion, and Morality
Cathleen Kaveny
WASHINGTON, DC: GEORGETOWN UNIVERSITY PRESS, 2016. 320 PP. $98.95 / $32.95

It is encouraging to read a book on the intersection of religion and law from an author as conversant with both fields as is Cathleen Kaveny. Reworking a number of columns that she wrote for *Commonweal* magazine, Kaveny offers her concept of a "culture of engagement" as an alternative to America's polarizing culture wars. She builds a vision of engagement—typified by Pope Francis's emphasis on the church's need to "encounter" all human beings—that welcomes the influence that religious traditions and the broader culture and its laws can have on each other.

Kaveny notes two ways in which the Roman Catholic tradition is particularly well situated to engage American culture and law. First, both American common law and the Catholic moral tradition use forms of "casuistry" to connect general rules with particular situations. Second, Catholic reluctance "to draw sharp lines between the pure and the tainted" can supply a salutary alternative to the Puritan tendency toward "prophetic indictment" (16).

In part 1, Kaveny argues that law has both pedagogical and pragmatic qualities. In part 2, she describes the nation's struggle to balance governmental interests and religious liberty in the context of the contraception mandate in the 2010 Affordable Care Act. She faults the United States Conference of Catholic Bishops for elevating the law's pedagogical role over its pragmatic function in their attack on the mandate. She herself leans toward pragmatism; she assumes that exceptions to laws of general applicability should apply only "in the most extreme cases" (116) and that the government—not the religious claimant—should determine when exceptions apply.

Kaveny also suggests that the bishops would do well to pay greater attention to the common good, as "it reflects the moral consensus of the community, which is accurately reflected in our democratic process of lawmaking" (90). Development of the grounds for this optimistic linking of a moral consensus and majority rule to the common good would have been an interesting addition to the book.

Part 3 is the heart of the work, exploring ways for American society to "move beyond a culture war mentality" (120). Kaveny resists the assumption that public discourse in a society torn by culture wars is served by pitting secular and religious voices against each other. She hopes instead for persuasion based on natural law. One is left wondering, however, how persuasion based on natural law could happen in America's ideologically diverse culture.

Part 4 explores the effect of America's ideological pluralism on discussions among American Catholics. Kaveny describes how the church's sexual abuse scandal has fed the growing sense of disconnection between church teaching and the expectations of the Catholic laity.

Part 5, a series of essays on difficult ethical controversies, hints at what interaction between the American and Catholic traditions might look like. Kaveny advocates "reframing the question" and hints at what reframing the contraception question might look like (221).

Some of the book addresses specifically Catholic questions. It is valuable in that respect. Its scope extends beyond any one religious tradition, however, as it offers a picture of engagement between equals: the American legal tradition and Catholic moral teaching. Nevertheless, Kaveny makes it clear that this sort of engagement can succeed only if the American legal community understands its need to reflect changing social values and the Catholic hierarchy moves away from insisting that "error has no rights" and toward acknowledging that people do have rights even when they are in error (257).

Allen Calhoun
PhD candidate,
University of Aberdeen

REVIEW OF

## The Promise of Martin Luther's Political Theology: Freeing Luther from the Modern Political Narrative
Michael Richard Laffin

NEW YORK: BLOOMSBURY / T&T CLARK, 2016. 272 PP. $121.00

Is Christianity antagonistic of the political, as Machiavelli, Rousseau, and Nietzsche have all claimed? Michael Laffin argues against this position for "the life-affirming, this worldliness of Christianity" by pointing to the "theologically saturated politics of [Martin] Luther" as one historical possibility (4). In particular, Laffin elevates Luther's notion of the three estates, the locus of sanctification in Luther's thought, and the Reformer's doctrine of the "two ecclesiae" as concepts holding together the "this-worldly" dimension of life with the theological tension of the fall and redemption. In this way, Laffin identifies a truly political life lived in community and a thoroughly theological politics extending from faith in the justifying God (3). Laffin defends Luther against charges of violent individualism (contra John Milbank) and quietism (contra

Jennifer Herdt) by highlighting the importance of the theology of the Word for Luther's treatment of *politia*. Per Laffin, Luther understands the Word as Christ's radically incarnate presence that transforms this-worldly communities by sanctifying the Christian's affections, which are then lived out in political relationships (chaps. 1–3). The *politia* therefore becomes a place of encounter with God in which the re-created human heart commits acts of moral beauty that are distinctively Christian (chaps. 4–5).

One strength of Laffin's argument is his thoroughgoing critique of the constructed narratives in contemporary political theology and philosophy that construe Luther as the harbinger of modernity's ills, as the inventor of the desocialized individual via his notion of faith and a proponent of quietistic authoritarianism in his elevation of human passivity in justification. By looking outside Luther's classic "political" texts, Laffin shows that careful study of Luther's broader writings on scripture, the sacraments, and ecclesiology actually reveal complex theological theories about the place of the political in realizing the good in human life and community. Both Laffin's critique of Milbank's ontology of violence and his assertion about human moral agency in the *politia* presuppose, however, that Luther's theological move from justification to sanctification includes the possibility for some kind of real, effectual change in the human person. This requires a metaphysical language capable of describing ontological change, something Laffin negates when he denies Luther's creative reliance on nominalism (39). Laffin wants to assume this ontological change that makes human moral agency possible but restricts himself from engaging the historical realities of Luther's intellectual life that make his assumptions plausible. Laffin's deft critique of Milbanks and Herdt would be strengthened by a more nuanced understanding of Luther's simultaneous critique *and use* of nominalist theology and philosophy for contemplating human action in both divine and political relations. Here real possibilities exist for showing how Luther used nominalist principles to construct a view of human moral agency for political relationships through the theological locus of sanctification (contra Herdt) by rehabilitating human persons in relation to God (contra Milbanks).

Despite this critique, Laffin's book opens up new questions about the historical narratives surrounding the secularization thesis and exactly what we mean by "political *theology*." Advanced political philosophers, theologians, and Christian ethicists must now reckon with the possibilities he creates for rethinking Luther's place in this narrative and the Reformer's ongoing relevance in current discussions. Laffin prompts these audiences to reconsider the extent to which the political and the theological can and do hold each other in tension, as he shows that Luther does.

Candace L. Kohli<br>Northwestern University

**REVIEW OF**

# Wisdom Calls: The Moral Story of the Hebrew Bible
Paul Lewis

MACON, GA: NURTURING FAITH, 2017. 99 PP. $18.00

Paul Lewis invites us into a thought experiment: What can we discern about moral development from a "naive" reading of the Hebrew Scriptures as narrative, starting at Genesis and working our way through to Chronicles? If we remove our presuppositions and eisegesis, ossified through centuries of familiarity, and read the stories at face value, what can we discern about character, virtue, and moral development via the human protagonists as well as God? In this book aimed at undergraduates and faith-seeking adults, Lewis provides an accessible introduction to both scripture and ethics, as well as a creative endeavor at the interface.

Using an eclectic hermeneutical approach, Lewis offers a fresh reading of the Hebrew Scriptures. Fundamental to his thesis are two points. First, even though the Hebrew Scriptures are made up of a variety of texts in different genres written by different authors over almost a millennium, at some point, they were collated into the canonical, three-part sequence (Law, Prophets, and Writings—the Tanakh, TNK) by redactors who shaped the collection with a particular directionality. Pivotal to this process was the Babylonian Exile, which Lewis considers a crucial lens for reading a narrative arc across the collection. Second, he reminds Christian readers that the structure and sequence of texts in the Christian "Old Testament" differs from that of the Jewish TNK. As a result, "TNK and Old Testament, by the way they order the documents that make them up, thus tell different stories" (9).

Lewis walks the reader through a series of ordered reflections on the three main sections of the Hebrew Scriptures. From Genesis to Chronicles, he charts a shift toward increasing moral complexity, finding in this narrative "a story of moral development" that begins with the need for and establishment of rules or laws (Torah—chap. 2), moves to the discernment of principles at the heart of the laws (Prophets—chap. 3), and culminates with a vision of wisdom captured in the multifaceted and sometimes conflicting texts in the Writings (chap. 4), complete with a controversial yet intriguing interpretation of Job. Wisdom, in his reading of these texts, is the practical skill needed to interpret the laws, rules, and principles of the tradition with the nuance necessary for the ever-changing sociocultural context of the "hard, cruel world" in which the Jews of ancient Palestine found themselves.

The book culminates with chapter 5, titled "Wisdom Calls," where he brings the multilayered Wisdom tradition (*chochmah*, in Hebrew) into conversation with the Aristotelian tradition of virtue and practical wisdom (*phronesis*), finding the analog for Aristotle's endpoint of *eudaimonia* in the Hebraic vision of *shalom*. *Shalom* is "the goal toward which wisdom strives and the good that it seeks to achieve" (p. 73). In a short appendix, he also brings *chochmah* into conversation with contemporary developments in the moral psychology of wisdom, drawing on the work of Darcia Narvaez and scholars at the Max Planck Institute, among others.

Lewis's reading brings the Hebrew Scriptures alive, reminding us how wonderfully messy, interesting, and complicated its characters and stories are. By way of critique, one might ask: Can one read a scriptural text too naively? At points, this reader wished for a bit more historical-critical interpretation as a way of enhancing the conclusions being drawn. Integration of the material on the moral psychology of wisdom into the final chapter, rather than as an appendix, would also have been welcome. In the end, *Wisdom Calls* provides an engaging starting point for students and congregations.

Therese Lysaught
Loyola University Chicago

**REVIEW OF**

## *Reading Kierkegaard I: Fear and Trembling*

Paul Martens

EUGENE, OR: CASCADE BOOKS, 2017. 130 PP. $18.00

The very first line of *Reading Kierkegaard I: Fear and Trembling* warns that "reading Søren Kierkegaard is a task that requires a relatively high level of intellectual investment" (ix). Yet the difficult task Paul Martens sets for himself, in keeping with the goal of the Cascade Companions series, is to provide a short introduction to Kierkegaard's thought for a nonspecialist readership. In this first volume, the primary text in focus is *Fear and Trembling* (*FT*), with a second volume to focus on *Works of Love*. More specifically, the threefold purpose of this volume is "(1) to illuminate the internal logic of the text in a manner that renders the text more accessible; (2) to highlight the links between *FT* and Kierkegaard's broader context in a way that helps one make sense of some of its more opaque sections; and (3) to attend to the theological themes that permeate and drive the text" (xi).

Martens helpfully follows the structure provided by *FT*, explicating each "chapter" in turn and highlighting the ways it relates to the others as well as to the argument as a whole. This approach is particularly helpful for the long and difficult Problem III "chapter" in *FT*, which Martens frames as an attempt by Kierkegaard's pseudonymous author Johannes de Silentio to perform the text's argument by demonstrating "that the whole investigation—any investigation, even an unlimited poetic investigation of characters and concepts—only leads to one conspicuous conclusion: Abraham is unintelligible" (54).

Attention to the links between *FT* and Kierkegaard's broader context is also helpful for unifying the seemingly disparate arguments in *FT*. In Martens's reading of this context, *FT* is to be understood against the broad backdrop of Kierkegaard's criticisms of nineteenth-century Danish Christendom and the particular backdrop of the Hegelianism that de Silentio finds within it. The overall task of *FT* is then "to raise the price of faith" (71).

Martens clearly attends to the text's theological themes with his repeated juxtaposition between "faith" as de Silentio sees it in the story of Abraham and "the ethical" as de Silentio sees it in nineteenth-century Denmark. Many theological themes are also highlighted and then brought into the reader's context in the discussion questions that follow each chapter.

In addition to the discussion questions, Martens provides an appendix, which includes a timeline of Kierkegaard's first authorship, a glossary of important terms that may be unfamiliar, and a list of suggested readings for further study. The glossary will be a particularly helpful tool for those less familiar with Kierkegaard. However, there are also several terms missing that are both significant enough and unclear enough to warrant inclusion. One thinks here of a figure like Socrates and concepts like the knight of faith and the knight of infinite resignation.

Similarly, another feature of the book that is both a strength and a weakness is its commitment to the text of *FT* rather than the scholarship surrounding the text. This is a strength because it keeps the book short and accessible for nonspecialists. It is also a weakness, however, because the reader interested in further study is not clearly pointed toward competing interpretations, despite the fact that some lines are ripe for a brief footnote providing such a reference— "Not all agree with me on this" (76).

Overall, the discussion questions and appendix, its short length and overall readability, and its commitment to the text make *Reading Kierkegaard I: Fear and Trembling* a significant pedagogical contribution to ethics and Kierkegaard studies as an entry point for nonspecialists.

Derek Hostetter
University of Dayton

■

REVIEW OF
# The Sermon on the Mount and Moral Theology: A Virtue Perspective
William C. Mattison III
NEW YORK: CAMBRIDGE UNIVERSITY PRESS, 2017. 290 PP. £75.00

Undergirding this book is a principle from the Catechism of the Catholic Church: the "analogy of faith" or "the coherence of the truths of faith among themselves" (241). The "truths of faith" under consideration are Matthew's Sermon on the Mount (SM) and the virtue ethics of Thomas Aquinas. Mattison aims to restore the SM to a more prominent place in Catholic moral theology by demonstrating the convergence between the teachings of the SM and Thomistic virtue ethics.

In this endeavor, the book largely succeeds, even if it occasionally over-reaches—that is, the SM is always shown to be in perfect harmony with Thomas's teachings on virtue ethics, in which some readers might see points of tension. For example, Mattison uses Thomistic action theory to argue that the Beatitudes (Mt 5:3–12) and the SM's concluding exhortations (Mt 7:13–29) both demonstrate an "intrinsic relationship" between action and eternal reward; that is, the "qualifying condition" (e.g., meekness) is itself constitutive of happiness and is thus an activity that continues in eternal life (22–25, 209, 221). Purity of heart works well in this framework, but Mattison struggles to make mourning fit. The Thomistic lens determines the sense of the text: Whatever mourning is, it is an activity that must persist in heaven, limiting the options for interpretation.

Mattison also aligns the seven virtues—faith, hope, love, prudence, justice, temperance, and fortitude—with the seven Beatitudes (following Augustine's reduction of the Beatitudes from eight to seven), with the seven petitions of the Lord's Prayer, and with sections of the SM as a whole. These latter, broad pairings are not always easy to find. Mattison matches the Beatitudes with the virtue of faith, and the six antitheses with the virtues of temperance and fortitude. The virtue of love pairs with Matthew 6:1–6, 16–18 (teachings on prayer, alms-giving, and fasting, sans the Lord's Prayer); prudence, with Matthew 6:19–34 (worry and money); justice, with Matthew 7:1–12 (judging, asking, the golden rule); and hope, with Matthew 7:13–29 (concluding warnings and exhortations).

Similarly, a virtue is assigned to each Beatitude (47) and to each petition of the Lord's Prayer (252). In the case of the Lord's Prayer, Mattison insists on a particular order of the virtues, following Aquinas's ordering (but reversing temperance and fortitude). But he does not use the same order of virtues for the Beatitudes or for the broader alignments with the whole SM (the orders are completely different for all three lists), raising the question of why Aquinas's order matters for one set but not for the others.

Mattison's alignments show both his indebtedness to patristic and medieval tradition and his innovation. Medieval commentators commonly matched sets of sevens (Beatitudes, virtues, vices, gifts of the Spirit), but (rather remarkably) none of them ever appears to have understood the seven petitions of the Lord's Prayer as requests for the seven virtues, as Mattison does. Likewise, Mattison's alignment of the Beatitudes with the virtues follows the practice but not the substance of previous lists; his pairings match neither Ambrose's nor Aquinas's. I would have found a discussion of the differences helpful.

The question is whether Mattison's alignments are fruitful or merely forced, and here readers may find the results to be mixed. Some are illuminating, such as the vice of presumption in relation to Matthew 7:21–23; others, such as the alignment of the six antitheses with the seven sacraments, "appear a bit of a 'stretch,'" as even Mattison admits (110).

Overall, scholars and graduate students interested in Thomistic virtue ethics, and in the relationship between scripture and Catholic moral theology, will find much food for thought here.

Rebekah Eklund
Loyola University Maryland

REVIEW OF

## Democracy, Culture, Catholicism: Voices from Four Continents

Edited by Michael J. Schuck and John Crowley-Buck
NEW YORK: FORDHAM UNIVERSITY PRESS, 2016. 350 PP. $105.00 / $35.00

*Democracy, Culture, Catholicism* is the product of a three-year, international project that started from a less specific inspiration. Originally begun at Loyola University Chicago's Joan and Bill Hank Center for the Catholic Intellectual Heritage in 2010 as a broad inquiry into the relationship between the Roman Catholic Church and politics, the project leaders eventually took a different bearing from events as diverse as the Arab Spring, the Occupy Movement, and Pope Benedict XVI's encyclical *Caritas in Veritate* to focus their project more squarely on democracy. Examining democracy from within the diverse experiences found in Lithuania, Peru, Indonesia, and the United States, the editors present us with a valuable snapshot of where the Catholic engagement with democracy as a cultural expression finds itself today in a global perspective.

Given the amount of material at play, the volume is a monumental achievement, if only for the clarity with which it presents its findings. Some essays are stronger than others. Still, the volume benefits tremendously from an apparent and unusual amount of editorial attention that sequences the essays and interrelates them with useful references to one another in such a way that *Democracy, Culture, Catholicism* escapes entirely the fate of so many volumes of collected essays. Here, the reader has the sensation of reading one coherent narrative, not twenty-three disparately connected, individual essays. This alone is impressive.

The volume possesses other strengths. Reflections emerge throughout that engage the deeper questions of democracy. Who are these people making decisions together? How can we understand the composition of a political community? Too much democratic theory overlooks the complex interweaving of history, memory, and identity that operates like a substrate of our consciousness beneath our reason while we are presuming ourselves to be rational decision makers using democratic procedures. The book's engagement not just with democracy and Catholicism but also with culture is important. These essays treat culture not only in different local expressions but also (and in a way that is deep, serious, and sustained) as a phenomenon of consciousness.

The American perspective always lurks in the narrative, threatening to dominate. This is inevitable not only because the project was managed in the United States but also because the polarizing obsessions of the church in the United States about how to acknowledge the norms of modern political arrangements have tended to dominate conversation in the church worldwide. The editors have shrewdly chosen to save the United States for the last part of this volume, allowing other voices to come forward first to claim their own space. This editorial decision, like so many others, improves the volume and keeps the narrative in good balance. Still, some questions linger in this reviewer's mind as the volume concludes.

What do we mean by democracy? Throughout, the authors treat this as a question that is largely settled. Democracy is identified with democratic values that the church accepts, and in Schuck's words, what is under way is "a critical conversation with the culture of democracy" (330). Yet procedural democracy cannot be severed from these values. Are democratic norms and values vindicated when majorities choose undemocratic values? A more careful drawing of distinctions between democracy, liberalism, and republicanism would expose the inner conflicts in which Catholicism meets modern political norms.

Perhaps most urgently for the subject matter of this book, are the claims of Catholic social teaching and Christian ethics a foundation for the democratic, participatory values of this secular age, as writers like Charles Taylor and David

Walsh have suggested? This also would raise questions about how culturally conditioned we should understand democracy to be, surely an important consideration for this very fine study.

Steven P. Millies
Catholic Theological Union

REVIEW OF

## Love and Christian Ethics: Tradition, Theory, and Society

Edited by Frederick V. Simmons and Brian C. Sorrels

WASHINGTON, DC: GEORGETOWN UNIVERSITY PRESS, 2016. 400 PP. $119.00 / $39.95

Fredrick Simmons and Brian Sorrels present an impressive, cohesive volume of essays by twenty-two leading scholars who engage different facets of love and theological ethics. Although dedicated to Gene Outka—thus setting the broad theme and establishing his work as a privileged point of reference throughout the volume—*Love and Christian Ethics* should not be confused with a Festschrift. It accomplishes far more in intellectual diversity and depth, making a significant contribution to scholarship.

The volume is organized into three sections: tradition, theory, and society. Across the first section, the authors address love within major sources and figures, treating scripture, Greek philosophy, Augustine, Aquinas, Kant, and Kierkegaard. Far from a textbook presentation, each essay marks out its own argument regarding the place of love in the respective subject. The second section is devoted to major theoretical questions raised within scholarship on love and ethics, addressing topics like the relation of eudaimonism to love (a running thread that emerges in the book), forgiveness, friendship, and evolution. The final section moves into the field of practice, application, and society, including an essay critically engaging implicit presentations of love found in the law, another treating love and international development, and one poignant essay by Mark D. Jordan calling for a moratorium on strong pronouncements in sexual ethics until ethicists can cultivate a loving knowledge of sex. This final section also includes reflections on love in the Jewish and Muslim traditions. Simmons's introduction and William Werpehowksi's afterword provide useful bookends. Although no single thesis blandly governs this volume as a whole—incorporating complementary, divergent, and competing positions—in constructing this volume, Simmons and Sorrels argue that love is not eclipsed in Christian ethics but has a rich and variegated tradition. Werpehowski appraises the volume as a whole, identifying key threads that emerge, like relations of love to eudaimonism and the theme of neighbor love.

The volume is admirable in its breadth and depth. It offers a robust encounter with major figures and questions, providing historical recovery as well as critical and constructive engagement. That said, depth can work against breadth, with essays like Oliver O'Donovan's demanding a familiarity with Augustine *Confessions* that will send the reader back to his or her bookcases. Missing too are other notable figures and topics, such as the Protestant Reformers, Christian mystics, and feminist ethicists. Nevertheless, these gaps do not diminish the volume as a whole. I found myself again and again excited by the insights offered by the contributors, unsettling easy assumptions regarding the relation between eudaimonia and love, illustrating the depths of accounts of friendship for thinking about polity and mediating institutions, and cautioning against overconfidence in sexual ethics as its boundaries destabilize.

*Love and Christian Ethics* would benefit scholars, teachers, and students alike. Its broad engagement with contemporary scholarship on love makes it a useful starting point for any researcher dipping or diving into this field. Introducing professors to key and sometimes obscured questions within figures and topics, it can round out lectures and help introduce students to the growing edge of scholarship on love. It would serve as a useful reference for any upper division or graduate course engaging with this significant, but often ignored, theme in Christian ethics.

Rare is it to find a book that embodies the very theme it presents. These essays on love are a scholarly gift of the best sort—one not diminished but enhanced in its sharing.

Michael Le Chevallier
University of Chicago

REVIEW OF
# *Calvin's Political Theology and the Public Engagement of the Church: Calvin's Two Kingdoms*
Matthew J. Tuininga
CAMBRIDGE: CAMBRIDGE UNIVERSITY PRESS, 2017. 258 PP. £69.99 / £27.99

In recent years, a vigorous debate has arisen within Reformed circles concerning the nature of the two kingdoms theology of John Calvin. Although all recognize that Calvin articulated a distinction between the spiritual kingdom of the church and the political kingdom of the state, there is disagreement over the nature of the engagement of Christians with the temporal kingdom and over what should guide the state in enacting civil justice and order.

The Kuyperian Neo-Calvinist movement holds a transformationalist understanding of the engagement of members of the spiritual kingdom with all vocations and spheres of life. Alternatively, two kingdoms Reformed theologians, such as David VanDrunen and Michael Horton, argue that the Reign of Christ is confined to the spiritual kingdom and must not be brought to bear directly on the temporal kingdom. Matthew Tuininga's book supports the latter view in his exposition of Calvin's political theology. Tuininga argues that Calvin articulated a sharp distinction between church and political society, such that politics is seen not as "a means of transforming society into the kingdom of God according to the dictates of Christian scripture, but as an endeavour to secure temporal order and civil righteousness in accord with reason, natural law, and the virtues of charity and prudence" (1).

Tuininga begins by situating Calvin and his two kingdoms theology in their historical and political context, indicating Calvin's concern for the autonomy of church contra government interference. The central chapters (3–6) present the eschatological basis for Calvin's two kingdoms doctrine and detail the development of this theme in Calvin's thought. The Kingdom of God is identified with the church and its spiritual authority. It is distinct from the state's temporal authority, whose role is to maintain civil righteousness and order. To support this distinction between the mandate of the two kingdoms, Tuininga presents in chapter 7 the novel, and debatable, claim that Calvin holds to two covenants of God with Israel: the covenant of grace made with Abraham and confirmed at Sinai and the narrower covenant of the law for Israel's national life, in which God's blessings and punishments were conditional on Israel's obedience and disobedience. Although this legal covenant—with its earthly and temporal character—is embedded in the broader covenant of grace, it is abolished with the fulfillment of the covenant of grace in the coming of Christ. Only the covenant of grace—with its heavenly, inward, and spiritual character—remains in force for God's people today.

Chapter 8 argues that Calvin's views on the mandate of the magistrate to protect religion and enact public justice is based not on appeals to scripture but to reason, the evidence of national laws, and natural philosophy. In chapter 9 Tuininga unfolds the implications of Calvin's two kingdoms theology for Christian political involvement in society. And in his conclusion, Tuininga unfolds numerous ways that this two kingdoms theology can guide contemporary Christians' engagement with modern liberal democracies.

This work is a welcome exposition of Calvin's political theology to support the two kingdoms theology. However, in addition to the novel, and debatable, claim that God made two covenants with Israel, this reviewer finds that Tuininga's exposition fails to incorporate key points in Calvin's thought: the failure of civil rulers' to enact natural law faithfully and consistently (2.2.13, 23; 3.14.2), the description of the calling of civil authority as "holy and lawful before God ... the most sacred and by far the most honorable of all callings" (4.20.4), and Calvin's claim that the best rulers are those governing according to *both* tables of the Decalogue (4.20.9–11). Nevertheless, this book is an important contribution to the ongoing debate and should be widely read.

Guenther ("Gene") Haas
Redeemer University College

REVIEW OF

# *Just Capitalism: A Christian Ethic of Economic Globalization*

Brent Waters

LOUISVILLE: WESTMINSTER JOHN KNOX PRESS, 2016. 260 PP. $40.00

In *Just Capitalism*, Brent Waters offers a wide-ranging defense of economic globalization, the market state, and the pursuit of affluence, which together provide a means to spread human flourishing around the globe. For Waters, the free-flowing economic exchange enabled by globalization does not inherently conflict with Christian tradition, and it can be harnessed in a responsible manner to share and communicate the goods of creation. He argues that breaking down global barriers to market participation expresses a preferential option for the poor and provides a means for achieving the work of the Spirit by spreading the materials goods that lift people out of poverty and alleviate suffering. The book's primary contribution is its broad explanation of recent work on the economics of globalization and Waters's ability to put this literature into a theological conversation. The argument is particularly timely for Christian ethicists who are concerned with developing the tools to respond to expanding movements toward isolationism and economic protectionism in the United States and Europe.

Part 1 of *Just Capitalism* claims that moral theology has not properly interrogated the common view that affluence fundamentally conflicts with the Christian tradition. By contextualizing both the biblical sources and the traditional theological voices that support this view, Waters shows that these sources assumed an economic model in which resources are scarce and wealth is built by exploiting the poor. Instead, Waters argues that our present economic system is based on increasing productivity, and therefore wealth is not necessarily exploitative. In fact, he claims that the pursuit of affluence can be beneficial for helping to lift people out of poverty. Rather than retreating from engagement with wealth and the market, Christians should recognize that free exchange is a necessary, though not sufficient, condition for human flourishing (15).

In part 2, Waters develops a notion of *koinonia*, whereby human flourishing depends on communicating the goods of creation in the associations of civil society. Responding to worries about the homogenizing forces of market economies that make individuals into producers and consumers, Waters offers the church as a communicative association that stands in tension with capitalist markets by cultivating reciprocity instead of consumption, breaking down barriers in a gathering community, and being nonterritorial in its scope (150–51). Because communicative associations like the church are essential to the vitality of civil society, the challenge is to "embrace the dynamism of global markets in order to promote more widespread prosperity," while establishing the requisite political stability that allows these associations to exist (159).

Nevertheless, Waters does not spend much time elaborating on specific moments when the church should come into conflict with capitalism—he notes that his reservations only give him "two-and-a-half-cheers" for globalization, rather than three (14–15). In his desire to show compatibility with globalization, he neglects to give a sense of when communicative associations could justifiably remove themselves from the system of exchange. This relates to Waters's final chapter on capitalist responses to environmental devastation, which relies on his earlier development of a stewardship model, one that seems to reduce creation to its instrumental value for human "delight" (89–90, 92, 111, 115). Waters admits that the pursuit of affluence requires short-term environmental damage, especially in developing countries; nevertheless, he thinks that affluent societies will better preserve the environment (through "national parks and wildlife preserves") (217), and some environmental exploitation is needed to form these affluent societies. This will probably be insufficient for environmental ethicists who resist the notion that creation's purpose is to be ordered to promote human flourishing (204). He is clear, however, that "Eden is a garden, and not a wilderness" (203).

Nicholas Aaron Friesner
Brown University

REVIEW OF

*War, Peace, and Reconciliation: A Theological Inquiry*
Theodore R. Weber
EUGENE, OR: WIPF & STOCK, 2015. 182 PP. $23.00

Weber's book makes a helpful contribution to enlivening more theologically grounded strategies for peacemaking through reconciliation. It is a careful, systematic work that takes as its foundation a distinctively Christian view of

God's nature and relation to the world. As a scholar and a pastor for over fifty years, Weber brings a much-needed, wise, and re-centered view to the questions entangled in war, peace, and reconciliation. He advises us not to look first into the realities of war for God, but to look to understand God as the context for all human conflict. He forcefully calls the reader to be a reconciler despite the intractability of conflict. The book is structured in three main parts, beginning with the theological context, then the political context, and, last, to peace, justice, and the church.

The "war" that Weber addresses is interstate conflict, representing the negation of the web of relationships constituting a healthy international system. War disrupts God's plan and ruptures the right relationship between humanity and God (43–44). Throughout, Weber embraces a kind of Christian Realism, one that takes seriously the loving nature of God, the sinfulness of humanity, and the limits and possibilities for peacemaking in a human world. Downplaying the pacifistic message of Jesus, Weber highlights the necessities within a fallen world. We cannot eliminate war as a category of existence under the conditions of sin (until the eschaton), but with right orientation and action we can eliminate some war.

Noting inadequacies of the just war tradition (though not dispensing with it), Weber identifies the need to ground it more firmly in theology, including enhanced attention to "just intention" as a primary criterion in evaluating the prosecution of war, displacing cause as the first question with which we must interrogate ourselves. Discernment about war and peace must be an ongoing conversation that should include people of faith as well as policymakers. Weber's theological and pastoral sensibilities, alongside his political savvy throughout, make the book a pleasurable and provocative read.

The definition of *reconciliation* deployed is broad and complex, and Weber marshals it for powerful work. Reconciliation "is God's work—the movement of Divine grace through history, engaging all aspects of brokenness and promise and reaching its climax of fulfillment and disclosure in the life, death, and resurrection of Jesus Christ" (3). Grace continually calls humanity to enter into the work of reconciliation. Here Weber introduces the idea of relational power; more nuanced than mere substantive power, it connects to the core idea of institution building and the critical emphasis on strengthening the social fabric in the interest of peace. It is the hallmark of the reconciling transformation from systems of dominance to relationships of consent.

The book raises questions regarding how to put reconciliation as described into concrete practice, responding to real cases and controversies. Also, there could be added discussion, against this theological backdrop, of what opportunities exist amid current US and global regime change to enter this reconciling activity more fully.

Ultimately, the Christian context is central to understanding the ethics that Weber advances. Weber recommends a biblical foundation, one in which we take the benefit of reading scripture backward from the Christ event. Such an exegetical strategy reveals that God has a plan for all of humanity, a vision of inclusiveness and reconciliation. It is from this vantage point of God's culminating vision, Weber illuminates, that we can understand and embrace human action throughout history and the meaningful, if incomplete, work of reconciliation to which we must commit ourselves, both politically and spiritually.

David H. Messner
Emory University

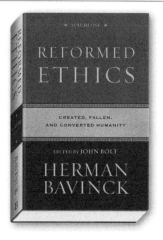
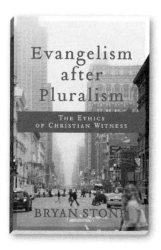
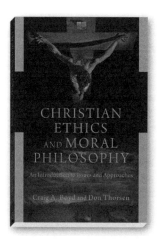

# The Journal of **Jewish Ethics**

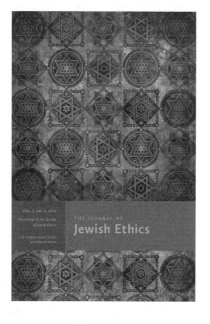

JONATHAN K. CRANE AND
EMILY FILLER, EDITORS

*The Journal of Jewish Ethics* publishes
outstanding scholarship in Jewish
ethics, broadly conceived. It serves
as a location for the exchange of
ideas among those interested in
understanding, articulating, and
promoting descriptive and normative
Jewish ethics. It aspires to advance
dialogue between Jewish ethicists
and ethicists working out of other
religious and secular traditions.
The journal welcomes articles that
engage contemporary moral and
ethical issues using philosophical
and theological methods, historical
and textual criticism, and other
approaches.

**Individuals** (2018 prices)
1 Year (2 issues): $49 (print or online)
1 Year (2 issues): $70 (print and online)

**Libraries/Institutions** (2018 prices)
1 Year (2 issues): $160 (print or online)
1 Year (2 issues): $233 (print and online)

ISSN 2334-1777 | E-ISSN 2334-1785
Biannual | Available in print or online

Submissions to: www.editorialmanager.com/jje

PENN STATE UNIVERSITY PRESS

www.psupress.org
journals@psu.edu

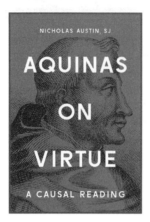
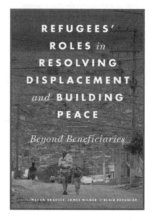
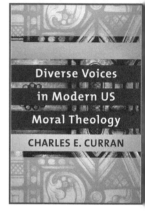

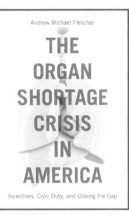

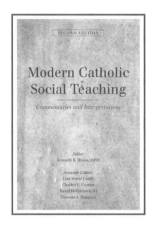

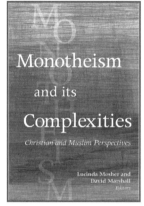

## The Organ Shortage Crisis in America
Incentives, Civic Duty, and Closing the Gap
**Andrew Michael Flescher**
paperback, $29.95,
978-1-62616-544-1
hardcover, $89.95,
978-1-62616-543-4

## Modern Catholic Social Teaching
Commentaries and Interpretations
**Kenneth R. Himes, Editor**
paperback, $49.95,
978-1-62616-514-4
hardcover, $149.95,
978-1-62616-513-7

## Monotheism and Its Complexities
Christian and Muslim Perspectives
**Lucinda Mosher and David Marshall, Editors**
paperback, $29.95,
978-1-62616-584-7
hardcover, $89.95,
978-1-62616-583-0

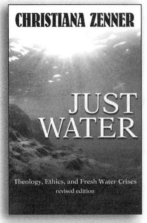
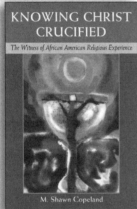
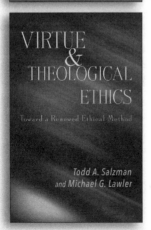

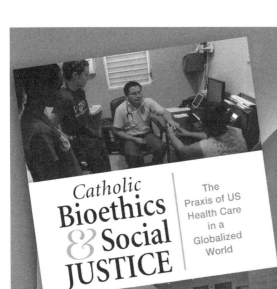

# Wabash Center
## for Teaching and Learning in Theology and Religion

Fully funded by Lilly Endowment Inc.
Located at Wabash College

**2018-19**
**Workshops & Colloquies**
- ❑ Early Career Theological School Faculty
- ❑ Early Career Faculty Teaching Undergraduates
- ❑ Colloquy on Writing the Scholarship of Teaching
- ❑ Teaching with Digital Media

Application Deadline:
January 15, 2019

**Grants up to $30,000**
Request for Proposals:
"Pedagogies for Social Justice and Civic Engagement"
Application Deadline:
February 15, 2019

**Resources**
- ❑ *Journal on Teaching*
- ❑ Teaching Resources
- ❑ Book Reviews
- ❑ Syllabi
- ❑ Blogs

## wabash.center